DATE DUE

NO 10 '95			

DEMCO 38-296

The Twilight
of Corporate Strategy

THE RUFFIN SERIES IN BUSINESS ETHICS
R. Edward Freeman, *Editor*

FORTHCOMING TITLES TO BE ANNOUNCED

The Twilight of Corporate Strategy

A COMPARATIVE ETHICAL CRITIQUE

❑ ❑ ❑

DANIEL R. GILBERT, JR.

New York   Oxford
OXFORD UNIVERSITY PRESS
1992

Oxford University Press

Oxford   New York   Toronto
Delhi   Bombay   Calcutta   Madras   Karachi
Kuala Lumpur   Singapore   Hong Kong   Tokyo
Nairobi   Dar es Salaam   Cape Town
Melbourne   Auckland

and associated companies in
Berlin   Ibadan

Published by Oxford University Press, Inc.,
200 Madison Avenue, New York, New York 10016

Oxford is a registered trademark of Oxford University Press

Library of Congress Cataloging-in-Publication Data
Gilbert, Daniel R., 1952–
The twilight of corporate strategy :
a comparative ethical critique /
by Daniel R. Gilbert, Jr.
p.   cm. (The Ruffin series in business ethics)
Includes index.   ISBN 0-19-506514-X
1. Strategic planning—Moral and ethical aspects.
I. Title.   II. Series.   HD30.28.G53   1992
658.4'012—dc20   91-35656

9   8   7   6   5   4   3   2   1

Printed in the United States of America
on acid-free paper

I dedicate this book to

Bretton Daniel Finch
New Canaan, Connecticut

Emma Wellen Freeman
Charlottesville, Virginia

Molly Wellen Freeman
Charlottesville, Virginia

Victoria Marie Gilbert
Allentown, Pennsylvania

Benjamin Wellen Freeman
Charlottesville, Virginia

Nicholas Patrick Meyer
Lewisburg, Pennsylvania

John Christopher Gilbert
Allentown, Pennsylvania

FOREWORD

One of the central tasks of business ethics is to show how recent advances in thinking about ethics are connected to the central metaphors of business. Dan Gilbert has done just that for "corporate strategy." He has made a compelling argument that our accounts of corporate strategy assume a dark and demeaning view of human nature. By applying the tools of ethical and literary theory to a host of real business examples, Gilbert causes us to question everything we thought we knew about strategy.

Once our idea of corporate strategy is in sufficient "twilight," we need a new way to think about the central tasks of the corporation and of business activity. Gilbert suggests that we put a theory of justice in the center and that we come to regard organizations as places where human beings enter into purposeful and pragmatic agreements with one another. It is our sense of justice that governs these interactions, not our sense of strategy as it has been developed in management theory.

This is a long and thorough book. It will repay many close readings. Gilbert's background as a businessman and a management scholar who has studied the central texts in philosophical and literary studies makes this a unique book. It deftly combines a practical concern with real managerial problems that comes with living with the problems as a businessperson, and a passion for creating a better way to understand business.

The purpose of The Ruffin Series in Business Ethics is to publish the best thinking about the role of ethics in business. In a world in which there are daily reports of questionable business practices—from financial scandals to environmental disasters—we have to step back from the fray and understand the large issues of how business and ethics are, and ought to be, connected. The books in this series are aimed at three audiences: management scholars, ethicists, and business executives. There is a growing consensus among these groups that business and ethics must be integrated as a vital part of the teaching and practice of management.

Corporate strategy will never be the same after Gilbert's book. Whether or not he convinces you, he shows us how to put our humanity at the center of business, making "business ethics" seem a great deal less contradictory.

R. Edward Freeman

PREFACE

This book presents a critical analysis of the concept of corporate strategy and the associated practice of strategic management research in ethical terms. The act of taking apart and reconsidering the meaning of strategic management research enables us to assess the worth of the corporate strategy concept as a commentary about the modern corporation. The criterion of worth that I employ is an ethical one, inasmuch as the corporate strategy concept can be understood as a commentary pertaining to persons, purposes, and interactions among persons at the corporation. In particular, my project is predicated on two premises that underscore the ethical possibilities for the concept.

First, the corporate strategy concept can support an uncommonly hopeful account of the modern corporation. That account can be hopeful by virtue of the place already accorded in strategic management research for questions about purpose and purposeful action that persons can take at the corporation. We can attribute to the concept, in other words, a decidedly "humanist" prospect: that distinct men and women can continually derive meaning, for their lives, from their actions at the corporation, and do so without interfering with one another's pursuits.

I adapt this liberal version of humanism principally from the arguments of Richard Rorty. For my purposes, I substitute "corporation" for "society" in Rorty's point, from *Contingency, Irony, and Solidarity,* that "the social glue holding together the ideal liberal society . . . consists in little more than a consensus that the point of social organization is to let everybody have a chance at self-creation to the best of his or her abilities" (p. 84). My point here is that the corporate strategy concept could guide a liberal endeavor, again in Rorty's words, to "equalize opportunities for self-creation and then leave people alone to use, or neglect, their opportunities" (p. 85). In short, I use "humanism" to convey a celebration of possibilities for the life of each distinct man and woman.

This liberal-humanist, ethical prospect (hereafter, simply "humanist") is uncommon by contrast to the bleak and cynical rendition of human activity that dominates conventional research in organization science and management theory. What I attribute to the corporate strategy concept is thus an unusual prospect, one that ushers the concept into an ethical territory with a humanist sense of hope for men and women and their endeavors. It is this rare prospect that warrants our willingness to ask whether contemporary strategic management researchers can deliver an account that fulfills such promise.

Second, my act of criticism turns on the premise that strategic management researchers routinely engage in activities that could serve as a vehicle for activating the ethical promise of corporate strategy and strategic management research. These researchers can be understood to seek a kind of dialogue with other persons through their writing, consulting, and teaching actions. In that dialogue, moreover, strategic management researchers can be understood to convey an account that they believe others will find useful as a guide for taking action at the corporation. With this interpretation, we can come to consider strategic management research as an effort to convey an account about the modern corporation whereby persons can "enter" that story as themselves, each with a unique past, present, and provisional sense of future. It is this worldly prospect—which complements the humanist, ethical promise of the corporate strategy concept—that further warrants our willingness to ask whether contemporary strategic management researchers do, in fact, make use of an account that fulfills such promise.

The title of this book reflects my concern about the ethical usefulness of strategic management research. To critique that research, and the associated corporate strategy concept, in worldly, ethical terms is to conduct the kind of critical assessment that nineteenth-century philosopher Friedrich Nietzsche called the *twilight* of worldly worth for a human practice. Thus this book can be understood as an inquiry about corporate strategy in a Nietzschean twilight.

The twilight metaphor implies a period of differentiation wherein our awareness of alternatives is heightened. In a Nietzschean sense, a period of twilight provides an opportunity to reflect on our choices in the past, the consequences of those choices in the present, and the alternatives from which we can choose for our future. Indeed, a central theme in this book is that strategic management researchers can exercise a choice about the accounts that they create and convey regarding persons acting at the corporation. In order to emphasize this choice in twilight, I organize the critical assessment of strategic management research to present a distinct choice between interpretations of the corporate strategy concept.

My line of inquiry could lead, on the one hand, to the conclusion that strategic management research proceeds on an interpretation that celebrates the possibilities for persons and their searches for meaning at the corporation. If this is the consequence of my critique, then all who make use of this interpretation can take heart in such an ethical justification of their pursuits. My line of inquiry could lead, on the other hand, to the conclusion that strategic management researchers convey an interpretation that proves unsuitable as a guide by which men and women can act purposefully at the corporation. If this is the consequence of my critique, then it is time to banish such an interpretation of corporate strategy to the deepening twilight—quite literally—of its usage and to begin anew with a reconstruction of strategic management research. In short, I write this book to place strategic management research on an ethical margin between the daylight of justifiable usefulness for distinct persons and the darkness of irrelevance for those persons acting purposefully at the corporation.

The central thesis of this book is that we have, in truth, good reason to begin anew in search of corporate strategy interpretations that celebrate human endeavor. My critical reading of strategic management research demonstrates that a broad and diverse spectrum of researchers continues to impart an idiosyncratic meaning to the corporate strategy concept. That meaning, which I interpret as Strategy through Process, logically and systematically frustrates persons in their searches for meaning through their own actions at the corporation. Ironically, these persons are the very partners in dialogue that strategic management researchers seek to persuade with their accounts. When assessed from an ethical line of inquiry, Strategy through Process is exposed as an unsuitable subject for that dialogue.

This book also introduces a logic for reconstructing strategic management research in ethical terms. Indeed, I conduct my critical practice by reinterpreting—which amounts to reconstructing—strategic management research as a kind of storytelling about men and women creating and re-creating their lives as they interact in a corporate context. In this regard, my inquiry can be considered an act of literary criticism in ethical terms. Acting as a literary critic, I show that Strategy through Process can be reconstructed as a coherent kind of ethical story that gives one kind of meaning to the corporate strategy concept. Through that same kind of reconstructive effort, I create what I call Strategy & Justice as a second kind of ethical story that strategic management researchers could use. This alternative story turns on assumptions drawn from a contractarian ethical argument, certain feminist critiques, and a modern version of philosophical pragmatism adapted from Rorty. The reconstructive efforts with which I produce Strategy & Justice are significant in three respects.

First, I create Strategy & Justice as a distinct alternative to Strategy through Process. To adopt one story is to eschew the other; I do this quite deliberately. In this way, I demonstrate that strategic management researchers can choose among very different meanings for the corporate strategy concept that they convey to others. Second, I create Strategy & Justice as a means for exposing the comparative weakness of Strategy through Process as a useful ethical account. Third, I create Strategy & Justice as a springboard for interpreting new stories about the corporate strategy concept, stories that can begin to fulfill the worldly, ethical promise of that concept. I conclude my reconstructive efforts by sketching one such story whereby men and women can jointly seek meaning at the corporation by means of conventions that they can create. In all three regards, my point—as a literary critic and an ethical critic—is that there is good ethical reason to continue telling stories with the corporate strategy concept, all the while there is dubious ethical reason for perpetuating the Strategy through Process story in particular.

The upshot is that *The Twilight of Corporate Strategy* can be read, singly or in combination, as (1) an ethical critique of the corporate strategy concept and strategic management research, (2) an ethical reconstruction of the corporate strategy concept and strategic management research, (3) a demonstration of the value of literary and ethical criticism for strategic management inquiry, and (4), by implication, a call for widening the ethical twilight to inlcude other unexamined concepts from the study of management and organizations.

Lewisburg, Penn.   D.R.G.
October 1991

ACKNOWLEDGMENTS

I received support, financial and otherwise, toward the completion of this project from the following sources: the Committee on Faculty Development, College of Arts and Sciences, Department of Management, Administrative Services, and Bertrand Library, all at Bucknell University; the Graduate School, Carlson School of Management, Wilson Library, and Strategic Management Research Center, all at the University of Minnesota; and the Olsson Center for Applied Ethics, as well as the Library, at the Darden School of the University of Virginia. The staff members at the Seven Corners Kinko's in Minneapolis provided their usual first-rate copying services.

Peggy and Ken Finch once again made available their dining room table in New Canaan, Connecticut, for several periods of furious writing and editing, for which I thank Peggy, Ken, and their loyal cat Rocket. Thanks also to Herb Addison, my editor at Oxford University Press, for putting up with the eccentricities of a writer. And I want to extend a special note of recognition to my noontime basketball partners at Bucknell. In the course of my association with them, I rediscovered what an intense hour of basketball can do to aging legs, a creaky shoulder, and a cluttered mind. More than once, my playing relationships with Bud Albee, Ken Ardrey, Julie Bachman, Tom Brett, Pete Cautilli, Terry Conrad, Jeff Crossland, Carl Danzig, Joe Dougherty III, Tom Fantaskey, Kathy Gailor, Rick Hartzell, Brad Hendrixson, Bob Hormell, Andy Jenks, John Link, Toby Lovecchio, Anne McGovern, Mike O'Connor, Tony Pierce, Caroline Shantz, Graham Showalter, Bob Sledzik, John Snyder, Jason Strayer, Joe Susan, and Jack Willoughby made this book easier to complete.

I prefer to think of this book as one destination in an intellectual journey that spans my initial and evolving understandings about corporate strategy, ethical inquiry, and poststructuralist literary criticism. This journey has hardly been a solo effort. Since I could also interpret this book as a commentary about the kinds of research stories that persons can and do share with one another, it is appropriate that I express my gratitude to those many persons whose willingness to consider my story has made this journey a memorable one.

Ed Freeman has been my storytelling colleague throughout this project and beyond. His friendship, generosity, uncommon commitment to autonomous action, search for handball partners, and appreciation of a crisp 4–6–3 double play helped make my four years at the University of Minnesota a turning point in my life. Without Ed's own evolving commitment to the value of twilight, I know what kind of strategic management research I would be conducting today. I shudder at that thought, and I shudder once again at how close I came to participating in such an uncritical, nonhumanist act. I am relieved that this book project is completed; Ed and I have a backlog of stories to tell.

I also consider *The Twilight of Corporate Strategy* to be a justification for, and extension of, the arguments that I helped make with Ed in *Corporate Strategy and the Search for Ethics* and with Ed, Ed Hartman, and John Mauriel in *A Logic for Strategy*. The present book is better for the questions that Ed Hartman and John Mauriel posed along the way. Furthermore, this book marks a complete revision and stronger poststructuralist justification for the arguments presented in the first third of my doctoral dissertation, "Strategy and Justice." I cannot say enough about the critical and crucial support that Ed Freeman, Balaji Chakravarthy, Paul Johnson, and Ken Roering gave to such an unusual kind of research story.

Over the years that led to the writing of this book, I participated in a number of episodes where conversation and storytelling had a profound effect on my interpretations of corporate strategy, ethical inquiry, and poststructuralism. Across this chronology, I want to thank many persons.

The first Seminar in Strategic Management (1984) in the doctoral program at the University of Minnesota: Barbara Edwards, Ed Freeman, John Guarino, Todd Hostager, Roger Hudson, Carol Jacobson, Paula King, Mike Rappa, and William Roering.

The first Organizational Ethics Seminar (1984), led by Ed Freeman, in the doctoral program at the University of Minnesota: Ron Dykstra, Barbara Edwards, Paula King, William Roering, and Shannon Shipp.

The Social Issues in Management Division Doctoral Consortium at the 1985 Academy of Management meetings in San Diego: Archie Carroll, Gerry Cavanagh, Sandra Christensen, Bill Frederick, John Mahon, Elaine Mosakowski, Martha Reiner, and Jim Weber.

The 1987 Liberty Fund Series Conference, "Wealth, Liberty, and Morality," in Fairfax, Virginia: James Buchanan, Robert Frank, David Kreutzer, Thelma Lavine, Jonathan Macey, and Lawrence White.

The 1989 Quality-of-Life/Marketing Conference in Blacksburg, Virginia, where fellow SIMians Steve Brenner, Phil Cochran, Ed Freeman, Tom Jones, John Mahon, Steve Wartick, and Donna Wood sparked a rich critique of my postmodern paper about the stakeholder concept.

Many others, although not participants in these particular conversations, have made a lasting contribution to my thinking about strategic management, social issues in management, and ethical inquiry:

Among the circle of regular partners in conversation and storytelling at the University of Minnesota were Hal Angle, John Bryson, Jeanne Buckeye, Ken Cooper, Janet Dukerich, Dawn Elm, Raghu Garud, Stephen Hoenack, Carol Jacobson, Robert Kudrle, Stefanie Lenway, Doug Polley, Peter Ring, Nancy Roberts, Pete Townley, S. Venkataraman, and Albert Wickesberg. Two remarkable Minnesota students, Kimberly Barron and Mary Nowicki, had a major influence on my early thinking about the ideas that appear here.

Beyond the University of Minnesota campus, my thanks go to John Aram, Doug Austrom, Jeffrey Barach, Norm Bowie, Paul Browne, Marta Calas, Max Clarkson, Robbin Derry, Tom Donaldson, Craig Dunn, Ed Epstein, William Evan, Susan Foote, Karen Gaertner, Barbara Gray, Ron Green, Diana Harrington, Michael Hoffman, Mariann Jelinek, Michael Keeley, Lance Kurke, Larry Lad, Jeanne Liedtka, Mary Mallott, Rick Molz, Richard Nielsen, Jean Pasquero, Mark Pastin, Jack Pearce, Jim Post, Lee Preston, Marjorie Richman, John Rutland, Robert Shively, Linda Smircich, Mark Starik, Ronald Storey, Charles Stubbart, Paul Tiffany, Manuel Velasquez, Sandra Waddock, Richard Weiss, and Tom Wilson.

At Bucknell, I have benefited from a widening set of conversations with Harry Blair, Doug Candland, Joseph Fell, Jim Gillespie, Mary Hill, Laurie Kutchins, Joe LaBarge, Chuck Longley, Gordon Meyer, John Miller, Larry Shinn, Doug Sturm, Tim Sweeney, Mary Evelyn Tucker, Jeff Turner, and Nancy Weida.

The discourse at Bucknell has another important cast of characters as well. This book was thoroughly influenced by my students, who listened to, endured, questioned, and reinterpreted for their own lives my line of postmodern argument about the corporation, from which this book is one destination. Among those who continue to make the Bucknell community a scholarly oasis for me, I take pleasure in thanking Pete Bandarenko, Stephanie DeMarco, Mia Fatta, Alan Fetzer, Michelle Flemming, Jennifer Froehlich, Kathleen Healey, Marcia Hoffman, Wendy Hyer, Mary-Ellen Judd, Bobby LeBlanc, Al Osgood, Anne Pusey, Steven Rocheleau, Laurie Scott, Linda Sein, Todd Singleton, Gary Sorin, Linda Treash, Todd Walrath, Janet West, and Tom Wyka (1987–1988); Barry Davis, Kelly Dekin, Steve Dwyer, Lee Hansen, Amy Harrison, Joe Joyce, James Lowe, Barbara Lowery, Tom Lupo, Kim Parsons, Mike Rapelyea, Kris Reed, Suzette Shaw, June Stratton, Stu Udell, Stu Weitzman, and Laura Williamson (1988–1989); Leo Abbe, Karen Accardi, Jen Adams, Rob Arndt, Jennifer Barlow, Robert Bates, Lisa Boudreau, Lori Coonan, Dan Fetzer, Martin Forken, Holly Hollister,

Gretchen Kamp, Kirsetin Karamarkovich, John Kennedy, Rachel Levenkron, Isabel Lopez, Kari Mason, Marcy McMann, Eric Molicki, Missy Morrill, Kathy Mullin, Christy Nill, Cathy O'Brien, Leonard Panzer, Brian Rhen, Linda Rourke, Marnee Schuermann, Margo Sipiora, Scott Strochak, Ann Sullivan, Glenn Van Alstyne, Margaret Wilkes, Laura Witmer, and Margaret Young (1989–1990).

The evolution of this book, of course, need not be confined to the months and years in which it took shape in printed form. I have come to realize that my humanist interests can be traced to the home that my parents, Joan and Daniel Gilbert, Sr., created for my brothers, Mike, Karl, and Chris, and me. I was privileged and rewarded to be included from an early age among the members of the unpretentious humanist community that I knew as Moravian College in Bethlehem, Pennsylvania, where my father has taught since 1953. I graduated from a school called Freedom High School, where Richard Jay, Ray Salabsky, and Robert Thompson influenced my evolving thinking about self, others, and community. My early education in strategy was likewise a humanist one. I am grateful for the encouragement extended in this regard by Samuel Banks and Anthony Mach at Dickinson College; Kraft Bell and John McNamara at Lehigh University; Don Herman, Daniel McCarthy, John Tomlinson, Elton White, and Vernon Yates at NCR and NCR Comten; and John McKeown and Stuart Weiner at Moravian College.

The evolution of this line of inquiry need not end, either, with the publication of this book. I write *The Twilight of Corporate Strategy* with the hope that the argument can contribute in some way to the day when discourse about the modern corporation, and the associated practice of strategic management, reads more like a novel, drama, poem, or autobiography, and less like astrology and normal social science. For this reason, I dedicate this book to seven members of the next generation. Someday, popular, professional, and academic discourse about the corporation might hold thoroughly humanist meanings for them. I pay particular tribute to Bretton Daniel Finch (son of Peggy and Ken Finch); Emma Wellen Freeman, Molly Wellen Freeman, and Benjamin Wellen Freeman (twin daughters and son, respectively, of Maureen Wellen and Ed Freeman); Victoria Marie Gilbert and John Christopher Gilbert (daughter and son, respectively, of my sister-in-law Cathy Gilbert and my brother Karl Gilbert); and Nicholas Patrick Meyer (son of Pat and Gordon Meyer). From Brett, who has taken his first steps, to John, who has completed the first grade, I am thankful for the eagerness of all seven to engage in the kind of free play at which children are masters and with which they amused me when diversion from this project was necessary.

CONTENTS

The Twilight
of Corporate Strategy

1

Strategic Management Research, Nietzsche, and a Different Question

> What does it matter if you're not playing for the highest stakes? You've got to prove yourself in the pinch, where the pressure is the greatest. You've got to go through the fire!
>
> CHRISTY MATHEWSON,
> in Eric Rolfe Greenberg, *The Celebrant*

Corporate strategy is an idea that can hold great promise. That promise is a logical consequence of the novel perspective on the modern corporation provided by those who study and convey—hereafter, strategic management researchers—the concept of corporate strategy. One particular premise distinguishes this concept from other contemporary vistas on the corporation: that the modern corporation can be understood in terms of human ambition and aspiration—yes, mission, and, even more, *purpose!*[1] The *corporate strategy concept* pertains to a kind of management practice whereby persons systematically attend to questions of purpose in a corporate setting, in anticipation of deriving lasting benefits—profits, market power, personal prestige, or whatever. Alfred Chandler specifies the span of this practice to include "the determination of the basic long-term goals and objectives of an enterprise and the adoption of courses of action and the allocation of resources necessary for carrying out these goals."[2] Chandler and the strategic management researchers who have followed him place the matter of purpose center stage in their accounts of the modern corporation. From this follows the great promise of corporate strategy and the practice of strategic management research.

The concept of purpose conveys generally the possibility that you and I can go about our lives with a sense of hope. More particularly, we can hope—if we think in terms of purpose—first to make sense of an uncertain and changing world and then to cope in progressively

3

more sophisticated ways with those complexities. Purpose thus can serve as a beacon by which we reason about our actions. As we learn to cope purposefully with our worlds, our lives can take on greater meaning for us. This, in turn, bolsters our confidence to weather difficult times and to pursue even more challenging purposes. When we act purposefully in ways that do not interfere with one another's pursuits of self-understanding, then purpose can be understood as a thoroughly *humanist* concept. Thinking about purpose and acting accordingly are endeavors that place great value—and even celebrate—our personhood.[3] My claim that the corporate strategy concept can be a promising idea turns on this hopeful, human-centered—hence "humanist"—conception of purpose.

As a link between persons and their hopes for meaning, on the one hand, and the corporation, on the other, the corporate strategy concept offers the prospect that our understanding of the modern corporation might come to celebrate what the nineteenth-century philosopher Friedrich Nietzsche terms "the profoundest instinct of life, the instinct for the future of life."[4] The promise of strategic management research, then, is that the modern corporation can be studied and managed as a means of fostering this "profoundest instinct" for persons who interact in a corporate context.[5] Persons can believe that their actions make a meaningful difference in a corporate setting by tracing the logical connection among purpose, hope, and corporate strategy.

Chandler's account adds credence to this belief. Through comprehensive attention—that is, "determination," "adoption," and "allocation"—and ongoing attention—that is, "long-term" and "carrying out"—to matters of purpose, men and women acting in Chandler's version of the corporation can ensure that questions of utmost human importance infiltrate corporate activity.[6] Chief among those questions is: Why are we doing this, and not that? In short, the concept of corporate strategy can promise a distinctly hopeful outlook on the modern corporation. This is the promise of a humanist perspective.

A DIFFERENT QUESTION

I wrote this book to assess the promise of corporate strategy as a humanist concept in the liberal sense of humanism as sketched thus far. Each year, strategic management researchers acquaint thousands upon thousands of undergraduates, M.B.A. and doctoral candidates, and consulting clients with the corporate strategy concept.[7] All these students are potential beneficiaries of the hopeful perspective that strategic management research can offer. So, too, are those who are affected by actions taken in the name of corporate strategy, even if they themselves do not practice the logic and techniques of corporate strategy. Given the wide reach of the concept, I aim to analyze how well suited it is for the promising task at hand. Accordingly, this book is an argument crafted around one question:

> Of what value is strategic management research as a humanist perspective on the modern corporation?

Plain and simple, I am interested in the intellectual justification for strategic management research as a human endeavor. It is with this "highest stake" in mind that I choose, for the epigraph to this chapter, an adage that Eric Rolfe Greenberg attributes to the baseball legend Christy Mathewson.[8] I choose to put the corporate strategy concept "through the fire" by questioning its worth as a promising commentary about human endeavor.

This is truly a different kind of question compared to the normal fare in strategic management research. Accustomed as they are to unearthing facts about corporate strategy and corporate performance, strategic management researchers do not routinely take time to debate the merits of the concept from which these fact-finding excavations logically follow.[9] Mine is a different question precisely because it is a question that throws open for debate that which has been heretofore undebatable. Thus I must explain carefully what I intend to do and why that plan is worthwhile.

In particular, I devote the remainder of this chapter to three questions implied by my different question:

1. Why assess the corporate strategy concept? (I address this issue in the section titled "Nietzsche, Twilight, and Strategic Management Research.")
2. What do I intend to argue about the value, or worth, of the corporate strategy concept and strategic management research? (I address this issue in the section titled "Strategic Management Research Beyond Mankind.")
3. How will I conduct this assessment of the corporate strategy concept and strategic management research? (I address this issue in the section titled "One Premise, Two Genres, and a Comparative Showdown.")

Taken together, my answers to these questions constitute my justification for the study. Since I have already, even at this early stage, staked a claim about the different—and, hence, potentially disturbing—character of this book, it is only fitting that I turn next to Nietzsche, a master provocateur.

NIETZSCHE, TWILIGHT, AND STRATEGIC MANAGEMENT RESEARCH

I intend to articulate and defend three compelling reasons for assessing
the worth of the corporate strategy concept and strategic management
research. That we need to consider even one reason to assess the concept might strike many strategic management researchers as more than
a trifle odd. After all, the study of strategic management has, over the
past quarter-century, quickly grown into a full-fledged—indeed, a
booming—enterprise. Journals are devoted to the subject. Hundreds
contribute to a burgeoning research literature. Researchers hold annual conferences and turn out research annuals. Strategic management
consultants reach virtually every corner of the globe. Thus extending
beyond the already impressive scope of attention to corporate strategy
in the business school curriculum, the focus on corporate strategy has
taken an honored place alongside accounting, marketing, finance, and
so on in the way we customarily talk about the business world. By all
conventional measures, strategic management research has "arrived" as
a line of inquiry.[10] So, with all the indicators "up," it might seem pre-
mature, if not preposterous and presumptuous, to talk about questioning the worth of the corporate strategy idea.

The problem is that these indicators can be deceptive. More particularly, those who appeal to these indicators can deceive themselves
through their willingness to idolize—that is, accept with admiration but
without questioning—the "up" signs. After all, the notion of "arrival"
is a contingent one. We cannot give meaning to arrival—whether we
are talking about research or mountain climbing—without reference to
some intended, or at least identifiable, destination. To put it bluntly,
we can always designate a sense of arrival if, and where, we so choose.[11]
We arrive because we seek arrival. Thus "arrival" begs a question about
possible destinations.

For strategic management researchers, the implications of this choice
about destination should be unmistakable. The indicators by which the
arrival of strategic management research has been touted might not
pertain to the kind of question that I pose for this book. What is commonly accepted on faith as "progress" for strategic management research might merely be signposts on a highway that I do not travel
here. In this section, I argue that there are three good reasons for
ignoring these conventional signposts—that is, three good reasons for
assessing the corporate strategy concept. As prelude to that argument,
I turn to Nietzsche, a keen commentator about human progress and
the worth of ideas.

Nietzsche and Progress Through Twilight

Nietzsche's name is seldom encountered among strategic management
researchers. Still, his anonymity need not mask the value to strategic

management researchers—and, for that matter, anyone else—of his concern with the meaning, or truth, of ideas we hold dear.[12] Most prominently, Nietzsche celebrates the possibilities for human thought and action. He argues that ideas and actions are worthwhile if they advance human aims: "My Ego taught me a new pride, I teach it to men: No longer to bury the head in the sand of heavenly things, but to carry it freely, an earthly head which creates meaning for the earth."[13] By placing meaning in an earthly, or worldly, context and in our hands, Nietzsche envisions hope for human endeavor not unlike the hope that I ascribe to the corporate strategy idea. For us to appreciate these possibilities, Nietzsche makes quite clear what the sobering alternative could be.

Nietzsche worries that persons—himself included—can be tempted all too easily to sidestep questions about the truth of their beliefs. We are susceptible to submit self-consciously to this temptation, Nietzsche cautions us, because we value intellectual comfort while we struggle with recurring episodes of doubt about our worth.[14] From the lure of comfort can follow our willingness to confer a permanence on our ideas, to cast them as idols—unchangeable and unassailable.[15] Comforted by idols, Nietzsche warns, we can lose the urge to question and thus we can willingly arrest our growth as persons: "One must invoke tremendous counter-forces in order to cross this natural, all too natural *progressus in simile*, the continual development of man toward the similar, ordinary, average, herdlike—*common!*"[16] From bouts of self-doubt can follow our eagerness to embrace idols that confirm these very doubts, idols valued in terms that transcend worldly activity. In other words, we can accept truths that do not contain a place for us as persons. Nietzsche brands these idols "beyond mankind."[17]

The tragic irony here is that, in our search for truths, we are all too capable of committing mass intellectual self-entrapment.[18] Nietzsche warns us that our choice to idolize beliefs "beyond mankind" can be a choice to suffocate as reflective persons capable of growth. We can always postpone our own efforts to question ourselves and others. We can always simply appeal to the idols, such as a god or rank in the hierarchy or slogan or whatever. To Nietzsche, then, idolatry of beliefs is the enemy of truth and, in turn, human progress.[19]

Nietzsche sketches a daunting solution to this problem. Our noblest endeavor, he argues, is to commit to testing regularly the beliefs to which we look for meaning: "All my progress has been an attempting and a questioning—and truly, one has to *learn* how to answer such questioning!"[20] Since Nietzsche places truth squarely in a human context, the appropriate test for an idea is manifested in what that idea can do for us as a guide for growth.[21] Hence, the promise of an idea is best assessed when the temptation toward idolatry is suspended, or made provisional. In Nietzsche's imagery, that provisional period during which a belief is put to the test of worldly significance can be understood as *twilight* between the idea's popularity—daylight—and its eventual demise—darkness.

In the Nietzschean perspective, then, "twilight" suggests transition between enduring usefulness and irrelevance. More broadly, as we engage new possibilities in our lives and new concepts that can help us, we can understand our progress in terms of passing through periods of twilight, or regular self-review: *to realize in oneself* the eternal joy of becoming—that joy which also encompasses *joy in destruction.*"[22] Since Nietzsche's line of argument addresses human endeavor generally, his logic applies straightforwardly to the concept of corporate strategy and the practice of strategic management research. The notion that corporate strategy can be understood as a worldly practice should come as no surprise to strategic management researchers. After all, in the course of teaching thousands of students about the concept, these researchers claim to their audiences, in effect, "here's an account of the (business) world with you in it."[23] If this were not the claim, then the teaching and research practices with which strategic management researchers occupy themselves would make no sense. The concept of corporate strategy "beyond mankind" seems to be a first-class non sequitur.[24] Crafted as it is around a question of worldly worth for the concept, this book is my attempt to put *corporate strategy and strategic management research in twilight.*

One Reason to Assess the Corporate Strategy Concept

Curiosity is one good reason for assessing corporate strategy as a humanist idea and, hence, practice. Curiosity is an issue in the first place because I pose a question that is virtually unknown in strategic management research.[25] My question is uncommon, in one respect, because I call attention to the very concept of corporate strategy. True, a handful of strategic management researchers do, from time to time, publish commentaries about strategic management research. Time and again, these commentaries leave the corporate strategy concept unscathed. This should hardly come as a surprise. These commentators do not make the concept an issue in the first place.[26] Rather, their analyses—predicated on the unchallengeable value of strategic management research—are concentrated on ways to "fine-tune" strategic management research.[27]

My question is uncommon, moreover, because I proceed on the premise that corporate strategy can be considered an accessible human practice—that is, conducted by men and women generally—and I pose my question in those terms. By contrast, the objects of discussion in the periodic commentaries about strategic management research are other researchers' current efforts and ways in which those efforts can be sharpened. The discussion rarely ventures outside this carefully guarded neighborhood.[28] On both counts, then, I raise a question that, by virtue of its uncommon themes which could lead us to draw uncommon conclusions, makes a prima facie case for following our curiosity.

The upshot here, in Nietzschean terms, is that the corporate strategy concept has never been thrust systematically into twilight.[29] Where strategic management researchers do discuss the meaning of their research, those discussions are held in "broad daylight." The very idea of corporate strategy is never made an issue—that is, designated as a destination for discussion. All this suggests just how idol-bound strategic management research has become.[30]

We can liken this situation to the case of a star baseball pitcher who, in the peak years of his performance, sustains a serious injury to his pitching shoulder. He and his employers might be tempted to assume that, after a suitable recovery period, the pitcher will resume performing at his previous level of prowess. Yet a shoulder injury is a nontrivial matter for any pitcher, so a case can be made for sending the pitcher briefly to the minor leagues for what amounts to a reevaluation of his skills. The shoulder injury—akin to my premise that the corporate strategy concept holds promise as a humanist idea—adds a new perspective to the pitcher's pursuits. That new twist alone does not provide sufficient reason for doubting the pitcher's recovery—or, by analogy, the promise of strategic management research. Still, there is reason to be curious.[31] The pitcher and his employers, just as you and I, might all learn something in the twilight.

Another Reason to Assess the Corporate Strategy Concept

Criticisms leveled at business school curricula and research underscore a second good reason for evaluating the corporate strategy concept. Although the critics rarely take aim at corporate strategy per se, we can follow their arguments toward a logical, and unflattering, prima facie case against strategic management research. The route to such a conclusion follows from the connection between the corporate strategy concept and the concept of purpose. In this way, the critics of business schools give further impetus—that is, more than general curiosity—for examining strategic management research as a humanist endeavor.

Consider three charges commonly voiced by critics of business schools.[32] First, business schools allegedly subordinate imagination and creativity to "number crunching" and other efforts to conserve organizational power structures.[33] Second, business schools allegedly emphasize the financial techniques of what Robert Reich calls "paper entrepreneurialism" at the expense of manufacturing, product quality, and customer service.[34] Third, business schools allegedly breed a "get mine first and always" approach to human interaction, thereby denying the value of a more expansive ethical disposition.[35] We can understand all three charges in terms of purpose. Accordingly, the corporate strategy concept could be indicted on each count.

Take first the argument about creativity. We could make a historical case that purposeful striving toward new and uncommon achievements—rather than striving for organizational control—is a recurring theme in American business history. Henry Ford reportedly fired his "number crunchers" as impediments to progress.[36] Alexander Graham Bell, the Wright brothers, Frank Lloyd Wright, and young Lee Iacocca likely did not fret over organizational charts and return-on-investment data. Understood in this framework, the subordination of creativity suggests an aversion to purpose as a liberating, humanist idea.[37]

Consider next the criticism that financial acumen and corporate management skills have become nearly synonymous. We could defend this criticism on the grounds that the purposes for business enterprise can routinely encompass interests—such as customers' claims—that range far beyond the seventeenth-century emphasis on shareholders holding property-rights claims on the corporation.[38] In this sense, the subordination of manufacturing and quality concerns suggests an aversion to thinking about purpose as a general human concern.

Take last the claim that ethical issues in business encompass much more than self-gratification. A defense for the act of infusing business school curricula with ethical study turns on the premise that civilized communities are vulnerable if purposeful pursuits are not restrained. Thus sketchy attention to ethical responsibility implies an aversion to thinking about purposeful action in contextual terms.[39] The critics could be understood to argue that business school curricula divorce purpose from the contexts within which purposes can flourish. A "me first" assumption logically follows from that separation.

Vulnerability for strategic management research. We can deduce, then, the following proposition that links these three criticisms of business schools: a restricted and diluted conception of purpose has infiltrated business school teaching and research. Here is where twilight can begin to encroach on the corporate strategy concept and strategic management research. If it stands apart from other business school concepts for its focus on purpose, then the finger of criticism could logically point at the corporate strategy concept.

That pointing could become all the more insistent when we add to this reasoning the fact that the culmination, or "capstone," of undergraduate business and M.B.A. programs is typically a course in strategic management and business policy. If business school professors use the corporate strategy idea to integrate the business curriculum, and if that curriculum is under fire from many quarters, then there is at least a prima facie reason for assessing the corporate strategy concept. In Nietzschean terms, others are moving closer to casting corporate strategy and strategic management research into twilight. A response from within the business school community might just be in order. By analogy, if a baseball team is scoring few runs, the team manager has some cause for evaluating the performance of the "clean-up" hitter. Furthermore, the manager might want to initiate the inquiry, rather than have members of the press or an impatient team owner do so.

A Third Reason to Assess the Corporate Strategy Concept

A persistent pall, a debilitating gloom, has fallen on the modern corporation as an arena for human endeavor. This pall provides a third, and compelling, reason for assessing the corporate strategy concept and strategic management research. A sense of hope about the opportunities for persons to engage in meaningful action at a corporation is as uncommon as it is sorely needed. Hopefulness about the corporation as an instrument of human meaning has drained steadily from the intellectual "neighbors" of strategic management research: management theory and organization science.[40] At the same time in parallel, the futility of human action at the corporation and in the marketplace can be read as a persistent theme in twentieth-century literature. Many writers have doubted the possibility for purpose and human meaning, if not altogether evicted them from their perspectives on the modern corporation. Corporate strategy, as a practice of purposeful action in a corporate context, can offer a way to reclaim purpose from the darkness into which many have tossed the idea. To determine whether corporate strategy is up to this stiff challenge, we must assess the very concept.

Management theory and organization science. A dark shadow on purposeful human endeavor has converged from two directions in management theory and organization science. Both streams of shadow are products of a modern fascination with the organization and, more particularly, the corporation as an entity. This fascination is manifest in researchers' efforts to idolize the corporation as something worth preserving.

One shadowy logical consequence of this fascination is the premise that workers must necessarily subordinate their purposes and pursuits to the "survival" of the corporation. There have been many expressions of this assumption.

Peter Drucker asserted in 1946:

> Because the corporation is an institution it must have a basic policy. For it must subordinate individual ambitions and decisions to the needs of the corporation's welfare and survival.[41]

The efficiency of an institution depends on . . . the extent to which it organizes man for his moral victory over himself.[42]

Daniel Katz and Robert Kahn claimed in 1966:

Since the individual is involved in a social system with only a part of himself, he might readily behave less as a member of any given organization and more in terms of some compromise. . . . There must be clarity of demands and constraints upon him so that he will give unto Caesar what is Caesar's.[43]

And Kenneth Goodpaster and John Matthews defend the notion of corporate social responsibility in terms of a corporation having a conscience. That conscience, they argue, exists apart from, and is more determinative than, the humans who reason in a corporate setting.[44]

Against this kind of backdrop, it should not be surprising that the grail, and eventual dependent variable, in management theory and organization science research is "organizational effectiveness." This proxy for organizational "survival" has nothing to do with distinct persons per se.

A second shadowy derivative of this idolatry is the well-known premise that persons possess very limited reasoning abilities and therefore need considerable assistance to function at the corporation. The corporation must, on this view, provide such assistance in "its" interest. In Nietzschean terms, this proposition marks the logic of a self-confirming argument about the corporation's worth "beyond mankind." A classic rendition of this proposition comes from Herbert Simon:

The behavior patterns which we call organizations are fundamental, then, to the achievement of human rationality in any broad sense. The rational individual is, and must be, an organized and institutionalized individual. If the severe limits imposed by human psychology . . . are to be relaxed, the individual must in his decisions be subject to the influences of the organized group in which he participates.[45]

Katz and Kahn discuss the problem in terms of controlling the limited range of human reasoning: "Much of the energy of organizations must be fed into devices of control to reduce the variability of human behavior and to produce stable patterns of activity."[46]

More recently, a host of organization scientists cast doubt on the meaningfulness of human reasoning in corporate settings.[47] Jeffrey Pfeffer argues that a research emphasis on individual decision-making "belies the facts" and yields "unproductive theory."[48] Gareth Morgan suggests substituting a "cybernetic" model of strategic management for a model centered on human choice.[49] Graham Astley rejects managers' decision-making autonomy in favor of a "collective strategy" account, and Andrew Van de Ven and Astley relegate human choice to one end of a "deterministic—voluntaristic" continuum.[50] The assault on human reasoning—and thus purpose—has long been under way in management theory and organization science research and teaching.[51]

Modern literature and human purpose at the corporation. More widely, a host of twentieth-century writers have, through fiction and nonfiction alike, cast doubt on business and corporate activity as meaningful for people like you and me. Studs Terkel, John Dos Passos, Arthur Miller, Theodore Dreiser, and Sinclair Lewis, to name a few, give us food for thought about the banal entrapments of a "business culture."[52] John Marquand, Sloan Wilson, Jan Kubicki, Upton Sinclair, George Lee Walker, and George Orwell, for example, acquaint us with the horrors, in humanist terms, of corporations and collectives.[53] Against this enduring and darkened backdrop—and in view of a similar drift in management theory and organization science—the idea that corporate activity can be organized around purpose and persons is a rare and fragile blossom.

The upshot here is that an assessment of the corporate strategy concept is justifiable for the same reason that a baseball manager goes to extra lengths to be patient with a star hitter mired in an 0-for-40 slump: the promise of extraordinary performance requires nurturing. So a journey by the corporate strategy concept through twilight can assure us that the promise of strategic management research can be fulfilled. Or it can signal the need for major rehabilitation. Either way, this assurance is crucial. Without the hopeful prospects implied by corporate strategy, management and the modern corporation become dubious— if not irrelevant—institutions for you and me.

Segue

I have defended an assessment of corporate strategy and strategic management research "in twilight" with three reasons that accumulate with an increasing sense of urgency. First, since such a review is new in strategic management research, who knows what might result? Second, with others from outside the strategic management research community aiming brickbats in the vicinity of the corporate strategy concept, there might be value in conducting a "friendly" preemptive analysis, one that follows from an understanding of the concept. Third, when we survey the intellectual context within which the corporate strategy idea has been shaped, we confront a sobering contrast between the hopeful promise of strategic management research and the overt skepticism in management theory and organization science regarding persons and purposes.

In short, the stakes are high. If we choose to view the corporation as a source of human progress rather than darkness and suppression, then we must be thoroughly convinced that strategic management research can satisfy this humanist longing. Thus before I push the corporate strategy concept well into twilight, I turn next to sharpen further the case for corporate strategy as a humanist idea.

PURPOSE AND THE HOPEFUL PROMISE OF CORPORATE STRATEGY

It is important that we reflect on just how thoroughly hopeful the concept of purpose can be. More specifically, we can derive a general message of hope not only from the concept of purpose, but also from several variations on that hopeful theme.[54] In this section, I examine three such variations and argue that each applies to everyday pursuits—citing cases from my own experience—as readily as to the practice of corporate strategy—citing issues that confront managers in the modern telecommunications industry. I pursue this line of reasoning in order to make two points.

1. We can build an even stronger justification for the premise that purpose is a hopeful concept by considering a range of applications of purpose.
2. We can better understand the humanist promise of strategic management research by drawing parallels between purposeful pursuits "outside" and "inside" the corporate context.[55]

Purpose as Possibility

A concern with purpose, first of all, can emphasize the alternatives, or possibilities, that we can choose to pursue. Purpose can serve as an invitation to believe that, as Hazel Barnes puts it, "the human being is a free consciousness facing an open future."[56] It is the potential for openness in that future, the availability of options, that gives reason for hope as we consider matters of purpose. I can aspire to develop an aesthetic sense through baseball, gardening, and photography. And I can aspire to participate with others in governance activities at my alma mater. I can adopt an optimistic stance toward my endeavors, in part, from knowing that options such as these are available.[57] This hopeful perspective is likewise pertinent for executives engaged in corporate strategy practice at American Telephone and Telegraph (AT&T). In the wake of the 1984 AT&T divestiture, these executives can draw a measure of optimism from the range of diversification and collaborative options never before available to them.[58]

Purpose and Worth

A concern with purpose, additionally, can call attention to the worth of our pursuits. We can usefully think of purpose as a standard that enables us first to clarify and then to evaluate what we do. Mark Pastin speaks to purpose and clarification: "Remember that purpose answers one of our most important questions: when you have collected the information and done the analysis, where do you stand to decide and act?"[59] To the question "Where do you stand?" Barnes adds a consideration akin to "Why is it worthwhile to stand there?" arguing that to act on purpose is to exercise "the will to live the life which may be reflectively appraised as holding in truth the greatest value."[60] What is hopeful here is the prospect that purpose facilitates our efforts to justify our lives to ourselves and others. With purpose as a standard of value, we need not choose haphazardly. I can consider abandoning the game of golf, for example, in terms of whether golf or handball is more worthwhile to me as a form of relaxation. At the same time, I can set up this choice about golf as a decision between the worth of my leisurely and professional pursuits. Either way, purpose helps me evaluate my actions, and I draw encouragement from the opportunity to do so.[61]

For executives at AT&T, the American market for long-distance telecommunications services provides a similar chance to evaluate purposefully. By any measure, AT&T's market share among residential long-distance users has been significantly eroded since 1984 by such competitors as MCI and US Sprint.[62] On the one hand, these executives can weigh the merits of various competitive responses in terms of regaining lost market share as a valued aim. Alternatively, they could capitalize on this situation to weigh the value of regaining market share versus seeking regulatory reform.[63] Either way, to apply the practice of corporate strategy here is to engage in the practice of assessing the very worth of actions taken in the name of AT&T. Executives can find encouragement in this act, competitive pressures notwithstanding, when they consider how much more difficult it is to act without a standard of worth.

Purpose and Continuity

A concern with purpose also suggests a continuity to our endeavors, a pattern that we can ascribe across what we have done in the past, do now, and value doing tomorrow.[64] Pastin notes, in this spirit, "Purposes persist. . . . Purposes are never completed; at a given time, they are either being lived up to or not."[65] Two reasons for optimism can follow from this persistence.

In one respect, the concept of purpose offers hope that we can entertain a stable sense of "who we are."[66] We can claim this sense of identity by retracing our actions in terms of a patterned attempt to fulfill our purposes. Operating then with a continuous sense of myself—that is, acting authentically—I can make more confident judgments of my progress as a friend, son, and tennis player. Robert Coles speaks to purpose, authenticity, and history as he recalls a session with a patient: "I explained that we all had accumulated stories in our lives, that each of us had a history of such stories, that no one's stories are quite like anyone else's, and that we could, after a fashion, become our own appreciative and comprehending critics by learning to pull together the various incidents in our lives."[67] The same connection between continuity and authenticity can be a source of encouragement for executives at the seven Bell regional holding companies (RHCs) created from the AT&T divestiture. More than a few regulators, consumer advocates, and customers have expressed concern that the Bells' predivestiture spirit of "universal service" has been diluted as RHC executives pursue nontelecommunications ventures.[68] With "universal service" in mind as a persistent theme, these executives can retrace their efforts since 1984 in terms of a continual saga of service. This, in turn, enables them first to thoroughly assess whether the critics have a point and then to justify to themselves and others the brand of service forthcoming from a RHC. Once again, the optimistic note is that the continuity of purpose can enrich our reasoned actions.

In a second respect, the persistence of purpose encourages us to think about our endeavors as a composite search for meaning. With search comes the hope that we can make progress—that is, seek out greater challenge and worth in what we do.[69] If I accept running as an activity in my search for diversions, and if I seek a pattern in my approach to running, then I can take heart that I have come to run less on a competitive impulse and more as a time to reflect. Hence, I no longer enter twenty-kilometer races, I run while planning segments of teaching and writing, and I believe that this historical pattern marks progress. Likewise, RHC executives can understand state and federal regulation in terms of their own search for fewer restrictions on RHC diversification. In this way, they can encourage themselves about the pattern of regulatory reforms approved by certain state commissions and U.S. District Court Judge Harold Greene.[70] Alternatively, absent a perspective of search, these executives could work themselves into a lather of frustration, and perhaps rash action, over the fact that the RHCs remain comprehensively regulated.

I have argued that the concept of purpose can inform and guide an option-filled, justifiable, and coherent search for meaning in our endeavors. On all three counts, purpose implies hopefulness, whether we practice scholarship, parenthood, or corporate strategy. It turns out that Kenneth Andrews, one of the pioneers in the study of the corporate strategy concept, paints a similarly optimistic portrait of the practice. To Andrews, the concept of purpose commands priority on an executive's agenda. He goes so far as to designate the executive as, among other things, the "architect of purpose."[71] To meet this architectural challenge, Andrews argues, the "prototype" executive must "mak[e] sure in what is done and the changes pioneered in purpose and practice that the game is worth playing, the victory worth seeking, and life and career worth living."[72] With his emphasis on possibilities ("changes pioneered in purpose"), purpose and value ("worth"), and purposeful action as a search ("playing . . . seeking . . . living"), Andrews offers endorsement in this passage for the premise that corporate strategy can be a thoroughly humanist practice. The promise of corporate strategy and strategic management research is that much more plausible. The problem, however, is that this promise is fast slipping from our grasp.

STRATEGIC MANAGEMENT RESEARCH BEYOND MANKIND

The centerpiece of this book is an argument that the corporate strategy concept, as strategic management researchers have shaped the idea over several decades, falls well short of the hopeful promise that it can deliver. Strategic management researchers have come to rely on premises that provide little assurance that the modern corporation can be a meaningful setting for persons. They have, in short, driven hope about the corporation from their theories and models and frameworks. More specifically, I will articulate and defend the following three-part thesis in this regard:

1. By means of an idiosyncratic—yet quite consistent—logic, strategic management researchers have nearly severed the link between the concept of purpose in a corporate context and the persons who can interact purposefully in that context. In other words, purposeful action by persons is quite circumscribed in that logic.
2. This idiosyncrasy is a widespread feature of strategic management research, reaching into many diverse corners of that enterprise and cutting across many ostensible boundaries among strategic management theories and models and frameworks.
3. This idiosyncrasy has an irrevocable logic that cannot be reworked to reconnect purposes and individuals at the corporation. Accordingly, this logic is largely unusable as a humanist interpretation of the modern corporation.

My analysis thus depicts a Nietzschean nightmare that pervades strategic management research: the corporate strategy concept pertains to a practice that strategic management researchers systematically and irretrievably place "beyond mankind." The nightmarish result is chilling twice over, once for explaining a human activity in terms that diminish the importance of human activity and, then again, for doing this to so central a human concern as purpose. My conclusion on this score is straightforward: we must begin anew in our thinking about corporate strategy and hence strategic management research as a human endeavor.

I say "begin anew" for one very important reason. My analysis gives us reason to reject the proposition that the widespread contemporary approach to strategic management research is a convincing humanist perspective on the modern corporation. yet my analysis does not necessarily enable us to close the curtains on—driving into darkness—the corporate strategy idea per se. In fact, there are good reasons not to eschew the corporate strategy concept, not the least of which are (1) the darkening pall about the corporation that we can read throughout the management theory and organization science literature, and (2) the premise that the corporate strategy concept can begin to drive away that gloom.[73]

For this reason, I answer the question that I pose for the book—Of what value is strategic management research as a humanist perspective on the modern corporation?—with the reply: *Not much, as currently interpreted.* This qualifier is crucial, for it underscores my line of argument throughout this study.

ONE PREMISE, TWO GENRES, AND A COMPARATIVE SHOWDOWN

I predicate my line of argument in this book on the premise that the corporate strategy concept is well worth nurturing. What is not worth nurturing, I argue, is the particular meaning given to the concept by a broad spectrum of strategic management researchers. So, in order to draw this distinction, I must develop my thesis about contemporary strategic management research in the course of justifying—that is, giving good reasons for—the corporate strategy concept. There is certainly an ironic twist to this effort: I reject, as insufficiently humanist, a broad swath of strategic management research *because* the corporate strategy concept can hold promise in humanist terms. The irony is deliberate. It is also quite defensible.

I defend the corporate strategy concept, as a prospective humanist idea, on the basis of four propositions. Given the absence of a research tradition in strategic management research circles for asking questions like the one I pose here, my search for—and defense of—these propositions takes me into a new territory of inquiry for strategic management. In that territory, spanning recent arguments in literary criticism and philosophy, the assessment of concepts and meanings is the primary research focus.

Corporate Strategy as a Literary Idea

If the corporate strategy concept is worth nurturing for its humanist promise, then it must pertain, at a minimum, to human beings acting on their own "turf" over time. The key here is not only the focus on the meaningfulness of action as a personal force, but also the element of time.[74] George Eliot reminds us about the danger of taking in but a glimpse of a person's endeavors: "The fragment of a life, however typical, is not the sample of an even web: promises may not be kept, and an ardent outset may be followed by declension; latent powers may find their long-awaited opportunity; a past error may urge a grand retrieval."[75] My point is that a humanist version of strategic management research must provide for persons coping with their ups and downs, with their achievements, failings, and recurring nemeses. If the corporate strategy concept can satisfy this condition, it joins company with a rich and timeless set of traditions whereby persons have pondered and written stories about the problems of human coping. Coles frames such coping in these terms:

> The whole point of stories is not "solutions" or "resolutions" but a broadening and even a heightening of our struggles—with new protagonists and antagonists introduced, with new sources of concern or apprehension or hope, as one's mental life accommodates itself to a series of arrivals: guests who have a way of staying, but not necessarily staying put."[76]

It is this ever-changing accommodation of "guests" that serves as the focus of storytelling traditions known as *literature*. To wit, a first step in the defense of the corporate strategy concept involves thinking about the concept as a literary idea.

Startling as this characterization might seem at first, the literary potential of corporate strategy can be readily explained. Coles asks us to think of literature as "renderings of life."[77] The novelist, the poet, the biographer, the critic, and anyone else who tells stories attempts to render certain aspects of our lives more understandable, more meaningful. Some write about the passage to adulthood. Others tell stories about love. Still others try to make sense of mortality. More than a few deal with family relationships. Each rendition can add meaning to the reader's understanding of a part of her life.[78] Each, in literary terms, provides an *interpretation* of adulthood, love, or whatever her subject may be.[79]

Literature, on this line of reasoning, is composed of a host of interpretations about persons' efforts to make sense, cope, and grow in line with their purposes. Since a constant in literary endeavors is the problem of, and hope for, human striving, there is no logical reason why the corporate strategy concept will be turned away at the door.[80] It so happens as Chandler notes, that it conventionally pertains to such matters as the determination and enactment of goals at the modern corporation, just as it so happens that a host of contemporary novelists deal with baseball as a context for learning about regret.[81] Both kinds of story can be literary. For corporate strategy to satisfy this literary condition, then, the concept must serve as an impetus for interpretations about persons and their lives at the modern corporation.

Corporate Strategy as Genre

If the corporate strategy concept is worth nurturing for its humanist promise—and, hence, for its literary vitality—then any interpretation about corporate strategy practice must apply extensively across a range of contexts in which persons strive to deal with their lives and one another. Put somewhat differently, the spotlight must shine in each "act" of the story on persons and their endeavors to cope at the modern corporation. By "act" I mean the assumptions, propositions, and conclusions that constitute an interpretation. Continuing with the theatrical metaphor, it is not enough to satisfy this condition by placing human striving off-stage in the wings. Nor is it enough to make a gratuitous reference to such striving with a grand wave of the hand and cape.[82] At issue here is whether the corporate strategy concept can serve as a rallying point for multiple and diverse stories about persons acting and interacting in a corporate setting.[83] In this way, my second condition supplements my first condition as it toughens the requirements for justifying the concept.

The literary value of the corporate strategy concept rests with attention to human coping in the first place. I now add a requirement that such coping be a persistent theme running across a host of stories about corporate strategy. If the first condition checks whether the concept provides an impetus for interpretations made with a human flavor, the second condition requires that particular kinds of ongoing concerns with persons must infuse interpretations about strategic practices. I include this second test, then, in a Nietzschean spirit, as another check on the temptation to render corporate strategy meaningful in some region beyond persons at the corporation. In short, the more persistent the interpretive emphasis on persons and their purposeful coping, the stronger the case for corporate strategy as a humanist idea.

In literary terms, a persistent interpretive theme is commonly known as a *genre*.[84] For our purposes here, we can think of a genre as a kind of recurring theme, or story line, about a particular kind of human concern. In this sense, a genre is an interpretation of a common thread that runs across a host of stories. The pertinence of genre for corporate strategy, although a novel connection, can be explained readily by sketching a parallel between strategic management research stories and other kinds of literature.

If we search for a recurring theme, for example, in a set of novels about immigrants' struggles to adapt to American life at the turn of the twentieth century, we can interpret one genre that attributes many of their difficulties to the power wielded by corporate tycoons.[85] We can expect multiple genres about a given literary theme as well. Thus with regard to the question whether corporate work assignments can satisfy individuals' creative drives, we can contrast the genre with which Tracy Kidder writes about the "Hardy Boys" engineers in *The Soul of a New Machine* with the genre through which Sloan Wilson portrays Tom Rath, a speechwriter, in *The Man in the Gray Flannel Suit.*[86]

In parallel, Chandler's argument that "structure follows strategy" has endured as a genre of strategic management research.[87] So, too, has a derivative genre to the effect that "effective" strategic practice turns on senior executives' abilities to read signs of change in a firm's environment.[88] At this point, of course, the issue of whether or not these and other possible genres about corporate strategy can be thoroughly infused with human concerns remains unresolved.

Corporate Strategy as a Pragmatist Idea

If the corporate strategy concept is worth nurturing for its humanist promise—and, hence, for its durability in terms of literary genre—then any preferred genre about corporate strategy must provide comparatively greater coverage of human endeavor than does some other genre about corporate strategy. Once again, this test of worthiness takes place where men and women are acting and interacting on the "turf" of their concerns at the modern corporation. By this third condition for justifying the corporate strategy concept, a genre about corporate strategy in terms of, say, anthropological concepts must be distinguishable from genres developed in terms of, say, biology and astrophysics. Moreover, the former genre must be preferred—by researchers and the subjects of their stories—to the latter two, if this condition is to be satisfied. I say this on the assumption that concepts from anthropology accord more favorable room for human reasoning as an impetus for human growth than do concepts from biology and astrophysics—and, for that matter, astrology.[89]

At issue therefore is whether, at any given time, we are working with the most generally human genre that can be concocted for making interpretations of corporate strategy. Given the broad scope of contemporary strategic management research, it is reasonable to expect that genres—for starters, those drawn from economics, sociology, and social psychology—will abound.[90] My third condition highlights a Nietzschean kind of concern with this flood of genres. It is one thing for a genre about corporate strategy to address persons' actions and inter-actions. It is still another for a particular interpretation to gain favor and persist. Yet even here, with my first two conditions specified for a justifiable corporate strategy concept, the temptation to become self-satisfied can arise. In Nietzschean terms, this is the temptation to idol-ize a genre simply for the coherent comfort that it offers.

It is still another matter, this third issue, as to whether any persistent stories about corporate strategy help us understand more richly—or even keep us "in touch with"—the changing course of human activity at the modern corporation. Unless provision is made for reviewing genres in a worldly context, such as at the corporation, strategic management research runs the risk of becoming a basement cluttered with familiar, but musty, stories.[91] For this reason, my third condition bolsters the first two criteria for defending the corporate strategy concept. A com-parative approach to defending the concept enables us to discard less extensive genres while not impeding a search for better genres.

This concern with the comparative, worldly relevance of ideas is a hallmark of a philosophical and literary tradition known as *pragmatism.* The overriding pragmatist criterion of worth for an idea is the useful-ness, or, to paraphrase Richard Rorty, the "cashability," of that idea for persons as they go about their activities.[92] A pragmatist perspective combines a persistent emphasis on worldly usefulness—hence pragma-tism—with an assumption that we are, again drawing from Rorty, al-ways "en route" in our searches for better ways to cope with our lives.[93] Accordingly, pragmatism implies a disposition to compare. If one idea fails to assist us make sense of the modern corporation, for example, then we can always hold out hope that another concept will enhance our understanding. Pragmatism provides, in short, the very kind of hopefulness that I seek in building a case for corporate strategy as a humanist idea.

Corporate Strategy as an Ethical Concept

Finally, if the corporate strategy concept is worth nurturing for its hu-manist promise—and, therefore, worthy for literary genre(s) that sat-isfy a pragmatist criterion—then any genre about corporate strategy must interpret strategic practice in ethical terms. As I sharpen my de-fense of the corporate strategy concept by moving from literature to genre to pragmatism, I add more and more to a kind of interpretation about corporate strategy that accords the most favorable status—a lib-eral humanist status—that we can provide for persons. For corporate strategy to support such humanist stories about the modern corpora-tion, it is necessary, but still deficient, to (1) stage the action in terms of persons striving, advancing, and regressing over time; (2) maintain the focus consistently and solely in such terms; and (3) defend the preferability of that kind of story over a contender. We can do better still.[94] What can be added to these three criteria is an explicit assurance that these stories about human activity are predicated on the dignity of those persons and the unabashed celebration of their struggles.[95] In search of this supplemental piece, I turn to the study of ethics.

Throughout ethical analysis and discourse, priority is given to persons, their purposes, and their problematic efforts at living peaceably with one another. As John Rawls notes so elegantly: "Justice is the first virtue of social institutions. . . . Each person possesses an inviolability founded on justice that even the welfare of society as a whole cannot override."[96] Human pursuits are celebrated by an ethicist in the same sense as a physicist celebrates the wonders of the atom.[97] Inquiry about ethics and physics proceeds from these respective premises about what is worthwhile. If the corporate strategy concept is to satisfy this stringent fourth condition, then stories about corporate strategy must give priority to human action and interaction. Certainly, there is nothing about the concept, as I have connected it to purpose, that logically impedes satisfaction of this criterion. So, through the possibility that corporate strategy and ethical analysis share a common concern with persons and purposeful action, we can interpret corporate strategy as an ethical idea—that is, an idea that bears ethical implications.[98]

Consequently, my search for reasons with which to justify the corporate strategy concept in humanist terms leads me to search for ethical genres about corporate strategy. This search, the culmination of interrelated literary, genre, and pragmatist considerations, will result in my rejection of a broad range of contemporary strategic management research along the way. This is an ironic, but fully defensible, conclusion that I develop as I sharpen my research question from, Of what value is strategic management research as a humanist perspective on the modern corporation? to read, alternatively.

> Of what relative value is strategic management research as
> an ethical interpretation of the modern corporation?

In other words, I write this book as an ethical analysis in search for a humanist conception of corporate strategy that strategic management researchers can use.

SUMMARY AND IMPLICATIONS

In sum, then, I construct my defense of the corporate strategy concept, and thus reject the drift of contemporary strategic management research, with reference to four propositions about the corporate strategy concept.

1. If the corporate strategy concept is worth nurturing for its humanist promise, then corporate strategy must pertain, at a minimum, to human beings acting on their own "turf" over time.
2. If the corporate strategy concept is worth nurturing for its humanist promise—and, hence, for its literary vitality—then any interpretation about corporate strategy must apply extensively across a range of contexts in which persons deal with their lives and one another.
3. If the corporate strategy concept is worth nurturing for its humanist promise—and, hence, for its durability in terms of literary genre— then any preferred genre about corporate strategy must provide comparatively greater coverage of human endeavor than some other genre about corporate strategy.
4. If the corporate strategy concept is worth nurturing for its humanist promise—and, therefore, worthy for literary genre(s) that satisfy a pragmatist criterion—then any genre about corporate strategy must interpret the concept in ethical terms.

Each proposition provides a partial, and provisional, answer to the question that I pose for this study: Of what value is strategic management research as a humanist perspective on the modern corporation? Each proposition sets a condition that, if satisfied, enables us to push the corporate strategy concept that much further along as a worthy humanist interpretation of the modern corporation. At the most challenging extent of this test for corporate strategy lies the possibility that the practice of corporate strategy can be justifiable for ethical reasons.[99] I have organized the chapters in this book to follow this line of reasoning, which is summarized in Figure 1.1.

Placing Corporate Strategy in Twilight

In Chapter 2, I discuss the enterprise of research generally in terms of literature, genre, pragmatism, and ethics. I move from talking about the corporate strategy *concept* in this way—an issue in Chapter 1—to interpreting what is means for *researchers* to interpret stories through genre in a pragmatist, ethical manner. On this basis, I defend the applicability of pragmatism and ethical inquiry to strategic management research and defend accordingly my analytical approach for the book. In short, I intend in Chapter 2 to defend my genre of Nietzschean inquiry about the corporate strategy concept and, accordingly, strategic management research.

In Chapter 3, I assess strategic management research in terms of literature, genre, pragmatism, and ethics. On a literary point, I argue that a wide range of strategic management researchers do, in fact, focus their analyses of corporate strategy on human "turf." I call this particular literary genre the *Problem of Strategic Management,* and I show

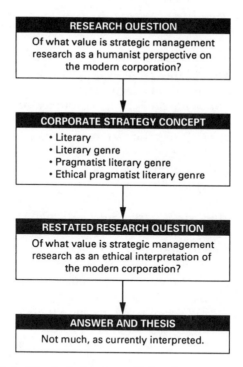

Figure 1.1. The logic for the twilight of corporate strategy.

that strategic management researchers tend to make three assumptions about the corporate strategy concept on that turf. For each assumption, I argue that the related concept of *strategy* provides a common thread.

By what I call the *Human Decision Assumption,* corporate strategy involves a program of decision-making that informs purposeful action at the corporation. As Andrews puts it: "Corporate strategy is the pattern of decisions in a company that determines and reveals its objectives, purposes, or goals."[100]

By what I call the *Interrelationship Assumption,* corporate strategy deals with what others "outside" the corporation are doing. Particular emphasis is given to competitors in this regard. Michael Porter begins his discussion of strategy with this in mind: "The essence of formulating competitive strategy is relating a company to its environment . . . the key aspect of the firm's environment is the industry or industries in which it competes."[101]

By what I call the *Advantage Assumption,* the whole point of practicing corporate strategy is to better the chances of gaining an enduring position amid forces "outside" the corporation that influence the enactment of a strategy. Porter observes: "The goal of competitive strategy . . . is to find a position in the industry where the company can best defend itself against these competitive forces or can influence them in its favor."[102]

The key part of this analysis is my argument that this logical structure for the Problem of Strategic Management is held in common across a diverse group of strategic management researchers. Thus I show that a powerful genre of writing about the corporate strategy concept can be read in strategic management research writings. In particular, I read twelve interpretations of corporate strategy, written by sixteen strategic management researchers, and interpret considerable support for these three assumptions about the Problem of Strategic Management. These writers include Kenneth Andrews; Igor Ansoff; Kathryn Rudie Harrigan; Lawrence Hrebiniak and William Joyce; Peter Lorange; Robert Miles; Raymond Miles and Charles Snow; Michael Porter; James Brian Quinn; Quinn, Henry Mintzberg, and Robert James; Alfred Rappaport; and Dan Schendel and Charles Hofer. This "group of twelve" is an important analytical device for the remainder of the study.

Moving further with the question of genre, I argue that, across the group of twelve, a particular genre about the Problem of Strategic Management enjoys wide popularity. Because these researchers hold in common an interest in the acquisition, or processing, of decisions about strategy, I call this genre *Strategy through Process*. I argue that Strategy through Process can be read as a pragmatist, ethical story about the Problem of Strategic Management. With Chapter 3, then, I defend my claim that the corporate strategy concept can pass muster on my four propositions.

In Chapter 4, I consider the Problem of Strategic Management from a different angle. The centerpiece of the chapter is a second genre about the Problem of Strategic Management. I interpret this genre from the standpoint of a contractarian tradition in ethical discourse. With pragmatist and ethical considerations in mind, I argue that this second genre—which I call *Strategy & Justice*—also provides a coherent rendition of the Problem of Strategic Management genre. Hence, this second genre is suitable for a comparative showdown with Strategy through Process.[103] With Strategy & Justice, the focus rests on the meaningfulness of a given strategy for the men and women who pursue and are affected by that strategy in their interactions with one another. The focus is not on how to acquire a strategy.

In Chapter 5, I conduct a comparative showdown. I argue that for each of the three assumptions that constitute the Problem of Strategic Management genre, Strategy & Justice provides a more persuasively humanist interpretation than does Strategy through Process. On the strength of this comparative assessment, conducted in the spirit of defending the corporate strategy concept, I conclude that Strategy through Process simply will not work for strategic management researchers, for pragmatist and ethical reasons. My plan for placing the corporate strategy concept in twilight is depicted in Figure 1.2.

In the Epilogue, after having disposed of Strategy through Process as a disappointing humanist conception of the modern corporation, I sketch the first steps toward reconstructing research about corporate strategy in terms of my Strategy & Justice genre. Although I do not argue extensively about corporate strategy interpreted in the ethical terms of Strategy & Justice, I take the Epilogue as an opportunity to suggest how we could thoroughly infuse strategic management research with humanist meanings.

I conclude the Epilogue with a brief discussion of some broader implications of this kind of research. By drawing a connection between management research and a line of inquiry known as the "humanities," I suggest that other management concepts might well be placed in twilight, too.

Implications

The concept of corporate strategy—and, thus, strategic management research—needs a thorough conceptual examination. Despite the uncommon promise that strategic management research holds as a humanist perspective on the modern corporation, strategic management researchers from all kinds of persuasions have shaped the corporate

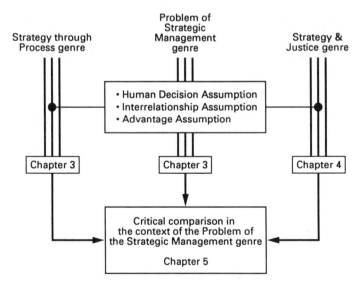

Figure 1.2. The corporate strategy concept in twilight: comparative critical analysis.

strategy concept in disappointing terms. Such an interpretation in a region "beyond mankind" must be counteracted, if the corporate strategy idea is to provide any sense of hope for human interaction at the corporation. If this trend is not first assessed and then reversed, we can abandon strategic management research as a humanist enterprise and, hence, corporate strategy as a usable concept. For this reason, it is appropriate to cast the concept of corporate strategy and strategic management research in twilight.

In the course of articulating and defending my primary line of argument, I aim to support three corollary claims. Although I confine discussion of these points to the Epilogue and the notes, each issue pervades the book.

First, if strategic management research, through the Strategy through Process genre, is a problematic source of hope about the modern corporation, and if corporate strategy is among the most *promising* management concepts in this regard, how much of the rest of management and organization research can be vulnerable in twilight? My study can thus pave the way for other assessments of the meaningfulness of management concepts—that is, critical assessments of those concepts.[104]

Second, I conduct the analysis as I do in order to suggest the powerful possibilities of ethical analysis for management research. In particular, I give reason to believe that ethical analysis can serve as a "scalpel" for cutting open our understanding of management practice and the corporation in humanist terms. Too often, what passes as ethical analysis in management research sidesteps questions of ethics, focusing on ethics instead as a problem of social science and measurement, not human growth, interaction, and connection.[105]

Finally, my analysis has been crafted to suggest how literary analysis can aid management researchers. To that end, I now turn to consider in greater detail my propositions that such "alien" notions as literature, genre, pragmatism, and ethics can assist the strategic management researcher in interpreting the practice of corporate strategy and the modern corporation as meaningful humanist institutions.

2

Research, Stories, and Strategic Management Research

Ideas should be judged by their descendants, not by their ancestors.

JON ELSTER, *Ulysses and the Sirens*

Corporate strategy is a concept with which we can bolster our confidence as we reflect on life at the modern corporation. By making a logical connection between the concept of corporate strategy and the concept of human purpose, we can begin to create a place for ourselves and others in our understanding of the corporation. As that connection is made and extended, we can begin to envision the modern corporation as a context where persons can act and interact purposefully and do so with the highest hopes for their respective lives. In this sense, the corporate strategy concept holds promise as a humanist supposition.

That prospect shines amid much skepticism, most certainly. We can read a gloomy, if not hostile, rendition of human activity at the corporation throughout management theory and organization science, as well as in the popular media.[1] That prospect also shines without any convincing justification of it coming from within the mainstream strategic management research community. Indeed, the practice of defending such a supposition is virtually unknown in that community. On both counts, then, there is a special urgency to defending corporate strategy and strategic management research in humanist terms.

The foregoing line of reasoning summarizes the argument that I articulated and defended in Chapter 1. In the course of making that argument, I set the stage for my eventual conclusion that a humanist conception of corporate strategy is plausible, even as the widespread contemporary conception of corporate strategy must be discarded due to its curious distaste for one kind of humanism that we might value. As I brought that line of reasoning to a climax, I argued at length that it is reasonable for us to interpret the corporate strategy concept in humanist terms—that is, as

29

1. An interpretation of human activity (i.e., literary).
2. An interpretation that can be devised with an enduring thematic clarity (i.e., literary through genre).
3. An interpretation of comparative usefulness to those men and women who are affected by worldly application of the corporate strategy concept (i.e., genre justified in pragmatist terms).
4. An interpretation that proves useful in terms that celebrate personhood (i.e., genre justified in ethical, as well as pragmatist, terms).

Still, I said very little about what it means for a strategic management researcher to devise such an interpretation in order to activate the humanist potential for the corporate strategy concept. I said very little, in other words, about the literary practice that can follow from the literary potential for the concept. I travel this route in Chapter 2 with the aim of connecting the humanist potential for the corporate strategy concept with the humanist potential for the practice of strategic management research.

I seek to articulate and defend this unorthodox connection for two reasons. First, the connection can provide a key piece in defense of the corporate strategy concept. The value of understanding the concept in humanist terms would do us little good if it were not possible for researchers—and managers, too—to unleash that potential. If it were not sensible to tell stories by means of a concept amenable to storytelling, then the corporate strategy concept might as well be enshrined in some Hall of Irony as a potentially humanist idea that no person could employ for humanist ends.[2] Thus I must give some good reasons for understanding strategic management research as a humanist endeavor to correspond to, and hence supplement, some good reasons for understanding corporate strategy as a humanist rendition of the corporation. One argument is stranded without the other.[3]

Second, I want to defend my plan for comparing the Strategy through Process and Strategy & Justice genres in Chapters 3, 4, and 5. It turns out that a defense of strategic management research as a humanist activity opens the door for me to justify my analytical approach. This opportunity arises because we can understand strategic management research and my plan for this book as two versions of the same kind of practice. Both strategic management research and my practice of placing corporate strategy in twilight can be understood as humanist endeavors.

I intend to assess, beginning in Chapter 3, the meanings that a group of prominent strategic management researchers have given to the corporate strategy concept. This means that I will comment on what others have strived to accomplish. I will tell a story, in other words, about others' stories. This particular kind of analysis, where one tells a story about the meanings in other writers' stories, is commonly known as *literary criticism.*[4] If I can show that this is the very same kind of activity that a humanist strategic management researcher would undertake—telling stories about the stories that others, as research subjects, create for themselves on their own "turf"—then I have justification for my undertaking a defense of strategic management research as a literary critic.[5] In making a humanist case for one activity, I make a humanist case for the other.

THE LINE OF ARGUMENT

I construct and defend the argument of Chapter 2 in four parts. First, I claim that we can readily connect the notion of humanist practice with a generic conception of what it can mean to practice research. To this end, I draw more extensively on the tradition of pragmatism, which I introduced in Chapter 1. My point is that pragmatism is a promising means for thinking about research, in general, in terms that accord priority to persons qua persons.[6] Accordingly, the section is titled "Humanism and Pragmatist Research."

Second, I turn my attention to articulating specific conditions for understanding research in pragmatist terms, while still considering research in a generic sense. I devise and defend four such criteria by means of a dialogue involving a researcher who adopts pragmatism and a researcher who adheres to the canon of orthodox management-research-as-science. Each criterion corresponds to one criterion for a humanist concept, as I developed that idea in Chapter 1. This dialogue serves two purposes. On the one hand, I call attention to the intellectual hurdles that researchers must clear if they seek to practice as pragmatists. I attribute the height of those hurdles to the canon of orthodox management science, a set of assumptions whose perpetrators vigorously resist the connection that I seek to forge.[7] On the other hand, I create the dialectic as a vehicle for proposing the opportunity to practice research—and, eventually, strategic management research—as a pragmatist. For all these reasons, the section is titled "Research Hurdles and Research Opportunities."

Third, I move the argument from a generic case for pragmatist research to the specific case of strategic management research. Using the four criteria from the previous section, I narrate a story ("Creating Research Stories") about three fictitious researchers. Each pursues an ostensibly different kind of research: history, meteorology, and strategic management. I argue that all three kinds of inquiry could be understood in pragmatist terms and, more importantly, that a strategic management researcher who so chooses can unleash the humanist potential for the corporate strategy concept.

I conclude the chapter with "A Justification for This Book," where I

draw a close parallel between a pragmatist strategic management research practice and my practice of placing corporate strategy in twilight. Along the way, I connect my efforts as pragmatist literary critic
with those of the orthodox management scientist who is concerned with
the standards of validity, reliability, and generalizability.

HUMANISM AND PRAGMATIST RESEARCH

By "humanist practice" I mean, generally speaking, an activity by which
a person chooses to include among her purposes treating other persons
with dignity for no other reason than their personhood.[8] The humanist
could accord such dignity, for example, to the judgments a person makes
about beauty, hence, an aesthetic humanism. Alternatively, she could
practice as a humanist by granting prima facie respect for the aspirations a person holds and the commitments he makes to those ends.[9]
We can think of this latter case as humanism in ethical terms. Either
way, one person's acknowledgment of another person's worth is central
to a humanist practice. But the acts of a humanist can encompass more
than granting respect unilaterally and from afar.

A humanist is also centrally concerned with the prospects for her
own life. She seeks to grow through her efforts to cope with her world,
all the while acknowledging the limits on her opportunities, resources,
and experiences. For reason of these limits and in anticipation of her
prospects, she seeks connection with others. For her to grow in her
understanding of herself, then, she seeks to grow in understanding
her connection to others. Hence, she requires a context wherein she
can expect that others will respect her pursuits, all the while she makes
it her purpose to honor theirs. Otherwise, "to include among her purposes . . ." has limited meaning for her.[10] In short, the humanist seeks
the company of other like-minded humanists. And this deliberate striving for growth through some sense of connection to other persons can
hold quite generally, whether the humanist acts as parent, teacher,
shortstop, or letter carrier.

In this sense, then, a humanist pursues her practice as a *joint act,* one
that turns on a kinship between herself and others who, like her, seek
and accord respect.[11] Robert Coles recalls what a mentor, William Carlos Williams, once reminded him about kinship and humanism, with
reference to their patients: " 'Their story, yours, mine—it's what we all
carry with us on this trip we take, and we owe it to each other to respect
our stories and learn from them.' "[12] This notion of a story as a means
of practicing in kinship with others can be readily extended to the practice of research in general and, eventually, to strategic management
research.

Humanist Practice and Research

A researcher conducts her inquiries in a humanist way insofar as she makes it her purpose to give thoughtful attention in her studies to the activities that others pursue for their own reasons. We can think of those pursuits as stories, or literature, for reasons that I gave in Chapter 1. In the course of conducting humanist research, then, she accepts *their* stories as prima facie interesting accounts. Coles reminds us on this count: "What ought to be interesting . . . is the unfolding of a lived life."[13] Still, the researcher makes it her own business to study the stories that others spin, rather than making it her business to draw editorial cartoons or trade bonds on Wall Street. She, too, wants respect for her story, her research account. She, too, wants to be understood as a "maker" of her meanings, as Adena Rosmarin puts it.[14] In search of this kind of respect, the humanist researcher seeks to participate in a dialogue of stories with others similarly inclined: perhaps her readers, perhaps her research "subjects," perhaps other researchers. In this way, we can extend straightforwardly the general idea of humanism-as-kinship to the generic practice that we commonly call research.

The upshot is that the practice of humanist research is open to those persons who are willing to understand themselves as no different from—and certainly no better than—the persons who are the subjects of that research, the readers of that research, and other researchers. As Richard Rorty writes on this point, the humanist sees others as "equal comrades with diverse interests, distinguished *only* by those interests, not by cognitive status."[15] In short, researcher, research subject, and reader alike can be understood as storytellers. This kinship holds whether the research involves medicine or education or poetry or philosophy. Each kind of inquiry could be pursued in a humanist manner.

Orthodox Management Science, Nietzsche, and Choice

Among the mainstream of modern management researchers, who fancy themselves as scientists, the proposition that research and storytelling have anything in common is as alien as the idea of a left-handed–throwing catcher is to a major league baseball executive.[16] The premise most foreign to the orthodox management scientist is precisely most central to a humanist—and, in particular, Nietzschean—rendition of worldly practice: the idea that the person involved in either kind of activity can exercise a choice about truth and meaning in his efforts.[17]

There is no room at the inn of orthodox management science for persons acting as interpreters, as makers of their own meanings, as creators of knowledge and truth in kinship with other persons. By that orthodoxy, neither a researcher's reasons for studying what he studies nor his style of writing about those studies can be permissibly under his control. If he does stray into such territory as *himself*, he invites the dreaded charge of "researcher bias."[18]

Nietzsche's characterization of the scholars of his day thus still rings true for the management-researcher-as-scientist: "But they sit cool in the cool shade: they want to be mere spectators in everything and take care not to sit where the sun burns upon the steps."[19] As spectator, a management scientist must act in the service not of himself, but of a Nature whose structure he is assigned to observe unobtrusively.[20] In the "cool shade," his own inclination to choose about meaning and knowledge remains obscured from everyone's view, including his own. And the self-imposed proscription on bias keeps him in the darkness.

A comment for future reference. I draw this sharp distinction between orthodox management science and a Nietzschean perspective as prelude to arguments further down the road in this chapter. Mainstream strategic management researchers fancy themselves as scientists abiding by the dicta of the orthodox management science canon. Among many public avowals on this point, Kathryn Rudie Harrigan makes explicit such scientific aspirations: "Scholars of strategic management follow rules of science in their research, and the care they exert in their research methodologies ensures objectivity in their results."[21] Dan Schendel and Karel Cool take the point further, lamenting that in the strategic management field "only a few vigilantes are in evidence to keep out the most obvious violators of the norms of scholarly, scientific research."[22] In short, we can assume that resistance runs deep among strategic management researchers to the idea of research as a humanist practice.

Pragmatism, Persons, and Choice

Nietzsche and his intellectual descendants approach the pursuit of knowledge in sharp contrast to the well-known canon of modern management science on this matter of a researcher's act of choosing. What engrosses Nietzsche most is a person's capacity to create, to be "value creating," her fallibility notwithstanding.[23] This celebration of human possibility, a principal premise of humanism, has been given prominent contemporary expression in the philosophical tradition known as *pragmatism.* To the pragmatist, a person creates, over and over again, through an act of choice in the context of others doing likewise.

The pragmatist gives special emphasis to each person's efforts—including her own—to cope with an uncertain, yet opportunity-filled, world. On this account, the pragmatist copes through acts of choice about how to make sense of her worldly endeavors. This choice to interpret, or tell a story, is the primary pragmatist vehicle for living and growing. Certainly, research qualifies as one such kind of self-conscious storytelling practice. To the pragmatist, a researcher is simply one more human being striving to lead a fulfilling life.

In a general pragmatist sense, then, literary—or storytelling—efforts offer you and me the opportunity to emerge from the "cool shade" that might bedim our parts as agents jointly engaged in search of knowledge and meaning. On a pragmatist account, we can exercise a host of choices, each enabling us to participate and collaborate actively in creating meaning for ourselves on our own turf. These stories are crucial, given the pragmatist's worldly focus. To the pragmatist, story-telling is our *only* means for coping individually and collaboratively. it is, in other words, "just us" when it comes down to questions of mean-ing. There is no independent Nature which we must consult for "The Truth."

For my purposes here, I can explain this pragmatist approach to hu-man choice in four accumulating regards. These choices apply whether the pragmatist acts as a moviegoer, political activist, teacher, game show host, coach, or corporate executive (but, not yet for this argument, as a researcher).

1. We can select a topic about which we want to make a connection to our lives, whether it is friendship, war, vanity, denial, or earth-quakes.
2. We can elect to tell our stories in this search by employing a host of (a) devices, such as voice, tense, character, time and place, meter, and plot; (b) kinds of narration, such as a novel, a poem, or auto-biography; and (c) themes with which to sustain a story line, such as feminism, Marxism, patriotism, monarchism, and egoism.[24]
3. We can select a group of other persons with whom to share stories in a campaign to champion, reject, or ignore different kinds of meanings. And we can use comparative storytelling devices to de-fend these preferences; for example, a feminist protagonist can be paired with a masculine voice bent on domination.[25]
4. We can elect, amid all the foregoing choices, the terms and condi-tions by which we want to understand ourselves and other persons, with all our aspirations and flaws. We can, in other words, elect to respect a person qua person.

Segue

I have traveled this route from humanism to humanist research to pragmatism in order to justify the following proposition: each of these four pragmatist choices opens a door to telling humanist stories in the course of practicing research, stories about persons and a world on which they jointly confer meaning. *I have traveled this route, in other words, to bring pragmatism to the doorstep of those who practice strategic management research*. In fact, I have moved the argument to this doorstep in two respects simultaneously: (1) my reasoning from humanism to humanist research to pragmatism; and (2) my articulation of these four choices such that each act of choice can produce a corresponding humanist understanding of a given concept, where those understandings are the very ones I developed in Chapter 1. In particular, these pragmatist choices can result in, successively, (1) a specific story, (2) a genre for that story, (3) comparative, worldly reasons for preferring that story, and (4) ethical reasons by which a comparative preference for that story can be justified.

Taken together, then, these choices and the literary consequences of acting on them can be connected to make a powerful case for the humanist potential for *any* research concept. Therein lies an opportunity for arguing that the practice of research, the practice of strategic management research in particular, and eventually the corporate strategy concept per se can hold considerable humanist promise.

RESEARCH HURDLES AND RESEARCH OPPORTUNITIES

The next task in capitalizing on this humanist opportunity for strategic management research is to more fully appreciate the hurdles—to use a track-and-field metaphor—that an orthodox management scientist can erect for making a case against a pragmatist conception of research. In each of the four sections that follow, I pose a question about the pursuit of knowledge. I tell a story first about how a pragmatist storyteller could reply and then about how a researcher trained in the tradition of orthodox management science could reply.[26] On each count, it turns out that the approach to meaning adopted by the orthodox management scientist sets up an intellectual impediment to the proposition that research in general can carry storytelling implications.[27] Once I have set up an array of four contrasting responses to my questions, I move to interpret how a pragmatist strategic management researcher, in particular, can transform these hurdles into opportunities and why, in a humanist sense, she must.

Interpretation and Research

In response to the question "From where does knowledge come?" the pragmatist storyteller responds simply, "My imagination, my passion, and my experience." She makes the choice to interpret a story as she encounters some problem, or puzzle, that has a bearing on the life that she wants to lead.[28] Her story is her interpretation of that puzzle and is a product of her imagination.[29] She chooses to create a particular story in terms of some anomaly that impinges on a part of her life for which she holds a passion.[30] And in creating her story, she is free to draw on her experiences in many past attempts to solve problems through storytelling.

To be certain, her choices can be significantly constrained. The historical context within which she moves can limit her choices. If she has never encountered a feminist argument about relationships among very different persons, then her choices are likely limited to familiar stories about warfare and domination. The cultural context within which she lives can likewise set limits on her choices. She might prefer to tell a feminist story but be coerced into not doing so, perhaps through the scholarly review process. These bounds notwithstanding, we can still look to a pragmatist as one who strives to create stories in search of ways to move her life ahead.[31]

The orthodox management scientist, in contrast, rejects interpretation as a fuzzy, undisciplined act.[32] In response to the question "From where does knowledge come?" he replies that Nature—that is, the real structure of the world—holds a store of information waiting to be probed, exposed, reflected, seen, and dug up.[33] As Rorty puts it, a researcher working in this tradition has long sought to know "what joints the world wanted to be cut at."[34] On this view, the management scientist is committed to finding those "true" joints. This is why the management scientist is so obsessed with *validity* and *sampling*. Validity serves as a check on whether the researcher is digging in the proper vicinity of a joint in Nature. Sampling is a technique for sifting the dross from the gems in the shovelfuls of data that the scientist unearths. To the management researcher conducting this kind of investigation, choice of interpretations and stories is, at best, a redundant exercise. The world is "there." Nothing about it can be chosen.

The opportunity here is to tell a story about strategic management research as a purposeful storytelling endeavor.

Language, Interpretation, and Research

In response to a second question, "In what terms is knowledge expressed?" the pragmatist storyteller responds, "A language that I choose to adopt in conjunction with others as a means of coping and growing in my life." To the pragmatist, a *language* is a pattern of meanings that enables her to communicate expeditiously with others. Language enables us to live interdependently, in other words.[35] A pragmatist considers language important as she encounters a life marked with contingency and surprise. Using language, Rorty argues, "is not having a special method but simply casting about for a vocabulary which might help."[36] To the pragmatist, a language is something that she can create in many enduring varieties—or *genres*—for purposes of telling stories. She can give meaning to her story through the language of, say, a historical novel in feminist terms, or a poem praising egoism. Regardless, the pragmatist storyteller takes language very seriously. She goes so far as to believe, as Rorty emphasizes, that "language is not a *tool,* but that in which we live and move."[37] To the pragmatist, then, the world has meaning only to the extent that she can choose and use a language *in* which to understand her place.

The management scientist, in contrast, responds to "In what terms is knowledge expressed?" with "Nature's voice, which I translate with my method." He refers, of course, to the scientific method.[38] On this view, the researcher's charge is to act on this method as faithfully as he can, lest the "voice" of Nature elude him or his biases garble the message.

For fear of the former, the management scientist worries about the *reliability* of his method.[39] He takes reliability measurements in order to assess how well he is perfecting his skill as a transparent conduit for the truth that Nature wants to reveal.[40] For fear of contamination by bias, the management scientist scoffs at the possibility of multiple and malleable versions of his method—that is, to him, language must be fixed and genre must be singular—and approaches warily the matter of writing about his studies. Rorty comments on the juncture of these concerns: "Writing is an unfortunate necessity; what is really wanted is to show, to demonstrate, to point out, to exhibit, to make one's interlocutor stand at gaze before the world."[41] Accordingly, the management scientist is easily frustrated by discussions about language, eager to pass them off as "semantic quibbling."

My opportunity here is to give an account of strategic management research as an exercise in using language, through genres, for purposes of creating and expressing meanings about certain worldly phenomena.

Community, Language, Interpretation, and Research

In response to a third question, "In what way is knowledge confirmed?" the pragmatist storyteller answers, "Interdependently, as I share stories with others who share their similar concerns and stories with me." This shared context within which pragmatist writers choose to interact is known as a *community.* What draws a community together is a common desire among some group of persons to interpret their lives in interdependence with one another. We can thus understand a community of free-market economists, a community of baseball sabremetricians, and a community of critical legal theorists.[42] Language and the genres that sustain language enter the picture as the coinage with which members of a community transact. Think of a community, then, as a group of persons who share a particular language. In a community, a language is something that persons create in their search for comparatively better meanings for living on their own turf. Rorty characterizes this joint search as a "horizontal" effort.[43] From a humanist perspective, horizontal interaction can have two important connotations.

First, members of a pragmatist community shape language among themselves, that is, horizontally across their membership. In this way, language is used to express and confirm knowledge in persuasive dialogues, rather than by coercive fiat.[44] Jerome Bruner makes the point about language, meaning, and community in this way: "Meaning is what we can agree upon or at least accept as a working basis for seeking agreement about the concept at hand. If one is arguing about social "realities" . . . the reality is not the thing, not in the head, but in the act of arguing and negotiating about the meaning of such concepts."[45] If a language no longer serves our common purposes—as, for example, feminists argue about much of contemporary society—then, on a pragmatist account, we negotiate a new and improved version.[46] Stanley Fish notes the value of this horizontal interaction in humanist terms: "But perhaps the greatest gain that falls to us under a persuasion model is a greatly enhanced sense of the importance of our activities."[47] We can grow, on a pragmatist view, as participants in jointly creating meanings by which we can live.[48]

Second, pragmatists negotiate their languages over time and in the context of past persuasive dialogues, some their own and some negotiated before their times. In other words, a pragmatist community has a history.[49] A sense of community can thus be horizontal in terms of time. On this interpretation, we can understand that the language we use today evolved from the problems that we and our ancestors once thought were important and, accordingly, from the languages negotiated to cope with those past problems.[50] This connotation of community is important in a humanist way because it enables us to accept each person in a community as a free and evolving participant, rather than a mere instantiation of present action.[51] We can thus understand a person growing through a sense of her own history and through the lessons she gains from dialogues with others doing likewise. The search for meaning can, in short, be understood as a lifelong project in a context of one's own search and the searches of others in the same community.[52] This conception of community storytelling is thoroughly humanist, for it keeps these searches in the spotlight. To a pragmatist living in a language, a community is *all* that she has as a way to confirm meanings.

The management scientist takes a very different view about how to accumulate knowledge. In response to "In what way is knowledge confirmed?" he responds, "Through a continual sequence of forays that move closer and closer to the truths that Nature holds." If the pragmatist confirms knowledge horizontally, the management scientist does so vertically.[53] With methods already a given and language redundant, he concerns himself with how deeply his techniques can penetrate the structure of truths that can stymie him. Thus he approaches the confirmation of knowledge in terms of how durably a particular technique can work. This is why the management scientist worries about the *generalizability* of his method.[54] If a technique exposes seam after seam of promising facts—that is, his digging can be replicated more and more generally—then he considers his work successful.

The management scientist has little use for "community" as a pragmatist talks about the idea. A management scientist can work with other scientists, but more in the sense of a blasting crew where members sign on to crack a vein of coal here this week and then scatter to other jobs the next.[55] Moreover, he has his methods and sees no point in dialogue with nonscientists about those methods. He sees himself as different from nonscientists.[56] For these reasons, the management scientist finds the notion of community redundant. Yes, management scientists can and do work together. No, the joint effort per se is not particularly meaningful in terms of amassing knowledge. After all, Truth is revealed by Nature, not by their conversations with one another.

The opportunity here is to give an account of strategic management research whereby we can understand the practice generally as a search for meanings through discussion and agreement in community among strategic management researchers, their research subjects, and their readers.

Ethics, Community, Language, Interpretation, and Research

In response to a fourth question, "How is the worth of knowledge evaluated?" the pragmatist storyteller replies, "In terms of whether it enables me and the persons who are affected by my story to advance our respective life pursuits." To the pragmatist, a story told in a language shared across persons in some community is worthwhile insofar as it enables the parties to the story to better understand themselves, individually and in relation to one another. Pragmatist knowledge, therefore, is always judged at the level of the individual person who is acting in connection with others.

This concern with self-justification can be understood to turn on a thoroughgoing ethical standard for the worth of knowledge. Hazel Barnes explains this act of self-assessment as "the choice to be ethical," which "involves the bare idea of the inner demand for justification as a self-imposed necessary relation between actions and judgments by and within the same individual."[57] Through telling stories, then, a pragmatist can activate this choice, or "inner demand," over and over again. Coles recounts how his students, in dialogue among themselves and in relations with the authors they read, make this connection between stories and self-knowledge: "Again and again, instructed by novelists, students reminded themselves of life's contingencies; and in so doing, they take matters of choice and commitment more seriously than they might otherwise have done."[58] Jean Baker Miller articulates this pragmatist logic in terms of a person's desire to be authentic: "To move toward authenticity, then, also involves creation, in an immediate and pressing personal way."[59] She situates that "personal way" in a larger context: "Personal creativity is a continuous process of bringing forth a changing vision of oneself, and of oneself in relation to the world."[60] To the extent, then, that the acts of telling, sharing, and revising stories can produce this kind of knowledge, knowledge that is set in a worldly and personal context, the pragmatist will choose to prefer it for ethical reasons.

The management scientist has a terse reply to my fourth question.[61] He says, "I have already answered that question." To the management scientist, if knowledge is found by means of a process that passes tests of validity, reliability, and generalizability, he has certified the worth of that knowledge. As Adena Rosmarin notes, the management scientist— as "theorist"—sees no reason for going any further: "When firm ground has been reached or, alternatively, when the mirror has been polished to perfection, the theorist stops and rests in the contemplation of truth."[62] Since he has excluded choice, creation, and hence persons—including himself—from the search for truth, the orthodox management scientist has no need for this fourth criterion of worth for knowledge.[63] He must believe, to do this kind of research, that a concern with ethics is independent of what he does.[64]

The fourth opportunity here is to give an account of strategic management research in ethical terms, as a search by researcher, research subject, and reader alike for knowledge with which to justify their respective pursuits in connection with one another.

Segue

The stage is now set. I have posed each of the four preceding questions as a hurdle separating a pragmatist's storytelling approach to knowledge from the orthodox management scientist's assumptions, which strategic management researchers routinely share.[65] Continuing with the track-and-field metaphor, I propose that a pragmatist humanist "running lane" is accessible beyond each hurdle for the strategic management researcher. By providing a guide to making each leap, I make a progressively stronger case for a humanist kind of strategic management research.[66] With each leap, a strategic management researcher can begin thinking in terms of what truths lie ahead for her and her fellow storytellers, rather than in terms of "natural" truths embedded beneath her feet.

Moreover, with each successive leap, the strategic management researcher can make a more enduring connection between her activities and the proposition that corporate strategy can serve as a humanist concept. This potential connection between a humanist research practice and a humanist concept is summarized in Figure 2.1. Thus in the epigraph to this chapter, Jon Elster highlights the choice facing a strategic management researcher: think about research as an act of choosing better and better stories about persons—that is, stories that "descend" from a choice to celebrate personhood—or think about research as an act of idolizing our tie to some primordial structure of the world and our method of digging it up—that is, our ancestry in Nature and science, respectively.[67] To choose the former over the latter is to make progress in a humanist way.

I make this case for a humanist strategic management research practice by means of a story. I create this story in a context that spans two kinds of contemporary inquiry: one kind of inquiry generally considered scientific but not pragmatist, and the other kind of inquiry generally considered pragmatist but not scientific.[68] In this way, I "bracket" strategic management research in order to highlight the choices available to the strategic management researcher.

In particular, I begin with a narrative about the research activities of two fictitious would-be protagonists who encounter these four hurdles.[69] LaFleur is a historian. Elan is a meteorologist. LaFleur is a would-be heroine, and Elan is a would-be hero in my story, because each could choose to clear the hurdles and practice as pragmatist. But each could hesitate as well. The same could be said about a third fictitious character in my story, Shepherd. Shepherd is a strategic management re-

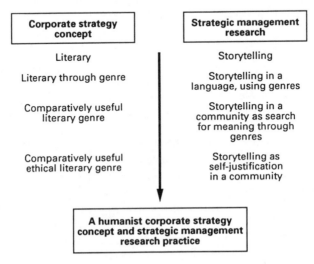

Figure 2.1. Connecting a humanist concept and a humanist practice.

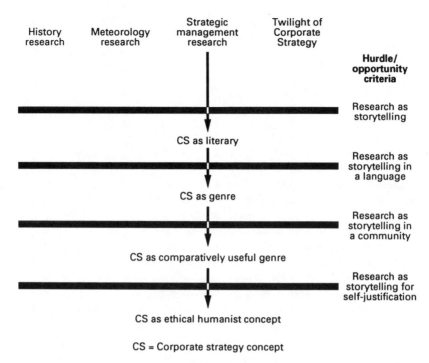

Figure 2.2. Toward a humanist practice of strategic management research.

searcher. He, too, is a prospective protagonist, a prospective pragmatist.

My story line is a simple one: each of these researchers can clear hurdles into storytelling territory if he or she chooses to do so. Some, or all, can go so far as humanist territory. That is, despite apparent differences in their crafts, I will work through a prima facie case for all three characters acting as pragmatist researchers. Along the way, I join them as a fourth character with my own story to tell: my intent to read strategic management research stories as a literary critic. My plan for this story line is sketched in Figure 2.2.

CREATING RESEARCH STORIES

Meet LaFleur, a historian. LaFleur studies the experiences of immigrants who settled in Pennsylvania steel-making regions before World War I.[70] LaFleur is particularly interested in the patterns of socialization as the descendants of these immigrants were influenced by American social institutions and vice versa. Lately, however, LaFleur has been puzzled about certain evidence for which her model of these socialization processes cannot adequately account.

LaFleur has been focusing, for some time now, on immigrants' participation in political processes, labor union activity, and the growth of local businesses ancillary to steel production. She now suspects that educational institutions, particularly private higher education, play a part in the socialization drama. She casts about to learn how others have tried to explain certain phenomena that she finds peculiar. LaFleur immerses herself in the works of other historians, education researchers, sociologists, political scientists, and those who study American civil religion. After a number of months in this pursuit, LaFleur is satisfied that she has modified her explanation as a blending of her earlier account and the "counsel" she adapts from the arguments made by other researchers who have gone before her into such territory. Then she puts her revised account through a series of tests.

LaFleur checks the relevance of her revised account across several seemingly diverse sets of conditions—such as different cities populated by immigrants at different periods—and reports her findings in a scholarly paper published in a history journal. She moves to still more diverse contexts and, satisfied that her explanation continues to hold, reports those results. Her papers receive rave reviews. Most prominently, her reviewers comment that LaFleur reports her studies in the form of biographies written across several generations in the specific families that she has followed. LaFleur pays special attention to the connection that these persons make between higher education, employment alternatives other than the steel mills, and satisfaction with their lives. All goes well until, months later, LaFleur begins to hear similar stories from immigrants' descendants living in cities where playground programs—particularly basketball—were popular among young men and women, but where private higher education opportunities were nonexistent. LaFleur ponders how this might be explained. The cycle begins anew as she returns to the drawing board.

Meet next Elan, a meteorologist. Elan studies tornado formation in the upper Midwest region of the United States. He concentrates on the post–World War II years when automobile ownership and use skyrocketed in that region, particularly in Chicago, in Minneapolis–St. Paul, and on the farms. Elan is particularly fascinated by the relationship between tornado formation and the development of large-scale thunderstorms called mesoscale convective complexes (MCCs).[71] Elan collects data about jet stream proximity, wind speed and direction at various levels of the atmosphere, air pollution composition, pressure gradients, and air temperature gradients.

In recent months, Elan has been reading others' studies about climate changes and the so-called greenhouse effect. At the same time, he has been casually perusing data about the movement of summertime weather patterns along the East Coast of the United States, where automobile use—a suspected contributor to greenhouse phenomena—is pervasive. Dissatisfied with his ability to use his model for tornado prediction, he takes steps to explain MCC formation in terms that reflect both local and continent-wide weather conditions. He prepares a paper for a conference attended by physicists, fellow meteorologists, geographers, and urbanologists. Their responses are encouraging. Elan moves to studying these climatic patterns more closely, with particular attention to smog and fog formation in the industrial regions of Pennsylvania, New Jersey, and New York State.

Meet Shepherd, a strategic management researcher. Shep, as he prefers to be called, studies European diversification prospects for U.S.-based telecommunications firms. He has become particularly impressed with joint venture opportunities. In each of the past twelve months, Shep learned about one more collaborative arrangement between a telecommunications company from the old Bell System and either a state-owned telecommunications monopoly in Europe or a diversified supplier of telecommunications products based in a European nation. Shep developed a well-known model of diversification processes for the industry, which he uses in consulting with executives and public policymakers on both sides of the Atlantic. Shep encourages his audiences to pay close attention to such variables as ownership stakes in joint ventures, processes of venture formation, complements between the venturers' European and American product lines, trends in government-to-government relations, and the availability of "native" managerial talent.

Shep has recently begun to wonder whether trends in U.S. antitrust policy might merit greater consideration in his explanations, while his longstanding emphasis on relations between national governments of the venture partners might be downplayed. As he ponders this substitution, and the consequences for the rest of his model, Shep talks with other strategic management researchers, international economists, political scientists, scholars studying European cultures, and antitrust legal theorists. In time, he revises his model and proceeds with his far-flung "teaching" activities.

A Translation

We can understand LaFleur, Elan, and Shepherd alike as storytellers by at least the first three meanings of pragmatist storytelling that I have developed in this chapter. Prominent across each story and all three stories is the extent to which choices made by researchers can serve as a coherent theme.[72] Across these three examples, then, we can apply a pragmatist's understanding in several areas.

First, LaFleur, Elan, and Shep each select a topic for their investigations. Implicit here is the availability of options. LaFleur can elect to concentrate on immigrants' experiences in steel-making towns instead of the Puritans' exodus to seventeenth-century Massachusetts. In Elan's research, we can understand his preference for tornadoes and thunderstorms over so-called lake effect snowstorms along the windward shores of Lakes Erie and Ontario. Shep could study leveraged buyouts as an approach to corporate restructuring in consumer food products industries. But he chooses otherwise.[73]

Second, LaFleur, Elan, and Shep each select a language, and genres with which to sustain that language, for their respective lines of inquiry. LaFleur reads, writes, and converses in a language of socialization processes and trends. She practices that language with a genre articulated in terms of political processes, labor union participation, and economic development.[74] Elan works in a language of mesoscale convective complexes.[75] That language, in turn, is shaped by Elan in terms of a genre of wind speed and direction, temperature, pollution, and humidity.[76] Shep chooses a language of global business.[77] His genre takes on meaning in terms of corporate governance, political economy, and product mix issues.

Each, however, could have chosen a different language and genre(s). LaFleur could write about immigrants' *resistance* to Americanization.[78] Elan could write about tornadoes from a topographic standpoint, or using a chemist's language. Shep could converse in a language of vicious competition, whereby alliances such as joint ventures are mere truces. Or he could employ a Freudian language.

Finally, LaFleur, Elan, and Shep each choose to interact with others who share a respective interest in the languages and genres they want to shape and with which they seek to make progress in their understandings. Moreover, each interacts with others in their community with an appreciation of the history of these shared uses of a language. LaFleur seeks out her peers among historians, sociologists, anthropologists, and the like. Furthermore, she acknowledges a kind of dialogue with those who have gone before her in that community, as long as she and her contemporaries find use for their ancestors' languages and genres.[79] LaFleur likely would not, however, find such comradeship if she chose to send her writings to her friend the astrophysicist. They probably could not find a language in common with which to converse about LaFleur's studies.[80]

Elan likewise interacts with a community of meteorologists and physicists, but probably not podiatrists. Shep's model takes on meaning through his discussions with other management researchers, economists, and political analysts. But he probably does not converse with either meteorologists or theologians. Both Elan and Shep, like LaFleur, are able to carry on these dialogues because of past dialogues that set the stage for their respective contemporary discussions and debates.

On each of these counts, and across each of these stories, we can understand LaFleur, Elan, and Shep performing the *very same kind of practice:* storytelling as a pragmatist whose inquiry becomes progressively more a humanist practice. Still, the most daunting of these four hurdle-cum-opportunities looms: the researcher's ethical choice for each story.

Ethics, Meteorology, History, and Strategic Management Research

Let's deal with Elan first. In my story about his research endeavors, I stopped short of including anything about persons—and, hence, an ethical genre—in the stories that he shares with his colleagues. The reason for this is straightforward. In my story, Elan chooses, as a meteorologist, to tell a story that has no provision in it for persons, their hopes, their regrets, and so on. This exclusion cuts two ways.

Elan and his fellow community members make no claim that anything you and I, specifically, do will influence tornado formation. My cutting the lawn and the growth of towering thunderheads have no connection in the meteorologist's story. In fact, Elan and company will eagerly brand such a connection an "old wives' tale," an "unscientific" genre that is unwelcome in their discourse.[81]

Likewise, Elan and his colleagues make no provision in their language and genres to the effect that thunderstorms and tornadoes have any bearing on us, as purposeful and striving human beings. Put somewhat differently, their dependent variables are more likely to include storm duration and intensity, rather than the effect of a torrential downpour on *my* hiking plans per se. Even if Elan were to choose something like "storm harm to personal health" as a dependent variable, he almost certainly does so in aggregated fashion—for example, so many deaths per gusty storm per year.[82] There is no distinction among persons implied by such a choice, a violation of the ethical criterion that I am defending.[83]

In sum, Elan can tell an entrancing story with the language of modern meteorology, even if he lacks the charisma of television announcer Willard Scott![84] Still, he makes his story largely ineligible as a humanist story, if we read it in terms of an ethical criterion that gives priority to personhood. His language will not permit it. Since there are no persons *in* his story, neither he nor his readers can engage in a search for worldly meaning by means of that story.[85] Thus Elan and his colleagues cannot clear this ethical hurdle with the kind of story that meteorologists have become accustomed to telling.

LaFleur could go either way with regard to the ethical themes in her story line, researching as a pragmatist or as a positivist scientist. In my story about her work, she acts as a pragmatist who produces a decidedly humanist story by weaving a theme of human hopefulness into her narratives. Moreover, she does so in terms that give respect to the stories told by her "subjects." Reading LaFleur's biographies is more like reading a novel than wading through a social science journal. A biography—a genre that LaFleur uses—is, by virtue of the writer's respect for that person on the latter's turf, a patent example of humanist research. On these terms, it is also an ethical genre.[86]

LaFleur perpetrates an ethical act first by choosing human opportunity and purpose as part of her language, in this case in a historical context "belonging" to the generations of family members whom she studies. She then goes on, through the act of telling another person's story, to welcome that person into her community. LaFleur could not write a biography, on a pragmatist account, unless she practices vicariously putting herself in others' shoes as an equal. When she accepts herself as no different from her subjects—that is, one storyteller engaging another—then LaFleur has perpetrated a second ethical act: respect for the comparable worthiness of that person's life.[87] In so doing, she commits a third ethical act by honing her skill as a humanist biographer, a skill that she could apply to her own life as an autobiographer. In sum, the practice of historical research could readily be understood as a pragmatist practice and, in view of my ethical criterion, a humanist one at that. History could thus be one of the "humanities."[88]

This brings me to Shepherd. Once again, I have deliberately chosen the cases of LaFleur and Elan to "bracket" the practice in which Shep engages and, accordingly, the humanist prospects for his work.[89] Clearly, we can interpret LaFleur's research activities in humanist terms. Just as clearly, the prospects for Elan doing so seem remote, although not impossible. He and his colleagues in their meteorology community would have to radically alter their stories toward treating you and me as much more than mere passive recipients of weather phenomena. Shep, even more than LaFleur, could be tempted to emulate Elan. This is especially so, given that the champions of mainstream strategic management research view themselves as faithful scientists. Thus by the string of four assumptions I previously attributed to orthodox science, Shep could[90]

1. Believe that his concepts, constructs, variables, and the like—for example, ownership stake, governmental relations, "local" management expertise—reflect the "objective" structure of truth about European joint ventures in the telecommunications industry.
2. Believe that his concepts, constructs, variables, and the like are natural and without reason for challenge per se. Thus he could believe that "the data speak."
3. Believe that, by adding antitrust trends to his model, he can move closer and closer to "the real" truth about European joint ventures in the telecommunications industry. In other words, he can believe that the new lineup of concepts, constructs, variables, and whatever

can be generalized across more data to produce more accurate representations of the problem he studies.[91]

4. Believe that he is assisting his clients, students, and readers of his articles solely by applying his research model validly, reliably, and generally.

Yet Shep need not do this. All these beliefs, and the research activities conducted in their name, are optional for Shep, when considered on a pragmatist account.[92]

I have given evidence for this optionality throughout my story about Shep. He can believe that he chooses to interpret European telecommunications joint ventures as *Shep*, strategic management researcher. Shep can believe that the meaningfulness of his model follows from the language that he selects and that he shares with others like him who choose to discuss European business topics, for example. So, at least on the first three pragmatist criteria that I have developed, Shep is no different from LaFleur and Elan as researcher–storyteller. We might even say that they can share such a language in their own community, if they so choose. The pivotal issue here concerns the matter of ethics in the language that Shep uses.

Certainly, Shep could travel the route followed by traditional social scientists and work with theories that rely on aggregate measures of human activity. Economists, sociologists, and organization scientists, to list a few, are wont to do this and then claim that they have something to say about "human implications."[93] But, from a pragmatist angle, Shep cannot easily get away with this, for two reasons.

First, he peppers his papers, lectures, and advice with references to chief executive officers, managers, government officials, and so on. If he means to do this sincerely as a storytelling device, rather than merely dropping names, Shep must create a way to include in his stories—that is, his models—the persons who occupy those roles. From a humanist perspective, he must go further to accord them, at a minimum, respect as holders of their own unique purposes and projects. Thus he must create a place for Robert Allen at AT&T and James Rill at the Department of Justice and others—all as themselves—who he is inclined to mention.[94]

More importantly, there is no reason why Shep cannot take this minimal ethical step of bolstering his already promising pragmatist practice with an enduring spotlight on human actors. He must watch these persons anyway, even if he fancies himself as a social scientist taking measurements to later aggregate into social data. Thus a humanist account of Shep's work, populated with specific actors here, there, and everywhere, is a viable option for him.

Second, Shep, perhaps even more than the historian LaFleur, can take part in a widespread dialogue that includes, among his contemporaries, the subjects of his research. For LaFleur, her subjects might be long dead. For Shep, he is "out of business" if he is not able to engage, in addition to his research colleagues, the students he teaches and the clients he consults with the language of strategic management research. If Shep is to carry out the humanist possibility for what he does in interdependence with his students and clients, then he must accord them respect in his stories as peers. What he cannot do on this score is to say to them, in effect, "I am telling you a story where you are so aggregated with others that your actions are inconsequential." To do so amounts to claiming that his story is meaningful to those who cannot act meaningfully as themselves in that story. With such a claim, Shep violates the criterion of creating conditions conducive for self-justification in a community.[95]

Elan has no such problem, at least with his current language. LaFleur can have this concern, as can novelists, philosophers, and poets. By virtue of the "outreach" activities in which Shep seems to want to participate, he can readily commit himself to the ethical act of inviting his peers into his community as peers. There is no reason why Shep cannot clear this fourth hurdle into a humanist running lane. In truth, if he wants to practice his craft coherently and authentically, he must satisfy this ethical criterion.

A JUSTIFICATION FOR THIS BOOK

With the foregoing argument, I have created the possibility of a community among practitioners of apparently dissimilar research traditions who can share a pragmatist, and even humanist, language about research. Now, on the eve of conducting a critical assessment of the corporate strategy concept and strategic management research in Chapters 3, 4, and 5, I claim full membership in this community as I make the following choices.

I choose to assess contemporary strategic management research in terms of the concept from which these researchers proceed, rather than, for example, in terms of the scope of this research endeavor or the string of resulting "knowledge." Indeed, I choose to claim that the *worth* of corporate strategy is a worthwhile question.

I choose to conduct my analysis in the customary language of strategic management research, which I interpret in Chapter 3 as a particular genre: the Problem of Strategic Management. I then interpret this genre in terms of three assumptions: Human Decision, Interrelationship, and Advantage. In the context of this genre, I interpret and compare two genres as options with which we can shape the Problem of Strategic Management: Strategy through Process and Strategy & Justice.[96]

I choose to conduct my analysis as a kind of dialogue among members of a community that could include a diverse group of prominent, contemporary strategic management researchers; a diverse group of researchers from other disciplines (principally, moral philosophy); and you, my readers. I interpret the Problem of Strategic Management in Chapter 3 as a genre that members of this possible community could understand. I then interpret the Strategy through Process and Strategy & Justice genres to sustain this dialogue.[97] With interpretation as our common activity here, I choose thus to "convene" what is known as an *interpretive community*. I expect that these persons might not choose to conduct the dialogue in this way. Nor would they all likely want to hear my conclusions. Still, I have made "arrangements" for them to participate, if they so choose.

I choose to interpret the Problem of Strategic Management, Strategy through Process, and Strategy & Justice as genres written in a language drawn from the study of ethics. In particular, I employ a contractarian language that highlights persons, their relationships with one another, and their respective purposes.[98] Moreover, I conduct my analysis on the premise that the corporate strategy concept is worth nurturing. In this way, I create an opportunity for strategic management researchers—myself included—to justify their efforts with regard to the concept. For these reasons, I practice as a literary critic who consistently applies a pragmatist, ethical analysis.

By crafting my study in this way, I have given reasons for justifying it in two related respects as a pragmatist, humanist endeavor. First, I have arranged my analysis akin to other pragmatist research—most prominently, the tack taken by pragmatist literary critics. It is the non–strategic management researchers, in the community that this book can bring together, who can best attest to this claim. Second, by interpreting a language that enables us to draw a parallel across what I intend to do as a researcher, what pragmatist researchers do more generally, and what strategic management researchers, historians, and even meteorologists *could* do, I claim credibility for my humanist study among the quite diverse community that I convene. If their pursuits are justified by pragmatist criteria, so are mine.

Still, to be prudent about all this, I want to go one step further and speak to concerns that might well linger among members of "my" community who still want "scientific relevance."

Pragmatism, Validity, Reliability, and Generalizability

I can further justify this study, specifically to those who are scientifically inclined, by means of a pragmatist interpretation of the validity, reliability, and generalizability concerns held by management scientists.[99]

Validity. My "data" for interpreting the genres of the Problem of Strategic Management, Strategy through Process, and Strategy & Justice are the writings—or *texts*—of other persons. So, to be "true" to these data in a pragmatist sense of validity, I simply seek support for my claims in terms of what these researchers have written. There is no magic to this aspect of literary criticism, although the data certainly read differently from those to which an orthodox management scientist is accustomed.[100]

Reliability. I substantiate my genres by repeatedly seeking support *in each text* for my interpretations. In this way, I am a dependable, or reliable, interrogator here. What I do is no different from asking each of my "subjects" to join in conversation with me in terms of what they could say, if *their* writings are reliable, about the interpretation of corporate strategy that I create. My study is conducted with reliability insofar as I "consult" these researchers consistently—each with the same questions—and continually—each on every aspect of the Problem of Strategic Management and Strategy through Process.[101]

Generalizability. I satisfy this test rather readily, since a major intent of pragmatists is to create stories that are useful for persons across more and more general contexts. The pragmatist is a competitor who accepts the possibility that, in the course of an interpretive dialogue, alternatives to her genres are possible. Bruner describes this discourse as "a *forum* for negotiating and renegotiating meaning and for explicating action . . . [and not] as a set of rules or specifications for action."[102] In such a forum, I conduct what might be called a *test of breadth* with respect to how far a pragmatist's account might reach. By such a test, we can "measure" how far a genre, such as Strategy through Process, can be pushed into the farthest regions of usefulness as an expression of the language of strategic management.[103]

I selected my "group of twelve" with just this ostensible diversity in mind. In Chapter 3, I apply this test with the following logic, referring to each text as a *case*.[104]

Suppose that I want to argue that the texts written by researchers Big and Small belong in the same interpretive community. I will have satisfied a test of breadth if

1. Another researcher has explicitly argued that Big and Small are two different kinds of cases, or
2. Other researchers have, by omission, implied this, and
3. I can interpret both the Big and Small cases as confirmations of my story.

From a pragmatist point of view, the number of such test cases is irrelevant, so sampling disappears as an issue. Instead, the diversity of those cases for the researcher's purposes is crucial. More formally stated, the issue is not whether the cases are drawn from a representative sample of Nature, but whether the cases replicate as much diversity of explanation as the researcher and her interpretive colleagues believe useful.[105] Pragmatism, in short, is all about generalizability.

Justification for This Third Justification

I go to the trouble of sketching this pragmatist interpretation of validity, reliability, and generalizability because a dyed-in-the-wool management scientist will likely feel uncomfortable with the notion that research can be conducted interpretively. Most often, this discomfort is expressed in a charge: "You are setting up straw men!" The clear implication in such an assertion is that pragmatist storytelling, whether humanist or not, amounts to license for undisciplined flights of fancy.[106] Fish seeks to bridge the gap between orthodox, positivist scientist and pragmatist on this score, noting that "the mistake is to think of interpretation as an activity in need of constraints, when in fact interpretation is a *structure* of constraints."[107] I offer my pragmatist rendition of validity, reliability, and generalizability as evidence of the constraints that I impose on myself for my storytelling efforts that now follow.[108] I enact these particular self-restrictions beginning in Chapter 3.

CONCLUSION

I wrote this chapter first to extend my defense of the corporate strategy concept as a humanist perspective on the modern corporation. I articulated and defended a thesis that the practice of strategic management research—that is, putting the corporate strategy concept to work for researchers, managers, and nonmanagers alike—can be understood as a practice with humanist possibilities. Although this potential for strategic management research might well mean that a strategic management researcher must make a long journey from the assumptions of orthodox science to the premises of a Nietzschean pragmatism, he can clear a variety of hurdles en route if he chooses to do so. I have defended that act of choice in this chapter.

This chapter defends the analytical approach that I will use in my endeavor to cast serious doubt on the humanist prospects for contemporary strategic management research. I defend my study in terms of (1) its appropriateness for the pragmatist question at hand (i.e., the worth of the corporate strategy concept); (2) its kinship to other kinds of research, including strategic management, that could be conducted in accordance with pragmatism; and (3) its satisfaction of three well-known tests of "good" research. By drawing a parallel among a diverse range of research practices, including strategic management research, I argue that my study can be read as a conversation among members of a far-flung community. I arranged the study so that the members of this community could share a language that eventually deals with the humanist and ethical worth of the corporate strategy concept.

3

A Genre About Strategy Through Process

But the poetry of industrialism, now there's a literary line where
you got to open up new territory.

T. CHOLMONDELEY FRINK,
in Sinclair Lewis, *Babbitt*

I explain in this chapter one specific sense by which we can choose to
give meaning to the corporate strategy concept as a literary, ethical
idea. I interpret that particular meaning in terms of a genre that I
create and call Strategy through the Means of Decision-Making Process, which I shorten to *Strategy through Process* (STP). The STP genre
is simply one way to employ the corporate strategy concept in our
thinking about human activity at the modern corporation. We can, in
the spirit of Frink, Sinclair Lewis's enterprising poet, think of Strategy
through Process as one kind of "literary line" about the corporation.[1]

My thesis here is that Strategy through Process can be read as a persistent, unifying theme in strategic management research. Furthermore, I argue that STP enjoys a time-honored popularity in ostensibly
diverse corners of that research tradition. This claim, it turns out, challenges a strand of popular wisdom which holds that strategic management research is still a nascent enterprise. In defending my thesis about
this research enterprise, I pursue the twin purposes of (1) substantiating my propositions from Chapter 1 regarding the literary and ethical
potential for the corporate strategy concept in general and (2) preparing for an eventual comparative assessment of the Strategy through
Process genre.

I accord the concept of *strategy* a central role here as I work through
my argument. More particularly, I emphasize the link between strategy
and purpose at the modern corporation. I begin by considering why
strategic management researchers believe that strategy is a worthwhile
concept in the first place. In a section titled "Why Have a Strategy?" I
explain that a host of strategic management researchers, working sep-

55

arately, have converged on an answer to this question. That answer can take the form of a genre that I create and call the *Problem of Strategic Management*. Think of the Problem of Strategic Management as one kind of literary rendition about the modern corporation.

I proceed to interpret three assumptions in this literary genre: a Human Decision Assumption, an Interrelationship Assumption, and an Advantage Assumption. In the process of interpreting these assumptions, I "consult"—carrying on a kind of conversation with—the authors of twelve prominent strategic management research models, theories, and frameworks for evidence of their "assent" to these assumptions.[2] Since this "group of twelve" becomes a crucial device as I advance my argument, I turn next to defending my choice of these twelve as "voices" that can "speak in unison" through the Problem of Strategic Management, and subsequently Strategy through Process. That section is accordingly titled "A Justification for My Group of Twelve."

Moving to the crux of the chapter, I derive next the Strategy through Process designation and genre. In this regard, I interpret how researchers across the group of twelve have moved from the premise that a strategy is vital at a corporation to the premise that the process of acquiring a strategy is a crucial endeavor. In the section titled "If a Strategy Is So Important, How Does a Firm Acquire One?" I explain that the logic of Strategy through Process turns on three provisos that correspond, point by point, to the three assumptions that give meaning to my Problem of Strategic Management story. By drawing this parallel to the Problem of Strategic Management as a literary genre, I confirm the literary implications of Strategy through Process.

The argument reaches a climax when I reinterpret Strategy through Process in ethical terms. Specifically, I claim that STP can be understood to turn on three premises that deal with persons and purposes, and hence can be clearly understood to bear ethical implications. Once again, I organize my argument in such a way that these three premises correspond point by point to the three provisos of Strategy through Process and the three assumptions of the Problem of Strategic Management. My point here is that a strategic management researcher must logically subscribe to these ethical premises if he is to approach the Problem of Strategic Management by means of the Strategy through Process genre. Since I take this culminating step in the spirit of defending Strategy through Process as one kind of ethical literature, I title this section "A Justification for Strategy through Process."[3] The chapter concludes with a comment about the implications of STP in light of the popular belief that strategic management research is a fragmented line of inquiry.

Throughout Chapter 3, I draw time and again on the statements made by authors from my group of twelve. Their meanings join mine in a kind of unfolding dialogue. I initiate the conversation and then invite concurrence from the group of twelve with regard to each central premise in the argument: (1) the Problem of Strategic Management, (2) Strategy through Process, and (3) Strategy through Process as an ethical genre. In this way, I can satisfy the pragmatist literary "equivalents" to scientific validity and reliability (Chapter 1), en route to my claim that Strategy through Process is a remarkably generalizable conception of the Problem of Strategic Management and, hence, the corporate strategy concept.

WHY HAVE A STRATEGY?

As a point of departure, consider these three stories.

1. In the closing thirty seconds of a tightly contested basketball game between the Blue Rockets and the Red Devils, the score is tied. A Red Devil player deflects the ball out of bounds and promptly asks the referee for a timeout. While the players huddle around their respective coaches, the television commentator makes this observation:[4]

> Rebound, the Red Devil coach, has called for a time out in order to discuss with his players a strategy for winning the game. He will probably instruct them to get the ball to West or East, who are accomplished shooters, in anticipation that the Blue Rockets will double-team Slim, who is the best shooter for the Red Devils.

Once the game resumes, West passes to East. The player guarding East slips, whereupon East scores the winning basket with time expiring. Rebound admits to an interviewer:

> I'm glad that we talked through our strategy during the timeout. That was a hectic finish, what with all the noise from the Blue Rockets fans. My assistants and I had been thinking about a final shot opportunity ever since we tied the game with three minutes remaining. More than anything else, I wanted for us to have the ball when the final seconds ticked off the clock.

2. The air has been filled with an unmistakable tension lately across the Blue Prairie College campus.[5] Within the past month, college administrators revoked their recognition of two fraternity chapters and one sorority chapter for a list of violations that include the provision of alcohol to minors and the staging of a talent show deemed—by administrators, several campus groups, and the local police—to be offensive to women and numerous ethnic minorities. During the same period, the college faculty voted overwhelmingly in favor of a resolution that would require the members of the ten remaining fraternities and so-

rorities to open their membership to women and men, respectively, or
risk revocation of their charters.

President Beleaguered of Blue Prairie has been petitioned by alumni
seeking preservation of the Greek system, by parents seeking a campus
atmosphere more conducive to academic pursuits by their daughters
and sons, and by a feminist caucus threatening to initiate a vote of "no
confidence" in her presidency. Students have hung protest banners from
residence hall windows. At the conclusion of an all-day, all-campus
meeting on this issue, Beleaguered announces that she and the trustees
will soon meet for three days to map out a strategy that will restore
calm to a tense campus atmosphere, ensure no ill effects for admissions
and development efforts, and generally preserve the integrity of the
college experience at Blue Prairie.

3. Potts, chief executive officer at Bison Ridge Telephone Company,
opens the annual shareholders' meeting with the following statement:[6]

> We spend a great deal of time talking about strategy at Bison Ridge. Our
> strategy is to serve the shareholders and customers of Bison Ridge by trav-
> eling two paths that sometimes strain our resources and attention. On the
> one hand, we aim to continue providing basic residential telecommunications
> services to our primarily rural customer base at the lowest rates possible.
> While under pressures to do otherwise, I am proud to report that the basic
> local telephone rate for a Bison Ridge residential customer is the same in
> 1990 as it was in 1970, even as our service fleet has grown threefold. So, we
> must continue to watch our costs diligently.
>
> At the same time, we are committed to rapidly enhancing the Bison Ridge
> network in order to accommodate the three multinational corporations that
> maintain significant presences in our local service area. We anticipate that
> their satisfactions with our enhanced services can help draw other such cus-
> tomers to this region. All this will require a program of capital expenditures
> that is unprecedented at Bison Ridge in terms of scale. In order for Bison
> Ridge to meet its obligations to its shareholders while continuing to serve
> this diverse set of telecommunications needs, we must pay close attention to
> competitive and regulatory forces that seem to change shape every day here
> in the region, at the state level, in Washington, and globally.

We can understand each of these three stories as a particular kind of
commentary about the concept of strategy. A first step toward address-
ing "Why have a strategy?" thus involves unpacking this commentary
for a possible meaning of "strategy." I do this now in three regards.

A Meaning for the Concept of Strategy

First, the principal characters believe that, in view of the stakes involved as they confront their futures, they must engage in an act of
thoughtful reflection about those futures. Each, in other words, at-

taches sufficient significance to the purposes at hand that he or she resists a whimsical approach. Rebound, the Red Devils coach, wants his team to win the game. To that end, he deliberates first with his assistant coaches and then with his players during the timeout. Beleaguered points to nothing less than the integrity of Blue Prairie as an institution as she prepares for a protracted discussion with the trustees. Potts's remarks indicate from the very outset his commitment to deliberating about customer service, en route to the commitment by others at Bison Ridge to provide customer service in two distinct markets. In all three cases, we can understand the central characters as interpreters of meaning for strategy as a kind of decision—about their respective purposes—that can subsequently inform their actions. Furthermore, we can extend this understanding to apply across a considerable time span, from the relatively hurried decision-making scenarios involving Rebound and Beleaguered to the relatively more leisurely pace at Bison Ridge.[7]

Second, the principal characters believe that such deliberations toward strategy decisions are made necessary partly by the presence of others and other forces that will likely influence their respective futures. Each character believes, in other words, that a relationship with what we might call "environmental forces" provides further impetus for thinking about strategy. Rebound takes into account the past defensive preferences of his rival coach and the incessant noise from the Blue Rockets fans. Beleaguered need look no further than the mail stacked on her desk and the banners hanging all over campus to acknowledge that she and the trustees will decide in a context that involves others. Potts makes explicit reference to dealings with residential customers, corporate customers, competitors, and regulators, believing that any strategy decision at Bison Ridge must be made in recognition of those ongoing relationships. None of these characters believes, in short, that thinking about strategy is merely a matter of clarifying one's own purposes.[8]

Third, the principal characters believe that they must devise a strategy if their actions are to advance their respective pursuits. Given the importance to each of them of their own purposes and given the relationships that can affect such pursuits, these characters believe that a strategy is an instrumental and downright essential means for having a chance to derive benefits in the futures that they confront.[9] Rebound links the timeout—and his preparatory discussions with his assistants—with the possibility that his players can have a chance to win the game. Beleaguered links the results of the trustees meeting with the hope that life can return to normal at Blue Prairie College. Potts links a Bison Ridge presence in two different marketplaces with the possibilities for satisfying shareholders and customers. In all three cases, moreover, the link between the achievement of purpose and the preparation of a strategy is accompanied by the hope that the potential benefits will endure. Rebound seeks a scoring opportunity for his players that also precludes a subsequent last-second opportunity for the Blue Rockets. Beleaguered announces her hope that a strategy can facilitate school-as-usual for some time to come at Blue Prairie. Likewise, Potts expresses hope that a strategy can contribute to the perpetuation of a long tradition of customer service by Bison Ridge employees.

Across all three cases, then, we meet persons who combine beliefs about (1) reasons for acting, (2) the context of their actions, and (3) the value of acting, all to produce a plan for purposeful action that is commonly called a strategy.[10] In short, all three stories can be interpreted as belonging to a common genre. What they hold in common is the following, and for now provisional, conception of strategy.

> *An Initial Interpretation of Strategy*
>
> A strategy is simply a set of decisions, the product of thoughtful reflection, that lays claim to a specific, enduring position in relation to an environment, in anticipation that those decisions can produce a benefit from that position.

The next step is to consider whether strategic management researchers have interpreted the concept of strategy in the same sense of deliberation about purpose, setting, and the necessity for having a strategy.

Strategy and the Problem of Strategic Management

My search for affirmation of the beliefs that Rebound, Beleaguered, and Potts hold in common about strategy leads, as a first destination, to the writings of Kenneth Andrews. In his book *The Concept of Corporate Strategy*, Andrews proposes that "a business enterprise guided by a clear sense of purpose rationally arrived at and emotionally ratified by commitment is more likely to have a successful outcome, in terms of profit and social good, than a company whose future is left to guesswork and chance."[11] We can readily unpack this elegant proposition in terms familiar to Rebound, Beleaguered, and Potts alike. First of all, Andrews draws a clear connection between strategy and thoughtful decisions ("a clear sense of purpose rationally arrived at . . .") as human concerns ("rationally arrived at and emotionally ratified by commitment"). He proceeds to locate this kind of decision in the context of others, more explicitly with reference to "social good" and less explicitly with regard to profits. Still further, Andrews leaves no doubt about the connection between strategy (the very antithesis of "guesswork and chance") and the prospects for desirable future benefits ("more likely to have a successful outcome"). On all three counts, then, we can read

Andrews's "assent" to the notions about strategy that integrate my stories about basketball, campus politics, and telecommunications services.

With Andrews's account at least provisionally joined to the conception of strategy that Rebound, Beleaguered, and Potts "helped" me develop, I am ready to cast my interpretive net more widely.[12] My next aim is to substantiate a claim that Andrews, several of his notable predecessors, and a host of his contemporaries *all* provide a common answer to the question "Why have a strategy?" As I extend this kind of dialogue about strategy, I will move to formally state that answer in terms of what I call the Problem of Strategic Management.

Strategy pioneers. Alfred Chandler and Chester Barnard, writing a decade and generation, respectively, before Andrews, both articulated conceptions of strategy that can be connected to what Andrews and my three story characters have to say on the subject. Chandler and Barnard crafted their arguments about the need for a strategy at the confluence of two concerns: (1) the pace of change in business environments, and (2) the degree of preparedness "inside" the firm for accommodating such change.[13] Chandler and Barnard can be understood to have argued in common that a strategy is crucial as a touchstone of preparedness in the face of an uncertain future world.

Chandler proposed a central role for the "visible hand" of professional managers whose decisions included perceptive consideration of what was happening beyond the firm: "Strategic growth resulted from an awareness of the opportunities and needs—created by changing population, income, and technology—to employ existing or expanding resources more profitably."[14] More particularly: "The visible hand of management replaced the invisible hand of market forces where and when new technology and expanded markets permitted a historically unprecedented high volume and speed of materials."[15] With these words, Chandler places the connection between careful decision ("visible hand" and "awareness . . . to employ") and the prospects for lasting gain ("more profitably") in the context of key relationships, which he characterizes in terms of population, income, technology, and market demand.[16] Chandler makes this connection more broadly in his well-known proposition that strategy decisions play a determining role in decisions about organization structure.[17] By means of this linkage among decisions about strategy and structure, executive reflection about the firm's circumstances can facilitate "the formation of an administrative structure to mobilize systematically the resources within each functional activity."[18] So mobilized, the firm stands prepared to meet the environmental challenge.

Writing in 1938, Barnard carefully delineated the "functions of the executive," most prominent of which was the generation of decisions about purpose at the organization.[19] Unless purpose was clear, he suggested, the executive could be stymied in the performance of his other principal functions: gaining employee commitment to that purpose and sustaining organization-wide communication about actions taken in the name of that purpose. Barnard set this purpose-driven challenge against a complex backdrop of (1) internal relationships, which he called the "organization economy,—and (2) an external "social economy": "The *social economy* consists of the organization's relationships (that is, power of exchange utilities) with other organizations and with individuals *not* connected with the organization in a cooperative way, which relationships have utilities for the organization."[20] The prospects for deriving lasting benefits ("utilities"), Barnard claimed, varied with the degree of satisfaction that a given organizational purpose held for those whose contributions of effort were necessary to fulfill that purpose. He referred to these prospects in terms of the "efficiency" problem of a cooperative system: "Thus, the efficiency of a cooperative system is its capacity to maintain itself by the individual satisfactions it affords."[21] This provision of satisfaction, clearly then, makes strategy a matter of human decision at Barnard's version of the corporation.[22]

Both Chandler and Barnard introduced versions of a proposition, more recently borrowed from the natural sciences, that has gained widespread appeal among strategic management researchers: survival of the firm varies directly with the "health" of the firm's internal systems.[23] On this account, the primary problem is to prepare the internal systems of the firm for the constant struggle to exist. A strategy is necessary, then, as a central decision around which the internal systems of the firm can be rationalized. To Chandler, this meant that a strategy was a source of the logic for resource commitments and organization structure.[24] To Barnard, decisions about purpose could serve as a rallying point to which employees could commit their efforts.

In sum, both Chandler and Barnard converged on a central theme: a strategy was necessary because chances were great that in the absence of one, environmental forces would find the firm unprepared. And, the reasoning continued, being adrift in a hostile environment foretold a mediocre future, if not extinction, for the firm. The environment could be confronted advantageously, on the other hand, Chandler and Barnard believed, through thoughtful deliberations that focused on questions of purpose.

Three assumptions and the problem of strategic management. The upshot here is that Rebound, Beleaguered, and Potts, as well as Andrews, Chandler, and Barnard, can all be understood as narrators of the same kind of story. Each believes it worthwhile to emphasize matters of human choice—or decision—amid a pattern of complex relationships, in anticipation that such choice can improve the prospects for deriving enduring benefits. In more formal terms, and cast in the context of the modern corporation with the assistance of Andrews, Chandler, and Barnard, I offer a three-part interpretation of this particular approach to the concept of strategy:

> **Human Decision Assumption:** *Purposeful action at the corporation requires, in part, that persons devote attention to questions about the purpose(s) for that action.*

> **Interrelationship Assumption:** *Purposeful action at the corporation requires, in part, acknowledgment of the influences that relationships with others "outside" the corporation can bring to bear on that action.*

> **Advantage Assumption:** *Purposeful action at the corporation requires, in part, that persons choose and actively seek a position of lasting benefit in relation to influential "outside" forces.*

By this logic, then, we can understand what I call the *Problem of Strategic Management* as the conscious effort to fashion a course of action on the basis of these three assumptions. Further, we can understand the concept of *strategy* as a product of human choice that provides for (1) the acknowledged influence of relationships with others, and (2) a plan of purposeful action that can improve the chances of deriving lasting benefits from acting in consonance with the plan in the presence of others.

My next task is to consider just how widely this story about strategy might be told.

Many Voices About the Problem of Strategic Management

I create and seek to give meaning to the Problem of Strategic Management as an avenue toward understanding the meaningfulness of contemporary strategic management research. Accordingly, it is imperative at this juncture in my argument that I substantiate the Problem of Strategic Management as a coherent kind of story line that reaches into many corners of strategic management research. I thus seek in this section to apply my discussion in Chapter 1 by showing how we can interpret this story as a genre about purposeful human action at the modern corporation. Since the credibility of my claim that the Problem of Strategic Management can be understood as a genre turns, in part, on the breadth of support that I can muster, I must portray this story as the outpouring of "many voices" in strategic management research circles.[25] That is my present task.

In the eleven subsections that now follow, I accord each of eleven voices an opportunity to join Andrews and one another in affirming their support for the Problem of Strategic Management as a genre.[26] I interpret these voices from the writings of many well-known strategic management researchers. Some of these voices belong to those writing alone. Others are raised in partnership. Either way, when added to Andrews's voice to make up my "group of twelve," these narrators join me in substantiating the proposition that the Problem of Strategic Management can give clear meaning to purposeful human action at the corporation.

Ansoff on the problem of strategic management. Igor Ansoff clearly links (1) attention to matters of purpose ("objectives") and (2) actions taken ("configure and direct") in pursuit of advantage ("attainment of objectives"): "From a decision viewpoint the overall problem of the business of the firm is to *configure and direct the resource-conversion process in such a way as to optimize the attainment of the objectives.*"[27]

He sets this decision ("selection") problem in the context of competitive relationships ("markets") with others: "Strategic decisions are primarily concerned with external, rather than internal, problems of the firm and specifically with selection of the product-mix which the firm will produce and the markets to which it will sell."[28]

Ansoff combines the concerns about the purpose of corporate action, relationships with others, and prospects for lasting benefit in terms of what he calls the "new corporate strategy": "Together with strategic planning, [capability planning and systematic management of discontinuous change] form a comprehensive and systematic approach to prepare the firm to benefit from future opportunities and to avoid future threats."[29]

Harrigan on the problem of strategic management. Kathryn Rudie Harrigan pays particular attention to choices that persons must make about key turning points in a firm's operation: "What strategies are best for businesses in decline?"[30] In this context, she provides a list of questions that address purpose ("opportunities") amid relationships with others ("rivals") and the prospects for gaining ("Does it pay?") from actions ("compete") taken in pursuit of those purposes: "How can I maximize the opportunities presented by market decline? Does it pay for me to stay in this business and dominate it? Which rivals seem best suited to remain in this industry? . . . If I do stay invested, how should I compete?"[31] Harrigan interprets "strategic flexibility" in terms of purposeful decisions ("reposition . . . change . . . dismantle") through which an undesirable outcome ("distasteful result") can be averted in relation to others ("customers . . . competitors"):

> This book is about *strategic flexibility.* It examines firms' abilities to reposition themselves in a market, change their game plans, or dismantle their current strategies when the customers they serve are no longer as attractive as they once were. It is a collection of essays about how competitive strategies often

ignore questions of strategic flexibility, with the distasteful result that firms get stuck in an obsolete strategic posture while competitors move on.[32]

Hrebiniak and Joyce on the problem of strategic management. Lawrence Hrebiniak and William Joyce connect attention ("series of . . . decisions") to matters of purpose ("long-term global objectives") with the actions ("means") that are proposed to satisfy those ends: *"Strategic decision making may be viewed as a series of means–ends decisions beginning with the determination of long-term global objectives (ends) and the development of shorter-term, more local actions to obtain these objectives (means)."*[33] They locate this concern with purpose in the context of an amalgamation of external relationships ("environmental contingencies"): *"Strategy formulation is a decision process focusing on the development of long-term objectives and the alignment of organizational capabilities and environmental contingencies so as to obtain them."*[34]

Lorange on the problem of strategic management. Peter Lorange offers a proposition that explicitly connects concerns with purpose ("best alternatives"), relationships ("environment"), and lasting benefits ("more advantageous directions"):

Strategic success in most instances will require that the firm systematically look for opportunities and/or threats in its environment to come up with the best alternatives for the firm to pursue. This outward-looking search is crucial to improve the firm's chances to take more advantageous directions and to employ its resources in such a way that they yield the best return.[35]

Miles on the problem of strategic management. Robert Miles poses two guiding questions that highlight decisions about purpose ("options") amid relationships with others ("extreme environmental stress"), where those decisions can offer the hopes ("adapting") of a lasting gain ("relative effectiveness"): "What is the range of strategic options available to complex organizations for adapting to extreme environmental stress? . . . What is the relative effectiveness of different patterns of strategic adaptation (of strategic variation) within an industry population?[36]

Miles and Snow on the problem of strategic management. Raymond Miles and Charles Snow interpret strategy in terms of a variety of decisions ("pattern") about the direction of purposeful activities at the firm ("possible future domains"): "Strategy is more of a *pattern* or *stream* of major and minor decisions about an organization's possible future domains."[37] They place such decision-making activities amid a complex set of relationships ("not a homogeneous entity"): "However, more specifically, the environment is not a homogeneous entity, but rather is composed of a complex combination of factors such as product and labor market conditions, industry customs and practices, governmental regulations, and relations with financial and raw materials suppliers."[38] Against this backdrop, Miles and Snow discuss the search for advantage in terms of achieving "an effective position": "The intent of this model is to portray the nature and interrelationships of the key problems that organizations must solve in order to achieve an effective position within their chosen environment."[39]

Porter on the problem of strategic management. Michael Porter proposes that advantages ("significant benefits") are to be gained through focused ("common set of goals") attention to decisions about purpose (*"explicit* process of formulating strategy") at the firm:

> The emphasis being placed on strategic planning today in firms in the United States and abroad reflects the proposition that there are significant benefits to gain through an *explicit* process of formulating strategy, to insure that at least the policies (if not the action) of functional departments are coordinated and directed at some common set of goals.[40]

He situates this search for advantage ("superior return") amid relationships in the marketplace ("competitive forces"): ". . . competitive strategy [is] taking offensive or defensive actions to create a defensible position in an industry, to cope successfully with the five competitive forces and thereby yield a superior return on investment for the firm."[41]

Quinn on the problem of strategic management. James Brian Quinn interprets strategy in terms of decisions about the purpose for corporate action ("overall direction of an enterprise"), the context of relationships ("most important surrounding environments") within which those decisions apply, and the hopes for benefiting from those decisions ("right directions"):

> *Strategic decisions* are those that determine the overall direction of an enterprise and its ultimate viability in light of the predictable, the unpredictable, and the unknowable changes that may occur in its most important surrounding environments. They intimately shape the true goals of the enterprise. . . . And they determine the effectiveness of the enterprise—whether its major thrusts are in the right directions—rather than whether individual tasks are performed efficiently.[42]

Quinn, Mintzberg, and James on the problem of strategic management. Quinn, Henry Mintzberg, and Robert James interpret the strategy process broadly in terms of the myriad external factors ("his world") that can influence a decision-maker's choices ("perceive and understand") about the possibilities ("guiding . . . through the unfolding future") for benefiting ("success") from action at the corporation:

Each CEO (Chief Executive Officer) shares with all other CEOs the challenge of guiding his organization through the unfolding future of the world about him. Success will depend on his ability to perceive and understand his world in all its subtlety, inconsistency, bureaucracy, and political maneuver as well as its rationality, in other words, in all of its *complexity*.[43]

Rappaport on the problem of strategic management. Alfred Rappaport interprets a "shareholder value" model of strategic management in which decisions about the direction of corporate action ("operating and financial analysis") are linked with the prospects for gain ("dollars of value"). He attempts "to integrate operating and financial analysis. In particular, the direct linkage between competitive strategy and shareholder value analysis is demonstrated by translating business strategies into the dollars of value they create."[44] He provides this model in contemplation of key relationships between the decision-maker and competitors ("competitive advantage") and shareholders: "As management considers alternative strategies, those expected to develop the greatest sustainable competitive advantage will be those that will also create the greatest value for shareholders."[45]

Schendel and Hofer on the problem of strategic management. Dan Schendel and Charles Hofer sketch a story line that revolves around a central ("at the heart") act of purposeful decision ("entrepreneurial choice") taken in recognition of relations with others ("consumer need") in hopes of a beneficial result ("excess . . . incentive [profit] to continue"):

> Any successful business begins with a "key idea" for: (1) supplying a product or service, (2) that will satisfy a consumer need, (3) and in so doing will lead to an excess of revenue over costs, (4) thereby supplying the originator of the idea with an incentive (profit) to continue to provide the supply. . . . The "key idea," that product of the entrepreneurial mind, is the central concept that is to be noted. Without it, there is no business, and indeed this same argument can easily be generalized to any type of purposive organization. This entrepreneurial choice is at the heart of the concept of strategy.[46]

Segue

The fact that these eleven lines of argument, when joined with Andrews's narrative, converge on the Problem of Strategic Management genre and my initial interpretation of strategy is a crucial step in my argument. It is crucial, since I will develop four interpretations on the basis of my foregoing interpretive efforts about the Problem of Strategic Management.[47] Later in this chapter, I interpret the Strategy through Process genre as one particular expression of the Problem of Strategic Management. I conclude the chapter with an interpretation of Strategy through Process as an ethical genre about the Problem of Strategic Management genre. In Chapter 4, I interpret the Strategy & Justice genre as another particular expression of the Problem of Strategic Management, and as an ethical genre in particular.[48] Finally, in Chapter 5, I interpret the relative advantages of Strategy & Justice over Strategy through Process in the context of the Problem of Strategic Management story about the modern corporation.[49] This progression of interpretations is depicted in Figure 3.1. On all four counts, then, both the logical coherence of and the breadth of support for the Problem of Strategic Management become central concerns of mine.

In this regard, it is just as important to understand that this fact of convergence by those included in my group of twelve is neither a coincidence nor an act of an unseen Nature. Quite to the contrary, this fact is a direct consequence of my choice to call on this set of voices. Since I will call on the members of the group of twelve time and again, it is appropriate that I now turn to justifying the composition of that assembly. To make my case, I draw on the arguments that I made in Chapter 2 with regard to how a pragmatist storyteller like me deals with matters of knowledge and truth.

A JUSTIFICATION FOR MY GROUP OF TWELVE

Recall that a pragmatist storyteller pursues knowledge through a self-conscious, self-directed quest for meaning about herself and the world of others in which she conducts that quest.[50] Her searches for meaning

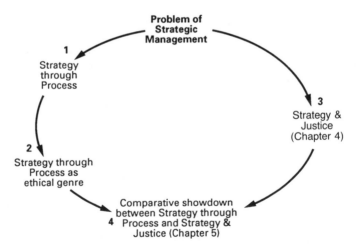

Figure 3.1. Four interpretations based on the Problem of Strategic Management genre.

are manifest in the stories that she spins about her world. In a pragmatist sense, "storytelling" pertains as readily to the more familiarly labeled craft of a novelist as the term pertains to the storytelling efforts of researchers LaFleur, Elan, and Shepherd in Chapter 2.

It is at the confluence of these individual, subjective quests that truths can be shaped and extended. Storyteller inevitably meets storyteller. Where their respective pursuits become entangled—as when LaFleur, Elan, and Shepherd begin to talk with others interested in steel towns, thunderstorms, and global business, respectively—they have reason to seek common understandings from which each can derive meaning.[51] These understandings are, on a pragmatist account, the truths that these persons use to connect themselves in a community and hence give meaning to their jointly created world. As a device for telling my story about strategy, I seek to connect the arguments made by the members of my group of twelve in terms of a set of truths about the modern corporation that they *could* hold in common.[52] To defend the possibility of understanding their eligibility for community status, I draw on my discussion in Chapter 2 about the connection between knowledge—and hence truth—and diversity.

Diversity, Truth, and My Group of Twelve

Diversity among interpretations about the world enters a pragmatist discussion as a profound source of evolving truths. As each person conducts her own quest for meaning, she travels a route to which no one else can gain admittance. Yet that quest is necessarily limited in scope. It is through engagement with others that we, as aspiring pragmatists, can learn more about ourselves. Jean Baker Miller makes this point, writing about diversity in terms of conflict: "In our individual lives, all relationships must encompass conflict. Whenever two people interact with each other, each person is presenting something new to the other, something different from what would arise from within herself or himself."[53] In this context, then, diversity presents an opportunity for a mutually meaningful connection between persons, which Miller states in terms of growth: "Our ability to engage with that new thought and feeling is the source of our growth and the growth of the relationship between us."[54] In this connection fostered by diversity, we can hope to create new truths that, held in common, enable us to move in our worlds.

Taking this cue from Miller, we can understand the worldly usefulness of a given story as a function of the diverse appeal that it can attract. *The test of usefulness is straightforward: the more diverse the membership of a community that is created around a particular story, the more credible is that story as an expression of human truths.* Worldly evidence abounds for this proposition. Economists of many persuasions have long maintained a common bond through their shared story about general equilibrium analysis.[55] Physicists, chemists, and engineers have joined in dialogues across generations by means of a story about the laws of thermodynamics. Musicians the world over pursue their respective crafts through shared truths about tempo, key, and harmony. And baseball fans and players alike, in Japan and in the United States, can distinguish a well-executed from an amateurish relay from the outfield by means of their jointly created truths about team defensive play.[56]

We can understand the evolution of each of these communities in terms of self-selected engagement among diverse persons who interact through a common story that strengthens the worth of their association. It is precisely this convergence of diverse interests, which I expressed at the end of Chapter 2 as a "test of breadth," to which I now appeal as I justify the membership ranks for my group of twelve.

Why These Twelve?

I selected these twelve well-known accounts of strategy and strategic management research for one basic pragmatist reason: *by virtue of the differences among them, this set of accounts can add persuasive possibilities for my argument.* To explain this reasoning, I now interpret these differences in terms of some "boundaries" between the theories, models, and frameworks that are commonly accepted as truths among strategic management researchers.[57] In particular, I chose a group of twelve accounts that can be understood to cut against the grain of four such distinguishing "boundaries" in strategic management research. By cutting against the grain not once, but in four different respects, I claim that much more credibility for my group of twelve as a diverse source of truths about the Problem of Strategic Management and related interpretations.

For the sake of exposition, I choose to explain these four boundaries, which I choose to override in selecting my group of twelve, in terms of four propositions:

> **Proposition 1.** *Strategy process research differs from strategy content research.*

Liam Fahey and Kurt Christensen have drawn the distinction in this way:

> Content focuses on the specifics of what was decided, whereas process addresses how such decisions are reached in an organizational setting . . . strategy content is defined as research which examines the content of decisions regarding the goals, scope, and/or competitive strategies of corporations or of one or more of their business units.[58]

Fahey and Christensen proceed to apply this distinction when they include the arguments made by Porter, Harrigan, Miles and Snow, Andrews, and Miles in the "content" contingent. Rappaport's recent thesis about strategies for shareholder wealth clearly belongs in this category as well. By contrast, Fahey and Christensen associate Ansoff with "the strategic decision process" and make no mention of the remainder of my group of twelve.[59]

Anne Huff and Rhonda Reger subsequently confirm this proposition by defining strategic process research to include Lorange, Schendel and Hofer, Quinn, and, by association, the thesis recently advanced by Quinn, Mintzberg, and James.[60] Moreover, Huff and Reger credit Ansoff and Andrews—alongside Chandler—with proposing the process–content distinction in the first place.[61] In short, my group of twelve clearly passes a test of breadth on this count. More particularly, I have already shown that a genre such as the Problem of Strategic Management renders the distinction between strategy content and strategy process unhelpful for my analysis.[62]

> **Proposition 2.** *Strategy formulation processes differ from strategy implementation processes, for research purposes.*

Within the domain of strategy process research, the dichotomy between formulation activities and implementation activities is well known. Andrews makes clear this distinction, referring to implementation in terms of converting plans into results: "The discussion of individual companies therefore matures into a consideration of *how to formulate* an appropriate pattern of purpose and policy and *how to convert* plans into results."[63] Schendel and Hofer give further impetus to this dichotomy by arguing that managerial attention must be directed toward "the *reconciliation* of social/political processes used in implementation with analytical/rational processes used in strategy formulation and evaluation."[64] More recently, Quinn, Mintzberg, and James extend this point about integrating strategy formulation and implementation, noting the "reality" of this connection: "In this text, as in reality, formulation and implementation are intertwined as complex interactive processes in which politics, values, organizational culture, and management styles determine or constrain particular strategic decisions."[65]

Across the decades that the three foregoing statements span, the work of Lorange, on the one hand, and the work of Hrebiniak and Joyce, on the other, vividly attest to strategy formulation and strategy implementation as different analytical concerns.[66] Even Porter, who is not generally considered a process researcher, finds reason to appeal to this dichotomy. He introduces his "competitive advantage" argument in the spirit of Schendel and Hofer and of Quinn, Mintzberg, and James: "The concepts in this book aim to build a bridge between strategy for-

mulation and implementation, rather than treating [them] sepa-
rately."[67] In particular, Porter argues that his "value chain" concept
can serve as a framework for implementation activities.[68]

In this second regard, then, I chose my group of twelve in such a
way that my interpretive efforts are not constrained by the formulation—implementation boundary.

> ***Proposition 3.*** *Strategy research about shareholder wealth differs from
> strategy research about perpetuating the firm and/or perpetuating the ten-
> ure of senior executives.*

Across the group of twelve, the desiderata for strategy formulation and
implementation activities vary widely. Rappaport stands alone as he argues unambiguously for a finance-based test of strategy: "Business
strategies should be judged by the economic returns they generate for
shareholders, as measured by dividends plus the increase in the company's share price."[69] Quite to the contrary, Quinn says nary a word
about shareholders in his claim that *"strategic decisions* are those that
determine the overall direction of an enterprise and *its ultimate viability*
in light of the predictable, the unpredictable, and the unknowable
changes that may occur in its most important surrounding environments."[70] Clearly suggested by Quinn here is the preservation of the
firm per se as the proper test of corporate strategy. In the same spirit,
references to shareholders are conspicuously scant, or absent altogether, in the arguments made by Hrebiniak and Joyce, Miles and Snow,
and Quinn, Mintzberg, and James.[71]

Andrews provides a third angle on this proposition by not only arguing against an axiomatic approach to shareholder wealth ("stereo-
type"), but actually proposing that strategies must be formulated to cor-
relate with the interests of senior executives:

> We should in all realism admit that the personal desires, aspirations, and
> needs of the senior managers of a company actually *do* play an influential
> role in the determination of strategy. Against those who are offended by this
> idea either for its departure from stereotype of single-minded economic man
> or for its implicit violation of responsibilities to the shareholder, we would
> argue that we must accept not only the inevitability but the desirability of
> this intervention.[72]

Harrigan likewise presents a mixed message, in comparison to Rappaport, on this subject. With regard to joint ventures, she openly advocates attention to wealth-creating activities.[73] At the same time, her discussion of strategies for declining industries suggests the importance of
executives wanting to keep playing the business game for their own
reasons.[74]

The upshot here is that the very reasons for worrying about strategy formulation and implementation and about strategy content and process vary significantly across my group of twelve. More specifically, I have shown that the wide appeal of the Problem of Strategic Management genre renders moot this distinction among desiderata, for purposes of understanding strategic management.

> **Proposition 4.** *Strategy research based on economic theory differs from strategy research derived from other disciplinary heritages.*

A perusal of the bibliographies, notes, and indexes provided by the group of twelve suggests a wide gulf between strategic management research writings based on economic theory and strategic management research that is not. Porter, Harrigan, and Rappaport, all of whom plainly approach strategic management research as a problem in applied microeconomics, make few, if any, references to the writings of such widely cited organization theorists as Herbert Simon, James March, James Thompson, Mancur Olson, Philip Selznick, Karl Weick, Peter Drucker, and Jeffrey Pfeffer.[75] Likewise, one will find few, if any, references to Richard Caves, Richard Rumelt, William Baumol, Edwin Mansfield, and Ronald Coase—all intellectual ancestors of Porter, Harrigan, and Rappaport—in the bibliographies and indexes offered by Lorange, Miles and Snow, Quinn, Hrebiniak, and Joyce, and Miles.

On either side of this divide, even if "cross-references" can be found, they play inconsequential parts in the arguments. The point, once again, is that my interpretation of the Problem of Strategic Management spans a set of arguments drawn on diverse disciplinary heritages.

I carefully chose my group of twelve arguments about corporate strategy in an effort to accentuate the diversity across these arguments. On four different counts, I showed how my group of twelve runs across the grain of—indeed, runs roughshod over—analytical boundaries that have been widely considered as meaningful for making sense of strategic management research.

It is within this context of diversity that I make a claim for the credibility of my interpretive efforts in this chapter. I already argued that these twelve diverse voices can be understood to "speak in unison" about the Problem of Strategic Management genre. As I now move to reinterpret that genre in terms of Strategy through Process, and subsequently Strategy through Process as an ethical genre, I elaborate on my claim that many different writers can share in the meaningfulness of a single story line.[76] As I progressively extend that story line, I take up Miller's challenge to create a sense of community in the midst of apparent diversity.

IF A STRATEGY IS SO IMPORTANT, HOW DOES A FIRM ACQUIRE ONE?

I devote the remainder of this chapter to articulating and substantiating a genre that I create and call Strategy through Process (STP). STP is an interpretation that I ascribe to each argument in my group of twelve. More particularly, I interpret Strategy through Process as one logical approach for dealing with the Problem of Strategic Management. By means of an extended "conversation" with my group of twelve, I will argue that all the ostensibly different arguments in that group can be interpreted to converge on STP as a "solution" to the Problem of Strategic Management.

In this section, I draw a connection between Strategy through Process and the Problem of Strategic Management by interpreting a logic for Strategy through Process in terms of three provisos.[77] I articulate each proviso in terms that correspond to one of the three assumptions that give meaning to the Problem of Strategic Management: the Human Decision, Interrelationship, and Advantage Assumptions, respectively. I conclude the section by summarizing the meaning of Strategy through Process at the confluence of these three provisos. This summary, in the form of a Reinterpretation of Strategy, gives new meaning to the Initial Interpretation of Strategy that I developed earlier in this chapter.

In the subsequent section, I reinterpret Strategy through Process as a kind of commentary about purpose at the corporation and, hence, as an ethical genre. I do this by reinterpreting each of the three STP provisos in terms of a corresponding premise about the pursuit of purposes in a corporate context. I conclude that section with a Reinterpreted Reinterpretation of Strategy that integrates the meanings of the three ethical premises to provide a meaning for the Strategy through Process genre in ethical terms. My plan for these two interpretations of the Problem of Strategic Management is diagramed in Figure 3.2, there the three provisos and three premises remain to be identified and defended.

The logical case for Strategy through Process is straightforward. By the Problem of Strategic Management, we can understand that each in the group of twelve argues for the advisability of the corporation *having* a strategy. I claim that those in the group of twelve then argue in their respective ways that, given the importance of having a strategy, careful attention must be given to how the corporation might *acquire* a strategy.[78] Given further that a strategy consists of many decisions (Human Decision Assumption) about the corporation, its place in a larger environment (Interrelationship Assumption), and its prospects for thriving in that position (Advantage Assumption), the acquisition problem becomes a matter of arranging a logical structure of activities through

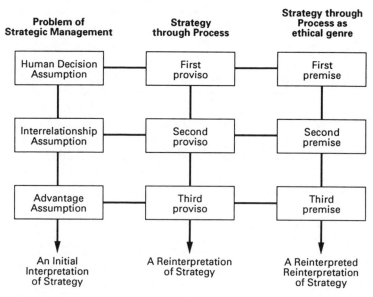

Problem of Strategic Management	Strategy through Process	Strategy through Process as ethical genre
Human Decision Assumption	First proviso	First premise
Interrelationship Assumption	Second proviso	Second premise
Advantage Assumption	Third proviso	Third premise
An Initial Interpretation of Strategy	A Reinterpretation of Strategy	A Reinterpreted Reinterpretation of Strategy

Figure 3.2. A sketch of the logical relationship between Strategy through Process and the Problem of Strategic Management.

which these decisions can be shaped, or *processed,* into a strategy for the corporation.

By this logic, the acquisition problem involves producing a *strategy through* the means of a decision-making *process.* For this reason, I call the genre "Strategy through Process." I now explain the logical coherence and appeal of Strategy through Process by means of a story about the Problem of Strategic Management. That story is written as a researcher guided by the logic for STP would write it. I situate this account at Bell Atlantic Corporation, one of the seven Bell Regional Holding Companies (RHCs) created in 1983 as a consequence of the AT&T divestiture.[79]

The Problem of Strategic Management at Bell Atlantic

Storm clouds gather as Raymond Smith, chairman and chief executive officer at Bell Atlantic Corporation, scans the Philadelphia skyline from his office window.[80] On this gray May morning, Smith would soon convene a day-long session with his senior officers and staff (hereafter, associates). The session is one more in a series of discussions about how best to deploy Bell Atlantic resources for the coming years. Recently, Smith and his associates fashioned a mission to make Bell Atlantic "a leading information and communications company."[81] They now set their sights on making the investments and arranging the organization structures that would enable the company to fulfill that lofty aspiration.

On the agenda today are six challenges. Five involve questions about committing resources to enhance Bell Atlantic's position in the telecommunications industry. The sixth hits closer to home. Smith and his officers want to be certain that they can convince Bell Atlantic's 80,000 employees to march along with the corporate mission. Unless a match can be forged between the mission and business plans derived from that mission, on the one hand, and the employees' desires, on the other, that mission could well become irrelevant. All in attendance that day know that this match is problematic, for many Bell Atlantic employees see dark clouds on the horizon, too.

A first challenge. The principal source of revenues for Bell Atlantic remains the provision of local telecommunications services through its seven Bell Operating Company (BOC) subsidiaries.[82] These subsidiaries are franchised as the providers of local telephone service to any residential and business customers who seek it. This franchise was reaffirmed as part of the divestiture agreement reached by American Telephone and Telegraph (AT&T) and Department of Justice officials in 1982.

The challenge for Bell Atlantic here is that the local franchise faces direct competition in a key marketplace. Technological developments, as well as federal policy governing "equal access" to the nation's telecommunications networks, have spawned a "bypass" industry that gains at the direct expense of Bell Atlantic's slowly growing revenues for local service.[83] Of particular concern to Smith and associates is the bypassers' grab for a share of the corporate market segment. It is there where the Bell Atlantic BOCs count on the combination of higher volume and higher rates—both relative to the residential market—for a significant revenue stream.[84] At issue here for Smith and associates are the investments that Bell Atlantic can make to plug the outflow of bypass revenues and reestablish the company's reputation among corporate customers as a dependable supplier.

A second challenge. Bell Atlantic has quickly become a major player in the mobile communications market. The company's principal product here is cellular telecommunications services, a fast-growing variation on local service. With a cellular presence in the populous northern New Jersey–Philadelphia–Washington, D.C., corridor, Bell Atlantic now ranks among the ten leading cellular providers in the United States.[85] To date, Bell Atlantic's service has been offered only in the Middle Atlantic region. Others have not been so bashful in playing out their ambitions, however. McCaw Cellular Communications, long the market leader and a national player, is busy consummating an acquisition of Lin Broadcasting's cellular properties. Other Bell Regional Holding Companies, most notably Pacific Telesis and Southwestern Bell, have invaded cellular markets outside their local franchise territories.[86] At issue for Bell Atlantic is how to fend off these market challengers and forge a sustainable position for Bell Atlantic in the cellular "big leagues."

A third challenge. All franchised providers of local telecommunications services—whether Bell BOCs or independents—are chartered to provide access facilities, to and from the local telephone network, for long-distance carriers such as AT&T, MCI, and US Sprint and their customers. As a supplier of "network access" to the long-distance industry, Bell Atlantic is situated at a key crossroads in the transmission of long-distance communications. Since the AT&T divestiture, the seven Bell Atlantic BOCs have invested more than $10 billion combined toward maintaining and upgrading the local network, including network access facilities.[87] Still, not all of the network switching equipment used by the local companies has been upgraded to state-of-the-art digital technology. Here is where the challenge arises for Bell Atlantic.

In the 1980s, the leading long-distance carriers began to accelerate the conversion of their transmission facilities to high-capacity fiber optic cable. Part of the appeal is that fiber optic cable enhances the clarity of voice and data communications. Even more alluring to AT&T, MCI, and US Sprint—engaged in their circle of vigorous rivalry—is the potential for "stuffing" their high-capacity nationwide "pipelines" with the transmission of voice, data, video, text, and whatever other information customers seek to send and receive. To realize that potential, these carriers argue, the local operating companies must convert completely to digital switches. At present, these carriers, as well as major corporate and institutional users, point to the local network access points as "bottlenecks" in the development of the information services market.[88] At issue here is how quickly Bell Atlantic converts to an all-digital local network, including access facilities. By doing so, Bell Atlantic can stay in tune with, and head off public pressures from, its access customers, such as AT&T. Moreover, Smith and associates are wary of the bypassers here, too. As antiquated access facilities remain in use, the possibility grows that corporate customers of Bell Atlantic access facilities will seek alternative access to the long-distance networks from bypass providers.

A fourth challenge. Smith and associates know full well that all three of the foregoing challenges are shaped, and even exacerbated, by the comprehensive regulatory environment in which Bell Atlantic operates. Of particular concern is the fact that the Federal Communications Commission (FCC), the principal regulator for Bell Atlantic's interstate activities, has long been prone to encourage competitive entry in the bypass, cellular, and long-distance markets. Moreover, beginning in June 1989, the FCC commissioners, acting on the premise that long-distance markets had become vigorously competitive, took steps to permit AT&T an unprecedented degree of pricing flexibility.[89] The significance of this move emerges in light of a second source of federal regulation of Bell Atlantic's activities.

Under provisions of the Modified Final Judgment, which spell out the terms of the AT&T divestiture and which calls for oversight by Judge Harold Greene, Bell Atlantic and AT&T compete on different terms. Bell Atlantic can sell, but not manufacture, telecommunications equipment. AT&T can and does engage in both activities. Bell Atlantic can provide access to information services but cannot generate that information. AT&T does both. Bell Atlantic cannot provide interstate long-distance services, whether for voice or for information transmission. AT&T, of course, offers these services. When this three-part imbalance is paired with AT&T's new pricing latitude, Smith and associates have reason to worry whether the "playing field is sufficiently level" for enactment of the company mission.[90] But the regulatory parameters for Bell Atlantic activities are more complicated still.

The seven Bell Atlantic local operating companies, such as Bell of Pennsylvania, operate within pricing, product, and service guidelines administered by state public utility commissions. Of particular concern to Smith and associates is the relatively conservative stances taken by these commissions in the Bell Atlantic service area. From Nebraska to Vermont to California to Texas, state utility commisioners have embarked on experiments in regulating the BOCs in an era of new competition and technological possibilities.[91] Most prominent among these regulatory reforms has been a movement away from rate-of-return limits on the BOCs toward greater freedom for the BOCs to set prices. This reform, the BOCs argue, can enable them to earn rates of return sufficient to provide the capital necessary for refurbishing the local networks. None of these reforms appears imminent in the Bell Atlantic franchise region. Nor, as Smith and associates know all too painfully, do they seem just around the corner in Pennsylvania, a bellwether market for Bell Atlantic. In a recent two-year period, Bell of Pennsylvania was investigated for a number of irregularities. The latest difficulty, involving fraudulent sales efforts, led to a $41.8 million fine against the BOC.[92]

At issue for Bell Atlantic are the twin questions of where and how to fight for the regulatory reforms that can improve the business climate for acting on the corporate mission.

A fifth challenge. Smith and associates, in their search for new opportunities in tune with the company mission, turned to two marketplaces in which they hope that Bell Atlantic's communications expertise can be extended. The first is the international telecommunications market-place. Bell Atlantic's participation there is unregulated by United States federal and state authorities. Yet Bell Atlantic has plenty of company in this arena. As economic and political barriers fall across Europe and, more slowly, in the Pacific Rim, AT&T and its long-distance rivals, along with the six other Bell RHCs, have converged in competition involving transoceanic transmission, refurbishment of national telecommunications networks, cable television, computer equipment and services, and cellular networks.[93] The second opportunity is the market for advanced network services in the Bell Atlantic service region. Already, Bell Atlantic has made inroads in this area by offering voice messaging, high-speed data transfer, and calling features such as caller identification.[94]

At issue for Bell Atlantic in both regards are the possible niches where the company can make further inroads. In the international arena, eager competitors, foreign regulations, and sheer distance all encumber the search for suitable niches. At home, the market for advanced network services has fallen well short of its much-heralded potential. Bell Atlantic must find a way to offset customer indifference toward these products.[95] Moreover, Bell Atlantic likely faces legal delays in expanding the market for caller identification services.[96]

A sixth challenge. Smith and associates know that they can make little headway in these five areas unless they can generate employee enthusiasm for the company mission and business plans. In four major respects, Bell Atlantic's management expects resistance. First, the employees are still going through wrenching adjustments in attitude made necessary by the shift from the Bells' monopoly protection of a decade ago to today's competitive circumstances. Within several years, Smith and associates hope that over one-half of Bell Atlantic's revenues will come from outside Bell Atlantic's quasi-monopoly local service activities.[97]

Next, the employees are also adjusting to the 1988 reorganization designed to better coordinate Bell Atlantic marketing efforts.[98] Even as the new structure is being enacted, Smith and associates know that this design might not accommodate what lies ahead. Moreover, they are keenly aware that they must proceed cautiously where integration of regulated and unregulated business activities is concerned. An attempt to coordinate activities across that regulatory boundary recently cost NYNEX, another Bell RHC, millions of dollars in fines and rebates.[99]

Third, these planning efforts have proceeded amid the lingering effects of a strike at Bell Atlantic and the other RHCs in mid-1989. Finally, Bell Atlantic employees are well aware that, across the industry, steps are under way to reduce labor costs. While AT&T has spearheaded this effort, Bell Atlantic has joined the campaign by closing its Chesapeake and Potomac Telephone headquarters in Washington, D.C.[100]

Looking toward the horizon. By the time he adjourns the session and returns to his office, Smith can see rays from the setting sun penetrate the still-angry clouds. To the east, jagged lightning flashes. That is an apt summary of the entire process, he thinks, and a harbinger of days to come. Early the next morning, Smith would begin a round of sessions with middle managers, supervisors, and groups of employees to explain the action plans agreed on today. Later in the month, he and his associates will reconvene to discuss details about organization structures and performance targets. "No picnic at all," he muses in the silence of his office, as he moves to the door.

Bell Atlantic and Acquiring a Strategy Through Process

The spotlight in this story about strategy at Bell Atlantic shines on the process by which that corporation can acquire a strategy. In the story, Raymond Smith and his associates engineer a set of activities by which they seek to translate and shape the Bell Atlantic mission—as a statement of purpose—into a plan of purposeful action—a strategy—at Bell Atlantic. I wrote this tale in such a way as to distinguish two principal activities in that process of acquiring a strategy.

First, Smith and associates—acting collectively as "senior management"—convene to *formulate* a set of decisions about an intended place and direction for Bell Atlantic in its environment. To this end, senior management decides on a corporate mission and prepares a plan of resource deployments consistent with that mission. Second, Smith and associates take steps to *implement* these decisions. In this regard, senior management moves first to persuade employees to act in accordance with the strategy. Subsequently, Smith and associates act to ensure that Bell Atlantic employees remain committed to the strategy over time. To this latter end, the senior managers arrange an organization structure and set objectives designed to guide the employees to act on that strategy.

This story line, which for obvious reasons I call Strategy through Process, should be familiar to anyone who has read even a smattering of books and articles about corporate strategy. Formulation and implementation activities are two well-known cornerstones in contemporary research about corporate strategy.[101] By STP, the logical combination of these two activities, when carefully linked and tailored to the corporation's particular circumstances, will result in a desirable "fit" between the corporation and its environment.

Smith and associates clearly act on the basis of this proposition in my story. On the one hand, they deliberate about five challenges as they formulate a plan of purposeful action designed to secure Bell Atlantic's place in the industry. On the other hand, they seek ways to enact that plan within Bell Atlantic. The key to this implementation problem is to match decisions that they formulate about Bell Atlantic's position in the environment with factors internal to the company, most notably the collective mood of the employees.[102] In my story, Smith and associates do all this in hopes that Bell Atlantic can achieve a favorable and lasting niche in the telecommunications industry. This well-known logic for acquiring a strategy through the means of a decision-making process is depicted in Figure 3.3.

Still, the formulation–implementation connection is not the only way to interpret my story about Bell Atlantic. I now turn to an interpretation that explains, point by point, how we can further understand Smith and associates dealing with the Problem of Strategic Management. In so doing, I connect Strategy through Process and the Problem of Strategic Management.

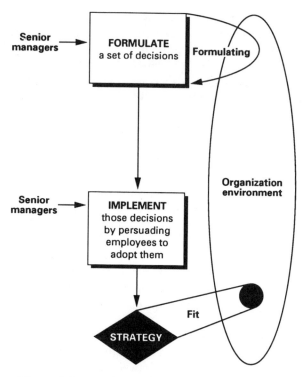

Figure 3.3. Acquiring a Strategy through Process.

STRATEGY THROUGH PROCESS AND THE PROBLEM OF STRATEGIC MANAGEMENT

We can understand Strategy through Process as a particular kind of commentary, or genre, about the Problem of Strategic Management. That commentary contains three provisos.

Specialization Proviso

> *Purposeful action at the corporation requires, in part, that senior managers, acting as decision-making specialists, devote systematic attention to questions about the purpose(s) for that action.*

The Specialization Proviso is one rendition of the Human Decision Assumption, from the Problem of Strategic Management, which holds:

> *Purposeful action at the corporation requires, in part, that persons devote attention to questions about the purpose(s) for that action.*

The connection here is straightforward. This first proviso for Strategy through Process is simply created by specifying "senior managers" as the persons charged with the responsibility for specializing in the act of making decisions about purpose at the corporation. The Specialization Proviso is evident in my story about Bell Atlantic.

It is Smith and associates who engineer, in systematic fashion, the process for acquiring a strategy at Bell Atlantic. They devote significant, specialized attention ("one more in a series of discussions") to shaping the corporation's strategy, doing so intensively ("day-long session") and widely within the company ("begin a round of sessions"). True, employees do enter this story as decision-makers in their own rights ("employees' desires"). Yet their role in the script is heavily circumscribed. They receive, react to, and are expected to acquiesce in ("march along with") the decisions that Smith and associates formulate and implement.[103] By the Specialization Proviso, then, the senior managers at Bell Atlantic act as the exclusive expert agents responsible for operating the process by which a strategy is acquired at the firm. They interact with others within Bell Atlantic, by this proviso, on the assumption that those others must be informed by means of, and even compelled to go along with, the decision-making process.

Supporting evidence for the specialization proviso. The Specialization Proviso is also evident in the arguments made by my group of twelve. I offer evidence of this convergence between my interpretation and their writings in Table 3.1. We can read vivid expression of the Specialization Proviso in the following instances.

Table 3.1. Concurrence with the Specialization Proviso

Purposeful action at the corporation requires, in part, that senior managers, acting as decision-making specialists, devote systematic attention to questions about the purpose(s) for that action.

Andrews

Strategic management is becoming recognized as the administration of operations dominated by purpose and by consideration of future opportunity, with explicit attention given to the need to clarify or change strategy as results suggest and to enter the future on a predetermined course.

The chief executive of a company has as his or her highest function the management of a continuous process of strategic decision in which a succession of corporate objectives of ever-increasing appropriateness provides the means of economic contribution, the necessary commensurate return, and the opportunity for men and women of the organization to live and develop through productive and rewarding careers.

Ansoff

Of these [management activities], we single out the process of decision making, since it is the cornerstone of successful management.

A firm's concern with the strategic problem is not automatic and . . . , in the absence of a trigger signal, most managements will focus their attention on administrative and operating decisions.

If it turns out that the new strategic thrusts are such that the historical strengths are inadequate and may indeed become weaknesses in the future, it becomes necessary to enlarge the perspective of strategic planning to *strategic management.*

Harrigan

Managers must ponder questions of greater importance than mere entry if they are to sustain strategic flexibility, especially given the rapidly changing arenas in which firms compete.

Successful implementation of endgame strategies will require timely commitments and informed tactics. The risk of erring could be formidable.

I argue that the dynamics of partnership relationships, which sometimes dominate joint-venture negotiations, should be subordinated to issues of competitive strategy. Preconceived notions about the competition must be reworked to recognize the interdependencies that may exist (and may be exploited) among the owners of joint ventures (and between owners and their venture) when managers face competitors with several strong backers.

Hrebiniak and Joyce

While formulation activities are generally most responsible for determining the ends of strategic action, and implementation activities are mainly responsible for the means, both decision processes represent *complementary portions of a recurring chain of means–ends relationships designed to factor large, complex, long-term objectives into smaller, less complex and manageable actions.*

Faced with this complexity [of implementation problems], and equipped with only limited information handling and decision-making capabilities, managers need a cognitively manageable implementation model or approach.

Lorange

In this opening chapter we have stated the overriding purpose of corporate planning as we see it and as we shall advocate it in this book, namely, to assist a company's line management to carry out its strategic decision-making task.

Table 3.1. *(continued)*

Planning is a vehicle for providing more effective managerial learning, so that the executive team of a company can systematically increase its strategic decision-making capabilities over time.

Miles
By now, it should be obvious that the role played by executive leaders is critical to the performance, adaptation, and persistence of complex organizations. This role includes the sensing of the nature of the enterprise and the total situation relevant to it, the development of organizational resources and environmental opportunities, and the articulation of the alignment among the essential elements of organizational character and strategy—all of which are ongoing role requirements.

Miles and Snow
The strategic-choice approach essentially argues that the effectiveness of organizational adaptation hinges on the dominant coalition's perceptions of environmental conditions and the decision it makes concerning how the organization will cope with these conditions.

This approach argues that organization structure is only partially preordained by environmental conditions, and it places heavy emphasis on the role of the top decision makers who serve as the primary link between the organization and its environment.

In our view, organizational adaptation is essentially composed of three broad problems requiring continuous top-management attention and decisions: the entrepreneurial problem (. . .), the engineering problem (. . .), and the administrative problem (. . .).

Porter
The book reflects my deepening belief that the failure of many firms' strategies stems from an inability to translate a broad competitive strategy into the specific action steps required to gain competitive advantage.

Competitive strategy is an area of primary concern to managers, depending critically on a subtle understanding of industries and competitors.

This book represents a comprehensive framework of analytical techniques to help a firm analyze its industry as a whole and predict the industry's future evolution, to understand its competitors and its own position, and to translate this analysis into a competitive strategy for a particular business.

Quinn
Since there is no objectively right answer concerning the proper ultimate ends for an organization, sensible practice dictates giving top priority to the *processes* through which such choices are made.

The most effective strategies of major enterprises tend to emerge step by step from an iterative process in which the organization probes the future, experiments and learns from a series of partial (incremental) commitments rather than through global formulations of total strategies. Good managers are aware of this process, and they consciously intervene in it. They use it to improve the information available for decisions and to build psychological identification essential to successful strategies. The process is both logical and incremental.

Quinn, Mintzberg, and James
Anyone in the organization who happens to control key or precedent setting actions can be a strategist; the strategist can be a *collection* of people as well. Nevertheless, managers—especially senior general managers—are obviously prime candidates for such a

role because their perspective is broader than any of their subordinates and because so much power naturally resides with them.

In this text, as in reality, [strategy] formulation and implementation are intertwined as complex processes in which politics, values, organizational culture, and management styles determine or constrain particular strategic decisions.

Rappaport
In today's fast-changing, often bewildering business environment, formal systems for strategic planning have become one of top management's principal tools for evaluating and coping with uncertainty.

The decentralization of the planning process is a promising development, but does not alter the essential purpose of the planning *process:* to provide managers with a systematic framework to think strategically and thereby shape the future of their business.

Schendel and Hofer
One of the major conclusions that emerges from this survey and its analysis is that a new concept of the general manager's role and responsibilities is developing, a concept we shall call *strategic management.*

However, since the end of World War II, major changes have occurred in the environment and nature of businesses that have required an explicit identification and understanding of the concept of strategy and its management.

There are six major tasks that comprise the strategic management process: (1) goal formation; (2) environmental analysis; (3) strategy formulation; (4) strategy evaluation; (5) strategy implementation; and (6) strategic control.

Note: Sources of quotations in all tables appear in notes to the text.

Andrews calls attention to the systematic aspect of strategic decision-making in terms of "the administration of operations dominated by purpose," "the need to clarify or change strategy as results suggest," and the "continuous process of strategic decision." He leaves little room for doubt about senior managers' specialization ("highest function") in this regard.[104]

Ansoff pronounces decision-making to be the "cornerstone" of management activities and makes a case for specialized attention to "the strategic problem" on the assumption that managers need to be prodded ("in the absence of a trigger signal") to perform that cornerstone role. He suggests that this role must be systematically fulfilled, inasmuch as strategic decision-making might well be "enlarged" in the event of poor results.[105]

Harrigan gives credence to the systematic aspect of strategic decision-making in terms of the scope ("questions of greater importance") and enduring attention ("timely commitments") required when managing firms in decline. It is in this context, as well, that she asserts that the specialized task of competitive strategy take priority over other managerial concerns, where joint ventures are concerned.[106]

Hrebiniak and Joyce clearly interpret a systematic decision-making process ("recurring chain of means–ends relationships") that is tailored to enable managers to specialize ("cognitively manageable") in the acts of strategy formulation and implementation.[107]

Lorange characterizes the strategic decision-making process as a systematic growth opportunity ("more effective managerial learning") for managers who bear specialized responsibility for that process ("carry out its strategic decision-making task").[108]

Miles assigns to executive leaders a specialized task ("role") of utmost importance to the firm ("critical to the performance, adaptation, and persistence") that consists of a number of systematic concerns ("ongoing role requirements").[109]

Miles and Snow identify a group of senior managers ("dominant coalition"; "top decision makers") who undertake the specialized task ("primary link") of arranging systematically ("continuous top-management attention") for the organization to adapt to its environment by means of three specialty concerns ("three broad problems").[110]

Porter argues that specialized attention ("subtle understanding") to the systematic problem of acting on an otherwise sound strategy ("translate") requires a specialized set of tools ("comprehensive framework of analytical techniques").[111]

Quinn accords "top priority" to the decision-making process that "good managers" orchestrate ("consciously intervene in it") in systematic fashion ("step by step").[112]

Quinn, Mintzberg, and James identify the role of the "strategist," who requires a specialized capability ("perspective is broader") to attempt to gain control over the systematic forces that make up the strategy process ("formulation and implementation are intertwined as complex processes").[113]

Rappaport seeks to provide those ("top management") who specialize in strategic decision-making ("to think strategically") with the means ("systematic framework") to address challenges to the purpose of corporate action ("evaluating and coping with uncertainty").[114]

Schendel and Hofer propose strategic management as a "new concept" that can inform the actions of decision-making specialists ("general manager's role and responsibilities") in a specialized ("explicit identification") and systematic way ("six major tasks").[115]

Struggle Proviso

Purposeful action at the corporation requires, in part, that senior decision-making specialists command a systematic decision-making process that acknowledges the potential antagonism that relationships with others "outside" the corporation can bring to bear on that action.

Stated in these terms, the Struggle Proviso is one variation on the theme set forth in the Interrelationship Assumption, from the Problem of Strategic Management, which holds:

> *Purposeful action at the corporation requires, in part, acknowledgment of the influences that relationships with others "outside" the corporation can bring to bear on that action.*

This second proviso portrays relationships with corporate outsiders, such as customers and competitors, in decidedly pessimistic terms ("potential antagonism"). Such anticipation of struggling through such relationships permeates my story at Bell Atlantic.

The very term "challenge" sets a fretful tone from the outset. Each of the five external challenges brings Bell Atlantic into relationships with others, where those links complicate the pursuit of Bell Atlantic's mission and business plans. In each complicated context, there is a strong suggestion that others' presences are hostile toward Bell Atlantic in the following ways: [116]

1. Bypassers "grab" for a share of the corporate market at the firm's "direct expense." In addition, the corporate customers enticed by the bypass alternative are presumably forgetful about Bell Atlantic's reputation, which needs to be "reestablished."
2. Cellular competitors are "not bashful" about "invading" others' traditional service areas.
3. AT&T and the other leading long-distance carriers are too impatient ("convert completely") about the pace of Bell Atlantic investments in digital switching equipment. The antagonism is evident as these carriers finger the Bell RHC facilities as "bottlenecks" in the burgeoning information services marketplace.
4. Regulators have assigned the Bell RHCs to a playing field that is not a "level" plane for engaging, most notably, AT&T. Federal regulators are all too willing to "encourage" competitors to Bell Atlantic's markets as well. Furthermore, state regulators seem prone not to enact "imminent" reforms to assist Bell Atlantic. Indeed, the reference to "reform" suggests that there is something amiss in the relationships between regulators and Bell Atlantic.
5. Bell Atlantic encounters "plenty of company" in overseas markets so as to "encumber" the firm's progress there. At home, "customer indifference" and "legal delays" deter sales orders for the corporation's advanced network services.

By the Struggle Proviso, then, across this range of business opportunities—called "challenges" for good reason—the presence of others is persistently troublesome for Bell Atlantic's pursuits.

Supporting evidence for the struggle proviso. The Struggle Proviso also has widespread support among my group of twelve. Evidence in each of the twelve cases is provided in Table 3.2. We can read the language of the Struggle Proviso in the following diverse interpretations.

Andrews argues for systematic decision-making effort ("continuous monitoring") aimed at preserving the firm as a "living system" that is vulnerable ("lest it falter, blur, or become obsolete") to powerful outside forces ("destroying and creating business opportunities").[117]

Ansoff situates strategic decision-making in an inherently uncertain ("turbulence") context where others' lack of appreciation of the corporation ("loss of social centrality") necessitates approaching larger environmental forces ("socio-political relations") with utmost care ("life-or-death importance").[118]

Harrigan tells a story of strategic decision-making in a vivid language of upheaval ("price warfare") where parties seek to "invade" and prevent invasion (" 'mobility barriers' ") amid the possibility of an unfortunate outcome ("unwanted bloodshed").[119]

Hrebiniak and Joyce argue that an "open systems" conception of an organization "forces" decision-makers to confront "problematic" dependencies that hold the potential for continually ("in both the short and the long term") threatening the organization.[120]

Lorange paints an ambivalent picture ("opportunities and/or threats") of the firm's environment where strategic decision-makers can hardly be comforted by the fact of "an increasingly violent and unstable environmental setting."[121]

Miles introduces us to decision-making specialists ("strategic managers") charged with the task of preserving the very organization ("survival potential") in an epic struggle to adapt the organization to "conditions of externally imposed stress and crisis."[122]

Miles and Snow argue that strategic decision-making must proceed under conditions complicated by myriad diverse factors ("its own unique way") that managers must struggle to understand and accommodate ("can . . . cannot").[123]

Porter concurs with Lorange's ambivalence about relationships with others outside the firm ("a blessing and a curse"). In the story that Porter tells, the firm's strategists struggle with a set of powerful ("collective strength") determinants that set the stage for competitive showdowns ("retaliation"; "moves and countermoves escalate") that might not help anyone ("all . . . worse off than before").[124]

Quinn pinpoints the greatest need for specialized decision-making ("genuine strategy") in a context where "intelligent opponents" can make things uncomfortable for the organization ("seriously affect the endeavor's desired outcome").[125]

Quinn, Mintzberg, and James place the strategy process in an environment subject to "continuous change" wherein they hypothesize that

Table 3.2. Concurrence with the Struggle Proviso

Purposeful action at the corporation requires, in part, that senior decision-making specialists command a systematic decision-making process that acknowledges the potential antagonism that relationships with others "outside" the corporation can bring to bear on that action.

Andrews
Change in the environment of business necessitates continuous monitoring of a company's definition of its business, lest it falter, blur, or become obsolete.

In any case, change threatens all established strategies, including those currently successful. We know that a thriving company—itself a living system—is bound up in a variety of interrelationships with larger systems comprising its technological, economic, ecological, social, and political environment. If environmental developments are destroying and creating business opportunities, advance notice of specific instances relevant to a single company is essential to intelligent planning.

Ansoff
In the following discussion we shall refer to the degree of changeability of environmental challenge as the level of *environmental turbulence*.

Thus, one of the consequences of affluence is the loss of social centrality for the institution that created it.

Thus, socio-political relations of the firm with the environment, which lay dormant during the Industrial Era, acquire a life-or-death importance to the firm. They become important as a source of information and opportunities for new commercial activities, as a source of new social expectations from the firm, and as a source of threatening constraints on the commercial activity.

Harrigan
It would be expected that price warfare or other forms of volatile competitive behavior would be more likely to occur in industries where there are several strategic groups (whose strategic postures are significantly asymmetric) which are competing for the same customers' sales in a shrinking market.

Past investments which these firms have made in developing these strategic postures define the "mobility barriers" which potential entrants would have to scale in order to invade a particular firm's market niche.

The firm may even be able to avert unwanted bloodshed if the industry consensus were (1) recognized among rivals and were (2) considered important to maintain for the mutual profitability of the participants.

Hrebiniak and Joyce
This view emphasizes that the external environment is simultaneously a source of opportunity (market expansion, new products) and threat (competition) for the organization. It indicates the points at which the organization is dependent on its environment, thereby identifying areas in which the dependencies could become problematic. The open systems view forces the top manager to look outside and consider the environmental factors that aid or threaten the organization, in both the short and the long term.

Lorange
It might be argued that this [strategic decision-making] task has taken on added dimensions of importance as a result of an increasingly violent and unstable environmental setting.

Table 3.2. *(continued)*

Strategic success in most instances will require that the firm systematically look for opportunities and/or threats in its environment to come up with the best alternatives for the firm to pursue.

Miles

This is a story of how complex organizations adapt under conditions of externally imposed stress and crisis. It focuses on the choices made by strategic managers of traditionally competitive corporations in a major U.S. industry to cope with a fundamental threat to the legitimacy of their right to do business.

Organizational adaptation is defined as the process by which an organization manages itself or its environment in order to maintain or improve its performance, legitimacy, and, hence, survival potential.

Miles and Snow

Each of these [environmental] factors tends to influence the organization in its own unique way: the behavior of certain environmental elements can be reliably predicted while that of others cannot; the impact of some conditions can be buffered while the impact of others cannot; and some factors are critical to the organization's operations while others are only incidental.

Porter

Competitors are both a blessing and a curse.

The collective strength of these [competitive] forces determines the ultimate profit potential in the industry, where profit potential is measured in terms of long run return on invested capital. Not all industries have the same potential. They differ fundamentally in their ultimate profit potential as the collective strength of the forces differs.

In most industries, competitive moves by one firm have noticeable effects on its competitors and thus may incite retaliation or efforts to counter the move; that is, firms are *mutually dependent.* This pattern of action and reaction may or may not leave the initiating firm and the industry as a whole better off. If moves and countermoves escalate, then all firms in the industry may suffer and be worse off than before.

Quinn

A genuine strategy is always needed when the potential actions or responses of intelligent opponents can seriously affect the endeavor's desired outcome—regardless of that endeavor's organizational level in the total enterprise.

Quinn, Mintzberg, and James

In this text, we have presented a wide range of different contexts, dealt with competitive economics plus the nature of power and politics, discussed structure and systems, and explored the relationship between continuous change in the environment surrounding an enterprise and its efforts to deal with that change by means of strategy.

H9. The more dynamic the environment, the more organic the structure.

H10. The more complex the environment, the more decentralized the structure. . . .

H12. Extreme hostility in the environment drives any organization to centralize its structure temporarily.

H13. Disparities in the environment encourage the organization to decentralize selectively to differentiated work constellations.

H14. The greater the external control of the organization, the more centralized and formalized its structure.

Rappaport

The case for why management should pursue this [shareholder value] objective is comparatively straightforward. Management is often characterized as balancing the interests of various corporate constituencies such as employees, customers, suppliers, debtholders, and stockholders. As Treynor points out, the company's continued existence depends upon a financial relationship with each of these parties.

The perpetuity method for estimating residual value is based on the foregoing competitive dynamics. It is essentially based on the assumption that a company that is able to generate returns above the cost of capital (i.e., achieve excess returns) will eventually attract competitors, whose entry into the business will drive returns down to the minimum acceptable or cost of capital rate.

Schendel and Hofer
The first of these changes is a significant increase in the rate of change of the environment in which businesses must compete. Moreover, the environment is much more interdependent than it has ever been before, leading to further complexities in the management of the firm. Thus, the birth and death of key ideas, that is of good strategies, must be expected to occur with much greater frequency.

Questions of the governance and function of the firm, and the manner in which it will be allowed to exist, are being raised today, forcing a reexamination of both enterprise strategy and the overall mission of the firm.

---

the strategist must struggle with conditions that are more or less "dynamic," "complex," marked by "extreme hostility," full of "disparities," and characterized by "external control." [126]

Rappaport argues that strategic decision-making involves keeping a wide cast of characters satisfied ("balancing the interests") such that purposeful action can be sustained ("continued existence") in a world of vultures ("attract competitors") looking for the spoils of competition ("drive returns down"). [127]

Schendel and Hofer portray purposeful action at the corporation as a monumental ("significant increase in the rate of change") struggle ("birth and death") over the very viability ("allowed to exist") of the corporation and business activity. [128]

Fitness Proviso

> *Purposeful action at the corporation requires, in part, that senior decision-making specialists systematically create an internal fit among decision-making processes about the purpose(s) for that action, so as to facilitate an external fit between that action and a composite of potentially antagonistic "outside" relationships.*

As such, the Fitness Proviso is one way to interpret the Advantage Assumption, from the Problem of Strategic Management, which holds:

> *Purposeful action at the corporation requires, in part, that persons choose and actively seek a position of lasting benefit in relation to influential "outside" forces.*

This third proviso specifies "lasting benefit" in terms of a match, or "fit," between purposeful corporate action and the relationships that compose the firm's antagonistic environment. The proviso goes on to specify "actively sought" in terms of senior management's command of a process of decision-making activities that "fit" together, so as to match the corporate purpose and factors within the corporation. One kind of fit requires the other, by the proviso. There is ample reliance on the Fitness Proviso in my story about the acquisition of a strategy for Bell Atlantic.

For each of the five external challenges, Smith and his associates seek to "enhance Bell Atlantic's position"—that is, "fit"—against the forces hostile to the firm's mission. In particular, they attempt to

1. Turn back the revenue "outflow" attributable to "direct competition" from the bypass suppliers, as well as "reestablish" the company's reputation against the composite skepticism among corporate customers.
2. "Forge" a sustainable foothold for Bell Atlantic against the forces that make up the cellular marketplace.
3. "Stay in tune with" the plans of network access customers.
4. Pursue an improved "business climate" by fitting the firm to regulations in new ways ("reform").
5. Find "niches" in overseas markets and in the market for advanced network services amid multiple competitive and/or regulatory barriers.

To arrange these postures, Smith and associates must seek internal compliance ("generate employee enthusiasm" and overcome "resistance") with the strategy that they are processing into shape. According to the Fitness Proviso, Smith and associates accomplish this by orchestrating a connected series of activities internal to the firm. Specifically, they

1. Establish a corporate mission ("a leading information and communications company"), a step already completed when my story begins.
2. Decide where to deploy the corporation's resources in the form of market and facilities investments.
3. Inform Bell Atlantic middle managers, supervisors, and employees about the mission, the planned resource deployments, and the link between the two sets of decisions.
4. Reconvene to plot the appropriate organization structure and performance targets that will ensure enactment of these decisions.

By the Fitness Proviso, then, Smith and associates improve Bell Atlantic's chances of achieving a lasting and favorable alignment with the telecommunications environment if they complete a rigorous ("no picnic") process of shaping decisions about the firm's place in that context. Without the latter concern for internal "fit," by this proviso, decisions about external "fit" become suspect ("that mission could well become irrelevant").

Supporting evidence for the fitness proviso. Each argument in my group of twelve converges on my interpretation of the Fitness Proviso. Their "concurrence" is detailed in Table 3.3. Once again, the language in support of this proviso is as vivid as it is diverse.

Andrews tells a story about an internal process ("Corporate strategy is an organization process") that can facilitate a fit ("optimal equilibrium") between the firm and its troublesome ("risk") environment by means of an internal match ("opportunity and corporate capability").[129]

Ansoff argues that the trick is to bring the internal fit ("capability matches its strategic behaviour") and the external fit ("behaviour matches the turbulence") into harmony ("optimal").[130]

Harrigan argues that vertical integration and joint venture activities can provide a vehicle for strategic flexibility if an internal fit ("recognizing *which . . . how to relate*"; "supplement internal resources and capabilities") can be found that enables a better environmental match ("accommodate new competitive conditions"; "responding faster to competitive challenges") for the firm.[131]

Hrebiniak and Joyce connect internal decision-making efforts ("process . . . results in agreement"; "interaction or participation") and the chances ("positive implications") for the organization's fit ("positioning") with the outside world.[132]

Lorange succinctly interprets the significance ("important relationships") that decision-makers can attach to connecting external position ("adaptation") with internal decision-making processes ("integrative challenges").[133]

Miles spins a tale about decision-making specialists ("executive leaders") attending to the match between internal processes ("formation"; "learn") and the possibility for an external fit ("effective, evolving alignments").[134]

Miles and Snow make the prospects for an external fit ("effective alignment") contingent on how well decision-making specialists attend ("how consistently") to affairs within the organization ("managing internal interdependencies"; "choices are integrated").[135]

Porter predicates his argument about competitive advantage on the possibility that an internal fit ("to build a bridge") among decision-making processes ("strategy and implementation") can beget a desirable external outcome ("create and sustain a competitive advantage").[136]

Quinn argues that a corporate purpose remains credible ("validity") if it can be systematically ("Constantly integrating") shaped and re-

Table 3.3. Concurrence with the Fitness Proviso

Purposeful action at the corporation requires, in part, that senior decision-making specialists systematically create an internal fit among decision-making processes about the
purpose(s) for that action, so as to facilitate an external fit between that action and a
composite of potentially antagonistic "outside" relationships.

Andrews
Corporate strategy is an *organization process,* in many ways inseparable from the structure,
behavior, and culture of the company in which it takes place.

The strategic alternative which results from matching opportunity and corporate capability at an acceptable level of risk is what we may call an *economic strategy.*

So far we have described the intellectual processes of ascertaining what a company *might
do* in terms of environmental opportunity, of deciding what it *can do* in terms of ability
and power, and of bringing these two considerations together in optimal equilibrium.

Ansoff
This hypothesis states that *the firm's performance will be optimal when its strategic behaviour
matches the turbulence of the environment and the firm's capability matches its strategic behaviour.*

Harrigan
Effective vertical-integration strategies mean recognizing *which* activities to perform in
house, *how to relate* these activities to each other, *how much* of its needs the firm should
satisfy in house, *how much ownership* equity needs to be risked in doing so, and *when* these
dimensions should be adjusted to accommodate new competitive conditions.

In summary, managers need to understand how joint ventures can help them supplement internal resources and capabilities to build strengths and bargaining power by responding faster to competitive challenges.

Hrebiniak and Joyce
If the process of assessment and analysis of relevant internal and external variables results in agreement, top management can more easily build on strengths and develop
plans to compensate for weaknesses when positioning the organization in its task environment. The study also suggests that the *process* of interaction or participation among
top-level managers and the resultant commitments to action plans and objectives hold
positive implications for the subsequent successful implementation of strategy.

Lorange
There are important relationships between the adaptation and integration purposes of
the corporate planning activities. While adaptation implies a focus on where the firm is
to go, integration focuses on how to get there in the most efficient manner.

As a consequence [of competitive pressures], today's planning challenge should be seen
in a dual perspective: It should enable the company to adapt better and quicker to environmental opportunities and/or threats. Also, however, it should facilitate the handling
of integrative challenges facing the firm.

Miles
Through the process of strategy formation, executive leaders can facilitate the development of effective, evolving alignments among the features of their organization and its
operating domain and institutional environment. Strategy formation—the interaction between the formulation and implementation of strategies—is also the primary process by
which organizations learn.

Miles and Snow
For most organizations, the dynamic process of adjusting to environmental change and
uncertainty—of maintaining an effective alignment with the environment while effi-

ciently managing internal interdependencies—is enormously complex, encompassing myriad decisions and behaviors at several organization levels.

Instead, adaptation occurs through a series of managerial decisions, the effectiveness of which hinges primarily on how consistently managers' choices are integrated.

Porter
The central theme of this book is how a firm can actually create and sustain a competitive advantage in its industry—how it can implement the broad generic strategies. My aim is to build a bridge between strategy and implementation, rather than treat these two subjects independently or consider implementation scarcely at all.

Quinn
The validity of the original strategy lies not in whether it is maintained intact, but in its capacity to adapt successfully to unknowable realities, reshape itself, and ultimately use resources most effectively toward selected goals.

Constantly integrating the simultaneous incremental processes of strategy formulation and implementation is the central art of effective strategic management.

Quinn, Mintzberg, and James
According to this idea, the various elements of organizations—their strategies, strategy-making processes, structures, support systems, cultures, and so on—tend to cluster together naturally to produce certain relatively distinct overall "configurations" appropriate to particular widely encountered situations, which we call "context."

Rappaport
Strategy formulation typically entails analyzing the attractiveness of the industry and the position of the business vis-à-vis its competitors. . . . In contrast, strategy valuation involves an estimation of the economic value created by alternative strategies. Successful planning requires sound analysis for *both* formulating business strategies as well as for valuing strategies.

Schendel and Hofer
Strategic management is a process that deals with the entrepreneurial work of the organization, with organizational renewal and growth, and more particularly, with developing and utilizing the strategy which is to guide the organization's operations.

The increasing interrelationships of governmental units and business enterprises over questions of legitimacy are forcing business firms to reexamine their role in society and to consider whether they can be insular in their decisions and actions.

---

shaped—in the hands of decision-making specialists ("central art")—to enable the organization to confront "unknowable realities."[137]

Quinn, Mintzberg, and James emphasize "configurations" as the focal points for integrating key "elements" of corporate action that, when taken together, can serve the organization well in a variety of "widely encountered" external situations.[138]

Rappaport proposes that the conjunction ("sound analysis for *both*") of the strategy formulation and shareholder valuation processes can be used by decision-makers to prepare ("Successful planning requires") an external fit for the firm ("position of the business vis-à-vis its competitors").[139]

Schendel and Hofer interpret strategic management in terms of internal processes ("entrepreneurial work"; "developing and utilizing") with which decision-makers can prepare to fit the firm, no longer necessarily "insular," within a context of increasingly unfriendly ("questions of legitimacy") linkages ("interrelationships").[140]

These three provisos encompass the logic of the Strategy through Process genre. This logic can be summarized in terms of a meaning for "strategy" that follows from STP.

A Reinterpretation of Strategy

A strategy is a set of decisions about the purpose(s) for action taken at the corporation—those decisions being the product of a systematic decision-making process directed by senior decision-making specialists—that lays claim to an enduring position that fits the corporation into an environment of many relationships which continually threaten that position.

Thus far, I have defended Strategy through Process for its logical connection, point by point, to the Problem of Strategic Management, and for the breadth of diverse support that Strategy through Process attracts from my group of twelve. In the process, I have shown one way to think of Strategy through Process as a literary account—that is, as a story about persons acting at the corporation.

Still, I am not finished with my interpretation of Strategy through Process. Since my purpose for the book is to critique the worth of STP as a commentary about persons and their respective purposes at the corporation, I must take the next step and give an account of Strategy through Process as an ethical commentary on the Problem of Strategic Management. Since I do this in the spirit of defending the coherence of Strategy through Process from a standpoint beyond mere connection to the Problem of Strategic Management, I present this account as a justification for Strategy through Process.[141]

A JUSTIFICATION FOR STRATEGY THROUGH PROCESS

I create in this section a different interpretation of my Strategy through Process genre. The principal difference is my choice to cast in ethical terms the STP line of argument about acquiring a strategy. I argue in particular that Strategy through Process and the study of ethics can be understood to share a common concern with the concept of purpose.[142]

The purpose that counts in the Strategy through Process genre is attributed to the particular corporation in question. As my group of twelve and I "agreed" throughout the previous section, the Strategy through Process story deals with a decision-making process that is applied by specialists in the executive suite to reach into all corners of the firm. Thus it should come as little surprise that "purpose" carries a collective connotation in the Strategy through Process story. We can understand this concern with corporate purpose as a hallmark of STP as an ethical genre, just as we can understand the emphasis on decision-making process as a hallmark of STP as an interpretation of the Problem of Strategic Management.

I wrote this section as a further show of support for the durability of the Strategy through Process story.[143] In the previous section, I made a literary case for STP by interpreting three points of connection between Strategy through Process and the Problem of Strategic Management. Since my aim for the book is to critique corporate strategy and strategic management research in both a literary sense and an ethical sense, I intend here to justify Strategy through Process as a coherent genre in the latter regard.

Like my previous interpretation of Strategy through Process, this new version of STP can be expressed in terms of three guiding premises. Unlike my previous interpretation of Strategy through Process, however, these three premises deal explicitly with the pursuit of purpose at the corporation in the course of acquiring a strategy for that corporation. Each of the three premises that I now articulate and defend corresponds to a proviso from STP and, accordingly, an assumption from the Problem of Strategic Management. This correspondence between Strategy through Process as a literary genre and Strategy through Process as an ethical genre is depicted in Figure 3.4.

Once again, I turn to my story at Bell Atlantic as a means for explaining my derivation of these three premises.[144] And once again, I call on my group of twelve to "concur" in their own diverse ways with this ethical rendition of the process of acquiring a strategy for a corporation. I conclude this section by showing that, when taken together, these three premises give me reason to restate my earlier Reinterpretation of Strategy as a Reinterpreted Reinterpretation of Strategy.

Injunction Premise

> *Purposeful action at the corporation requires, in part, that senior decision-making specialists be enjoined, as they command a structured decision-making process, by that process from distinguishing between the corporate purpose(s) derived from that process and their own respective purposes.*

The Injunction Premise can be understood as one possible version of the Specialization Proviso. In particular, senior managers acting as

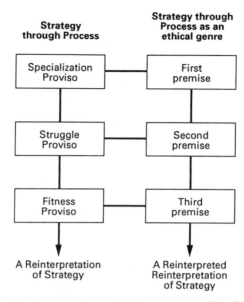

Figure 3.4. Strategy through Process as an ethical genre.

decision-making specialists are charged with the responsibility of arranging the strategy acquisition process in such a way that "corporate
purpose" remains the sole subject of the process. In this way, the premise circumscribes just how far senior managers can proceed in considering "questions about the purpose(s)" of action at the corporation, from
the Specialization Proviso. This premise clearly turns on the assumption that senior managers entertain purposes of their own that will not
necessarily coincide with the purpose(s) for corporate-wide activity.[145]
Given this possibility for divergence, the injunction becomes necessary.

We can make further sense of the Injunction Premise if we interpret
it as one rendition of the Human Decision Assumption. The decision-
making process of Strategy through Process is "human" inasmuch as it
is entrusted to senior managers who are presumed capable of reasoning at the helm of a specialized process about purpose and strategy.
Yet the line on "human" involvement is drawn at that point. By this
premise, the purposes chosen by Smith and associates to guide their
own endeavors cannot enter the story line *unless* those purposes happen to coincide with the corporate purpose. Even then, the Injunction
Premise implies that the purposes of Smith as Smith, for example, are
redundant and thus unnecessary in the Strategy through Process story.

In both regards, the Injunction Premise can clearly be understood as
an ethical imperative. In particular, it is an imperative to reason impartially about purposeful action at the corporation. At the juncture of the
Injunction Premise and the Specialization Proviso, senior decision-making

specialists are compelled to provide a systematic means for screening "stray" considerations—that is, those at odds with the pursuit of corporate purpose. At the juncture of the Injunction Premise and the Human Decision Assumption, the premise sets a clear boundary whereby "human" ends must coincide with corporate ends. In short, senior decision-making specialists can act impartially if they arrange the strategy acquisition process such that their own preferences are channelled into deriving a corporate purpose.

Evidence of the injunction premise. The Injunction Premise has a prominent place in my story at Bell Atlantic. To begin with, the very mission for Bell Atlantic is stated in terms that compel Smith and associates to focus on corporate purpose. It simply makes no sense for any one person to conduct her life according to a maxim to become "a leading information and communications company."[146] Throughout the story, Smith and associates oversee a decision-making process that leaves no room for their own private deliberations about the merits of one purpose versus another.[147] It is no accident that they meet in a "day-long session." And no sooner than that session is over, Smith moves to further sessions with employees before all the officers reconvene. This pattern of continual activity carries a clear implication: "There's no time left for reflecting on your own preferences about the purposes of all this." In sum, the Injunction Premise clearly makes provision for the meaningfulness of corporate action in the Strategy through Process story. As such, the premise ushers STP into ethical territory. At the same time, the premise just as clearly enjoins Smith and anyone else at Bell Atlantic from separating corporate purpose from their own ends.

Supporting evidence among my group of twelve. Each argument in the group of twelve supports my interpretation of the Injunction Premise. Their respective expressions of support are presented in Table 3.4.

The most intriguing case here—and the case most crucial to my claim for support—concerns the argument made by Andrews. Andrews, more than any other in the group of twelve, seeks to incorporate a senior manager's preferences into the process of acquiring a strategy. Indeed, Andrews champions such a connection, noting that "it will remain true" that executives' "personal values, standards of quality, and clarity of character" play a crucial role in executing strategy—as a "human construction"—at a "high professional level."[148] Yet Andrews circumscribes this link between values and action in two significant regards.[149] First, he distinguishes between values and "reasoned decisions" and warns against an "imbalance" in favor of the former. Second, he clearly enjoins a person's effort to act on her own values with his "congruence"

Table 3.4. Concurrence with the Injunction Premise

Purposeful action at the corporation requires, in part, that senior decision-making specialists be enjoined, as they command a structured decision-making process, by that process from distinguishing between the corporate purpose(s) derived from that process and their own respective purposes.

Andrews
It will remain true, after we have taken apart the process by which strategy is conceived, that executing it at a high professional level will depend upon the depth and durability of the chief executive's personal values, standards of quality, and clarity of character.

Strategy is a human construction; it must in the long run be responsive to human needs. It must ultimately inspire commitment. It must stir an organization to successful striving against competition. Some people have to have their hearts in it.

It is entirely possible that a strategy may reflect in an exaggerated fashion the values rather than the reasoned decisions of the responsible manager or managers and that imbalance may go undetected.

It is as much a matter of enlightened self-interest as of responsibility to provide conditions encouraging the convergence of the individual's aspirations with those of the corporation, to provide conditions for effective productivity, and to reward employees for extraordinary performance.

Ansoff
The benefit of the doubt is given clearly to the "traditional" approach of the economist, but with the addition of a long-term view of profitability. At the same time, the influence of the key managers is admitted as a modifier to the final system of objectives.

This hypothesis states that *the challenges from the firm's environment determine the optimal mode of behaviour.*

Therefore, for a given change in culture and power, *the resistance by managers will depend on the strength of their convictions, their preparedness to defend themselves, their power drive, and their predisposition to learn and change.*

We shall refer to this method of introducing change, which uses power to overcome resistance, as a *coercive change process.*

Harrigan
In practice, managerial exit barriers make implementation of endgame strategies difficult. Overcoming these exit barriers is a part of the challenge of managing a profitable endgame.

Barriers to entry (and exit) represent mental baggage that managers carry with them into problem solving. These barriers are the established way of looking for solutions to a problem. They are the traditional excuses for why actions are not undertaken. They are a mind-set that inhibits firms' strategic flexibility.

Usually their reasons include heavy previous investments (. . .); big differences between book value and liquidation value; fear of image loss in the business community; emotional attachment to a line of business; feelings of responsibility to employees, suppliers, and customers; and fears of customer reprisals against *other* company products. All these are forms of *exit barriers.*

Since ventures are a means to an end, their owners need to create a system of incentives among their respective managers—both as partners and as owners—to cooperate in ventures.

Hrebiniak and Joyce
The need, then, when implementing strategy is to try to ensure that desirable outcomes at the individual level are consistent with and support positive outcomes at the organizational level.

Similarly, given individual rationality, it is unwise to allow individuals to benefit at the expense of or detriment to desired organizational outcomes.

Lorange
The concept of corporate planning rests upon the premise that managers are motivated and willing to work together in a shared direction toward a long-term strategic position advantageous to the firm. For this to be possible, there must be at least some degree of congruence between the personal goals of each individual key manager and the corporation's goals.

Thus, there is a natural tendency among many managers to wish that there will be no major environmental changes affecting their businesses so that they can keep on doing business in the future in the way they have done it before.

The nature of the strategic task at hand should be reflected in the incentive system so that managers can be motivated in a way which facilitates congruence between the strategies to be pursued by the organizational unit and the manager's personal goals.

Miles
Perhaps the most important finding of this study will be judged to be the demonstration of the relatively enduring construct of corporate character and the variety of ways in which it may be shaped or capitalized upon by executive leaders who guide the strategy-formation processes of an enterprise.

In the cases where the values and beliefs of key decision makers representing different functions in the executive cadre—manifested in the strategic choices they made over time—departed significantly from the distinctive competences and strategic dispositions of the firm or the requirements of its operating environments, performance "gap" eventually occurred.

Miles and Snow
That is, if management chooses to pursue one of these strategies, and designs the organization accordingly, then the organization may be an effective competitor in its particular industry over a considerable period of time.

Can this theoretical framework aid managers in diagnosing the current adaptive posture of their organization? The answer is guarded . . . second, because it is difficult for managers to suspend their past perceptions and behaviors and view their organization's condition and needs objectively.

Porter
The personal values of an organization are the motivations and needs of the key executives and other personnel who must implement the chosen strategy. Strengths and weaknesses combined with values determine the internal (to the company) limits to the competitive strategy a company can successfully adopt.

The three generic strategies are alternative, viable approaches to dealing with competitive forces. The converse of the previous discussion is that the firm failing to develop its strategy in at least one of the directions—a firm that is "stuck in the middle"—is in an extremely poor strategic situation.

Quinn
Effective goal processes . . . operate at three levels: (1) They define broadly what the organization intends to be and what it should accomplish. (2) They ensure that each key person's role goals are designed to support these conceptual thrusts. (3) They obtain maximum identity between people's personal goals and their role goals.

Table 3.4. *(continued)*

Effective organizational goals satisfy a basic human need. They enable people to develop an identity larger than themselves, to participate in greater challenges, and to have influences or seek rewards they could not achieve alone.

Quinn, Mintzberg, and James
Here, *strategy is a perspective,* its content consisting not just of a chosen position but of an ingrained way of perceiving the world.

In effect, when we are talking of strategy in this context, we are entering the realm of the *collective mind*—individuals united by common intention and/or action.

In fact, the CEO must be the focal point for optimizing the long-range health of his or her enterprise.

Rappaport
In Chapter 1 providing maximum return for shareholders was established as the fundamental objective of the business corporation.

There are, however, a number of factors that induce management to act in the best interests of shareholders. These factors derive from the fundamental premise that the greater the expected unfavorable consequences to the manager who decreases the wealth of shareholders, the less likely it is that the manager will, in fact, act against the interests of shareholders.

A well designed compensation system in itself represents a source of value by aligning management incentives more closely with shareholder interests.

Ultimately, it is necessary to translate qualitative, and hopefully creative, strategic analysis into plans that specify resources required and expected rates of return.

Schendel and Hofer
The "first" task in the strategic management process is the formulation of a set of goals for the organization.

The essence of the problem that any goal formulation process must solve is making sense out of a collection of individual organization member's personal goals, as well as those of the parties and actors that can influence the organization. Some consistency among these goals is necessary before effective behavior can result. Such consistency may be achieved through a variety of means, including sequential attention to goals, quasi-reduction of conflict, or by making personal and organizational goals congruent.

---

requirement.[150] The upshot is that strategic decision-makers, in Andrews's view of the firm, must remain true to a process of "reasoned decision"—lest a strategy become "exaggerated" by a person's preferences—that requires them to make sure that their ends are consistent with the corporate purposes. What is even more significant here is that Andrews makes the best case, among the group of twelve, for admitting managers' values to the discussion in the first place. In short, if his argument supports the Injunction Premise, we should not be surprised that the other eleven do as well.

Ansoff admits that managers' values can "modify" strategic decision-making, but he argues that forces in the firm's environment "determine the optimal mode of behaviour." To that end, managers' "resistance" to such optimal behavior must be enjoined through a "coercive" process.[151]

Harrigan provides a clear rendition of the injunction against managers' acting for reasons that diverge from corporate purpose, such as "emotional attachment" and "feelings of responsibility" to others. In particular, she pinpoints managers' preferences as "exit barriers" and "mental baggage" that must be overcome and aligned with corporate purpose through a "system of incentives."[152]

Hrebiniak and Joyce clearly argue that, in the process of strategic decision-making—in particular, "when implementing strategy"—it is imperative that decision-makers' ends be "consistent with and support" organization purposes, lest persons "benefit at the expense of or detriment to" those purposes.[153]

Lorange explains the need for an injunction in terms of managers' "natural tendency" to avoid strategic considerations. On this account, the strategic planning process must include an "incentive system" that pushes managers toward "congruence" with the organization's purposes.[154]

Miles portrays organization purpose in terms of "corporate character," which can be "capitalized upon" by executives as they look for guidance in their decision-making. If these persons stray from certain manifestations of that corporate character ("distinctive competences and strategic dispositions"), an unsatisfactory "performance 'gap'" can befall the organization.[155]

Miles and Snow propose that there are certain kinds of pure "adaptive postures" by which the organization can last as an "effective competitor," if only "management" is enjoined to "pursue" such strategies. This injunction is made necessary by decision-makers' tendencies to prefer their own "past perceptions and behaviors" to applying these pure strategic postures "objectively."[156]

Porter, like Miles and Snow, assumes that strategies come in certain recurring "generic" and "viable" varieties which decision-makers must be enjoined to follow if they want to avoid becoming "stuck in the middle" of a "poor strategic situation." Moreover, Porter asserts that the "motivations and needs" of decision-makers help to set the "limits" on what a firm can do with a generic competitive strategy.[157]

Quinn explicitly bounds decision-makers' preferences first by referring to "what the organization intends to be" and then by subordinating "each key person's role goals" to that intent in such a way that "maximum identity," or congruence, can be achieved. In this way, decision-makers can grow "larger than themselves" if they act in accordance with "effective goal processes."[158]

Quinn, Mintzberg, and James argue that those decision-makers at the "focal point" of strategic processes ("optimizing") can interpret strategy as "perspective" on the world, where that "ingrained" approach informs a standardized ("collective mind") pattern of action at the organization.[159]

Rappaport asserts that maximizing shareholder value is "the fundamental objective of the business corporation." While there is room for "creative" approaches to enacting that standard of purpose, Rappaport stresses the wisdom ("source of value") of finding ways ("aligning") to ensure that strategic decision-makers do not lose sight ("induce") of that corporate end.[160]

Schendel and Hofer designate "goals for the organization" as the point of departure in strategic decision-making processes.[161] Against this standard, decision-makers must "solve" the problem of creating "consistency" between a complicated "collection" of their own goals—which require "making sense"—and the organization's goals. Schendel and Hofer suggest a variety of means for systematically ("sequential attention") deflecting attention from the decision-makers' own goals, which create "conflict" for the organization.[162]

Impediment Premise

Purposeful action at the corporation requires, in part, that senior decision-making specialists command a systematic decision-making process to impede the potential constraining influences that relationships with others "outside" the corporation can bring to bear on that action.

Stated in these terms, the Impediment Premise provides one interpretation of the Struggle Proviso. In particular, the premise translates the need to predicate the strategy process on potential antagonisms in the firm's relationships (Struggle Proviso) into an imperative to prepare countermeasures that can impede those constraining forces.[163] As such, the premise injects, across the entire strategy-acquisition process, a disposition to draw battle lines in defense of the guiding purpose(s) and resulting strategy at a given corporation. The premise amounts in short to a "call to arms" in anticipation of troublesome relationships.[164]

Likewise, the Impediment Premise can be interpreted as one kind of commentary on the Interrelationship Assumption. Unmistakable here is the guiding assumption that relationships with others in the firm's environment serve as conduits for difficulties in enacting a plan of purposeful action at the corporation. Relationships with others, such as competitors and customers, can all too readily "get in the way." Accordingly, senior managers must acknowledge (Interrelationship Assumption) the influences of relationships with others through the act of preparing countermeasures designed to impede the advance of those influences.

In this sense, then, the Impediment Premise can be understood as an ethical imperative. In particular, the premise compels senior managers to act with prudence as they consider, throughout the strategy-acquisition process, how to approach the many relationships between the firm and its context. "Prudence" here carries two connotations.[165] One involves wary, circumspect acknowledgment of the corporation's relations (Struggle Proviso). The other provides for shrewd, calculated responses to combat the threatening tenor of those relationships. By this premise, then, we can understand Strategy through Process to provide for the protection of corporate purpose through prudent stewardship of the process.

Moreover, this requirement of prudence complements the impartiality imperative from the Injunction Premise. In both cases, senior decision-making specialists are implored to counteract forces that can shackle the pursuit of corporate purpose. In the case of the Injunction Premise, the threat comes from within if senior managers are distracted from their specialized task of considering purpose in corporate terms. In the case of the Impediment Premise, it is relationships with others that bear wary scrutiny. In this way, the Impediment Premise fortifies the Injunction Premise by reminding senior decision-making specialists that the process of protecting corporate purpose faces both internal and external threats.

Evidence of the impediment premise. The Impediment Premise is manifest throughout my story about the strategy-acquisition process at Bell Atlantic. I articulated each of the five external issues faced by Smith and associates in terms that indicate this imperative to mitigate the effects imposed through relationships with external actors. The footprints of this imperative lie in my choice of verbs.[166] Each connotes wary responsiveness to problematic relationships. That is, Smith and his officers must consider the following:

1. In the case of local network bypass, how to "plug" the outflow of revenues drained by bypassers as well as "reestablish" the company's reputation among corporate customers.
2. In the cellular marketplace, how to "fend off" market entrants and "forge" a better position for Bell Atlantic.
3. In the network access context, how to "head off" the dissatisfaction of long-distance carriers.
4. In the regulatory setting, where and how to "fight" for more favorable rules.
5. In the overseas and advanced network services markets, how to "make further inroads" and "offset" customer indifference.

In all five cases, Smith and associates must prepare to act in opposition to the effects of others across a set of uneasy relationships that constitute the corporation's environment. By the Impediment Premise, these senior decision-makers are ordered to view relationships between the firm and the environment with the regret, "If only ___ weren't there," and then to lessen the impact of those presences.

Supporting evidence among my group of twelve. Support for the Impediment Premise comes from each of the diverse corners of my group of twelve, as seen in Table 3.5.

Andrews argues that it is the "economic mission" of the corporation to "maximize strength" while minimizing vulnerability ("organizational weaknesses") in preparation for impeding the "risk" of competition. This process of building strength is all the more important when we consider the "conflict" that others ("steadily rising moral and ethical standards") have injected ("complexity") into strategic decision-making.[167]

Ansoff proposes that decision-makers incorporate an "aggressiveness" in the firm's strategy in order to prepare the firm to "attack" market forces that can impede the firm ("turbulence").[168]

Harrigan argues that it is "expected" that competitors behave in a manner that pits one "against" another, often through efforts to erect "steep mobility barriers" that impede the influences of others ("preserve their advantages").[169]

Hrebiniak and Joyce portray strategic action as the pursuit of survival for the organization, whereby decision-makers are well advised to seek "control" over the influences that are transmitted between organizations ("exchange process").[170]

Lorange proposes that a disposition for "innovation and change" must permeate strategic decision-making in a world of hostile forces ("survival of the fittest"). Strategists can prepare the firm to "adapt" in ways that impede the "threats" of others either in offensive ("take advantage"; "creation of new opportunities") or defensive ("ameliorate") ways.[171]

Miles portrays organizational adaptation as an interventionist process in which decision-makers can find themselves "adding to, subtracting from, or even trading off threatening environments," seeking to "adapt the environment" to the organization's goals, attempting to "overpower" those who pose a "legitimacy threat" to the organization, and competing in "zero-sum conditions." What Miles finds remarkable is that strategists can do this "simultaneously."[172]

Miles and Snow portray relationships with outsiders in terms of three kinds of adaptive processes ("a series of characteristic actions") that are intended to impede ("manipulate the environment itself") what the outsiders are doing. In particular, the Prospector approach involves "enthusiastically" acting as "creators of change and uncertainty" for others ("their competitors").[173]

Porter's story is rife with military metaphors (e.g., "best battleground") and the accompanying implication that the "ideal" strategic moves are those that either directly impede what others are trying to

Table 3.5. Concurrence with the Impediment Premise

Purposeful action at the corporation requires, in part, that senior decision-making specialists command a systematic decision-making process to impede the potential constraining influences that relationships with others "outside" the corporation can bring to bear on that action.

Andrews

The way to narrow the range of alternatives . . . is to match opportunity to competence, once each has been accurately identified and its future significance estimated. It is this combination that establishes a company's economic mission and its position in its environment. The combination is designed to minimize organizational weakness and to maximize strength. In every case, risk attends it.

The emerging view in the liberal-professional leadership of our most prominent corporations is that determining future strategy must take into account—as part of its social environment—steadily rising moral and ethical standards. Reconciling the conflict in responsibility which occurs when maximum profit and social contribution appear on the same agenda adds to the complexity of strategy formulation and its already clear demands for creativity.

Ansoff

For optimal success, the aggressiveness of the firm's strategy must match the turbulence of the environment.

But many other discontinuities challenge not the basic attractiveness or feasibility of a market, but the ways by which firms will have to attack that market if they are to remain successful in it.

Harrigan

It would be expected that each firm would bring to the endgame its most successful competitive techniques and use them, if they are effective, against other competitors.

Successful strategic postures can emanate from differences in the attributes of firms' products or variations in their means of distributing them, and successful firms often preserve their advantages by developing steep mobility barriers.

Hrebiniak and Joyce

To survive, the organization must engage in this exchange process; it must give something to get something.

Rationality demands that managers take actions to control elements of these environments to allow economic efficiency in the face of ambiguous or shifting competitive situations.

Lorange

Consequently, if a formal system for strategic planning does not support innovation and change, it is a failure.

Similarly, competitive pressures seem to be as strong as ever in calling for efficient modes of operation; today more than ever there seems to be a survival of the fittest.

For each critical [environmental] factor, we might ask whether there is anything we can do to take advantage of a potentially positive development in the environment, to ameliorate a potentially negative environmental development.

Assisting the firm to *adapt* to environmental opportunities and threats, identify relevant options, and provide for an effective strategic fit with the environment. This should be interpreted in a broad sense. The strategic behavior of successful companies deals with the creation of new opportunities through development of superior product systems, through interaction with government and society at large, and so on.

Table 3.5. *(continued)*

Miles

Organizations may adapt by adding to, subtracting from, or even trading off threatening environments or environmental segments for ones more receptive to their needs, goals, strategies, resources, skills, competences, modes of operation, and outputs (including their by-products and wastes). Or organizations may attempt to adapt the environment to their goals and methods of operation or to restructure the patterns of interdependences that link them to elements of their environment.

This [domain defense] response required a major departure from the traditional competitive relations among rivals in the tobacco domain, who began to coalesce around the issues posed by the legitimacy threat in an attempt to influence or overpower antismoking elements in the institutional environment.

Since they were faced with a pernicious decline in domestic cigarette-market growth, significant market-share gains by one firm would have to come in large measure from the traditional market shares of its five competitors. Indeed, by the later stages of the smoking-and-health controversy, domain-offense strategies were being developed under virtual zero-sum conditions.

Thus, the Big Six were able to partition their traditional domain into political and market arenas, and to simultaneously engage in collaborative domain-defense strategies and competitive domain-offense strategies.

Miles and Snow

These managers are viewed as being in a position not only to adjust organization structure and process when necessary but also to attempt to manipulate the environment itself in order to bring it into conformity with what the organization is already doing.

In other words, when presented with a change in its environment, the Defender, the Analyzer, and the Prospector all set in motion a series of characteristic actions aimed at incorporating the change into the organization's ongoing behavior.

Thus, in direct contrast to the Defender, which insulates itself from environmental change, the Prospector enthusiastically searches for new entrepreneurial ventures in an effort to manipulate the competitive arena in its favor.

Thus, these [Prospector] organizations often are creators of change and uncertainty to which their competitors must respond.

Porter

Assuming that competitors will retaliate to moves a firm initiates, its strategic agenda is selecting the *best battleground* for fighting it out with its competitors.

The ideal is to find a strategy that competitors are frozen from reacting to given their present circumstances.

Another key strategic concept deriving from competitor analysis is creating a situation of *mixed motives* or conflicting goals for competitors.

If a challenger's strategy creates mixed motives for a leader, it will inhibit the leader's ability to retaliate. A leader that must undermine its past strategy to match or respond to the challenger faces mixed motives.

Quinn

Exxon faced different opponents from Xerox or Chrysler. . . . Each force was powerful. Any untoward move by Exxon could create a new coalition among these forces, and individual players could be both brilliant and extremely hostile. The company had to be very responsive at local levels, yet able to use its full force to maintain some control over its destiny in international relationships. Single errors could be very costly for Exxon or its opponents.

[Xerox] defended itself against threats with patents, through a very large R&D endeavor, and through incrementally developed diversification moves. As long as these defenses existed, Xerox had the lead times needed for more structured formal strategic planning.

Quinn, Mintzberg, and James
As plan, *a strategy can be a ploy* too, really just a specific "maneuver" intended to outwit an opponent or competitor. . . . Likewise a corporation may threaten to expand plant capacity to stop a competitor from building a new plant. Here the real strategy (as plan, that is, the real intention) is the threat, not the expansion itself, and as such is a ploy.

But strategy as position can be extended beyond competition. Indeed, what is the meaning of the word "niche" but a position that is occupied to *avoid* competition.

Rappaport
This value creation objective is achieved by firms that can obtain funds at competitive rates from capital markets and then invest these funds to exploit imperfections in product markets. For example, a leading firm in an industry may enjoy high entry barriers due to factors such as economies of scale, product differentiation, large switching costs, substantial capital requirements, and favorable government policy.

A second barrier to entry is product differentiation which can be accomplished by exceptional customer service, advertising, and actual product differences.

Schendel and Hofer
Business strategy deals with the question, "How should a firm compete in a given business?" That is, how should it position itself among its rivals in order to reach its goals? Alternatively, how can it allocate its resources to achieve a competitive advantage over its rivals?

---

do ("competitors are frozen") or create protracted confusion ("mixed motives") in an effort to "undermine" what competitors seek to accomplish.[174]

Quinn tells a tale of relationships marked by environmental "threats" from "brilliant and extremely hostile" actors who decision-makers engage with "full force to maintain some control" over the organization's "destiny" by erecting "defenses" (e.g., patents).[175]

Quinn, Mintzberg, and James provide one interpretation of strategy whereby the goal is to "outwit" and "stop" competitors from pursuing their ends in a "ploy" to "avoid" the unwanted influences of competitive relationships.[176]

Rappaport argues that the success of value creation can hinge on decision-makers' efforts to build "entry barriers" that deter others' influences through specific strategic decisions (e.g., "economies of scale"; "actual product differences") that can be used to "exploit" forces in the marketplace.[177]

Schendel and Hofer succinctly interpret "business strategy" as an effort to mitigate the influence of others ("in order to reach its goals") by taking steps ("allocate its resources") to find a position that dominates others' efforts ("competitive advantage over its rivals").[178]

Institution Premise

Purposeful action at the corporation requires, in part, that senior decision-making specialists, by means of an internally coherent decision-making process, seek a fit between the corporation and potentially antagonistic "outside" relationships such that the corporate purpose can become institutionalized.

The Institution Premise supplies the Fitness Proviso with a criterion by which senior decision-making specialists must direct the strategy-acquisition process. In particular, the premise holds that a proper "fit" is one that holds promise for the perpetuation of the corporate purpose and associated resource commitments. This promise, moreover, must compel senior decision-making specialists to arrange a decision-making process (internal fit) that positions the firm against its environment (external fit) to create self-sustaining practices informed by the purpose. Senior managers are thus charged with the task of transforming corporate purpose into the kind of central self-perpetuating practices that compose what is commonly called an institution.[179]

A parallel can be similarly drawn between the Institution Premise and the Advantage Assumption, from the Problem of Strategic Management. By the Institution Premise, the continuity of a particular corporate purpose, nurtured through senior management's specialized guidance, can be taken as the measure of "a position of lasting benefit" (Advantage Assumption) for the corporation. In other words, the premise clearly specifies that it is advantageous for the corporation if the strategy-acquisition process implants a lasting purpose at the corporation.

In both these connections, the Institution Premise imposes on senior managers, as decision-making specialists, an ethical imperative to exercise due diligence while conducting the acquisition process. If the corporate purpose is to become ingrained in action across the corporation, then these managers must persevere in their dedication to the process. In this sense, the imperative sets an overarching tone that can encompass the Injunction and Impediment Premises. On this account, senior managers are reminded that neither the focus on corporate purpose nor the preparation of countermeasures can be viewed as once-and-done endeavors. In this way, the three premises provide a logically connected blueprint for senior managers as they address the meaningfulness of corporate action.

Evidence of the institution premise. The Bell Atlantic story illustrates five examples of the Institution Premise. First, I set the entire story about strategy acquisition at Bell Atlantic in order to stress the importance of institutionalizing the *Bell Atlantic* mission. Next, the very mission implies an unfolding process requiring unswerving executive guidance, since the mission deals with making the company a leading industry player. Third, Smith and associates pay close attention to the human relations climate—their sixth challenge—in recognition of the fact that their institutionalizing efforts are constrained by other institutional factors. Among these constraints are (1) the lingering "Bell System" approach to customers and markets, (2) the organization structure implemented in 1988, (3) the tone of labor–management relations at the firm, and (4) employees' expectations about job security, also a likely carryover from the "glory days" of the Bell System.[180] Fourth, Smith and his colleagues use resource deployments as a route for translating corporate purpose into a lasting beacon, thereby highlighting the temporal element implied by a diligence imperative. Finally, Smith in particular has his calendar dominated by the continual process of decision-making about purposeful action at Bell Atlantic.

Across all five aspects here, the senior managers at Bell Atlantic are busily engaged in arranging a pattern of internal activities in search for an external fit that will be congenial to the maturation of Bell Atlantic's purpose into an institution.

Supporting evidence among my group of twelve. Each argument in my group of twelve concurs with my interpretation of the Institution Premise. This support is seen in Table 3.6. Of particular note is the concurrence, among these diverse arguments, with the idea that it is worthwhile to pursue the institutionalization of purpose at the corporate, or organizational, level of analysis.

Andrews proposes that a comprehensive choice process ("purpose rationally arrived at and emotionally ratified by commitment") bodes well for the future of the enterprise ("successful outcome"). On this account, the elusive ("continue to evolve") goal is to embody strategy across a range of activities that persons pursue at the corporation to confront the "concrete" realities of the environment.[181]

Ansoff proposes three decision processes under the strategic management rubric that must be applied if the firm is to "succeed and survive" as an institution.[182]

Harrigan links decision processes internal to the firm ("takes pains to select"; "takes steps to focus") with the problem of environmental fit ("better enabled to confront") in pursuit of more prosperous "fortunes" for the business in an endgame situation. She reinforces the desirability of the firm as an institution with the clear assumption that "decline" is an undesirable condition that shrewd, specialized decision-making can mitigate.[183]

Hrebiniak and Joyce are concerned with perpetuation of the orga-

Table 3.6. Concurrence with the Institution Premise

Purposeful action at the corporation requires, in part, that senior decision-making specialists, by means of an internally coherent decision-making process, seek a fit between the corporation and potentially antagonistic "outside" relationships such that the corporate purpose can become institutionalized.

Andrews
None of these alters the fact that a business enterprise guided by a clear sense of purpose rationally arrived at and emotionally ratified by commitment is more likely to have a successful outcome, in terms of profit and social good, than a company whose future is left to guesswork and chance.

Furthermore, a unique corporate strategy determined in relation to a concrete situation is never complete, even as a formulation, until it is embodied in the organizational activities which reveal its soundness and begin to affect its nature. Even then it will continue to evolve.

Ansoff
The basic proposition of strategic management is that: *To succeed and survive in an industry, the firm must match the aggressiveness of its operating and strategic behaviours to the changeability of demands and opportunities in the marketplace.*

Strategic management consists of: formulating strategies, designing the firm's capability, and managing implementation of strategies and capabilities.

Harrigan
If upper management takes pains to select appropriate business managers for declining business units and takes steps to focus their attentions on the desired behavior for managing in decline (through corporate policies, compensation, and other structural elements), the firm should be better enabled to confront the problem of declining demand squarely and to guide the endgame units' fortunes more precisely.

Hrebiniak and Joyce
However, the complexity of organizational environments and technological developments in most industries suggest that poor planning and a lack of integration of short- and long-term needs present a poor prognosis for success. In fact, research suggests that the ability to remain effective and prosper over time depends to a large extent on strategy formulation and implementation, including the integration of long- and short-run concerns.

Lorange
What we have aimed at is a concept of planning which is explicitly fit to deal with today's turbulent environments—by seeing a set of plans as an initial bench-mark which then will be modified as needed in a way consistent with what surfaces through the subsequent monitoring. Thus, our planning approach is attempting to turn the firm into a self-corrective system, entirely analogous to a rocket honing in on a target.

Miles
In summary, it is primarily through the strategy-formation process guided by executive leaders that the operating domains and institutional environment of an enterprise become defined. It is primarily from the character-formation process, also guided by executive leaders, that the formal aspects of organization, typically referred to as structure or design or systems, and the informal organization, including its myths, norms, and rituals, evolve and become institutionalized or deinstitutionalized. Moreover, it has been demonstrated repeatedly in this study that these two developmental processes are highly interactive.

Miles and Snow
Subsequently, it became clear that a given market strategy was best served by a particular type of organizational structure, technology, and administrative process—an internal pattern that not only supported the existing strategy but also tended to perpetuate it.

Organizational survival may be said to rest on the quality of the "fit" which management achieves among such major variables as the organization's product-market domain, its technology for serving that domain, and the organizational structures and processes developed to coordinate and control the technology.

Organizations must also constantly modify and refine the mechanism by which they achieve their purposes—rearranging their structure of roles and relationships and their decision making and control processes.

Porter
Competitive strategy is the search for a favorable competitive position in an industry, the fundamental arena in which competition occurs. Competitive strategy aims to establish a profitable and sustainable position against the forces that determine industry competition.

Competitive advantage grows fundamentally out of value a firm is able to create for its buyers that exceeds the firm's cost of creating it. Value is what buyers are willing to pay.

The crucial question in determining profitability is whether firms can capture the value they create for buyers, or whether this value is competed away to others.

Quinn
Consequently, the essence of strategy—whether military, diplomatic, business, sports, political, or eleemosynary—is to *build a posture* that is so strong (and potentially flexible) in selective ways that the organization can achieve its goals despite the unforeseeable ways external forces may actually interact when the time comes.

The essence of formal strategic planning is (1) to establish the enterprise's goals at a level that provides the greatest satisfaction to all critical stakeholders and (2) to create a pattern of commitments and psychological rewards that will achieve the greatest advance toward these goals at the least expected cost.

Quinn, Mintzberg, and James
The concepts of the strategist as managing process more than content, strategy formation as a learning process, the emergence rather than the formulation of strategies, and the emphasis on the mutual interactions of structure, systems, and environments, all flow together into a cohesive approach to the strategy process, another of our configurations.

Here we see the full flowering of the "emergent strategy" concept. We also see a strategic leadership less concerned with "formulating and implementing" strategies in the classic sense than with establishing the types of processes in which specific action strategies will grow of their own accord around individual innovations.

Rappaport
If the company does not satisfy the financial claims of its constituents, it will cease to be a viable organization. Employees, customers, and suppliers will simply withdraw their support. Thus, a going concern must strive to enhance its cash-generating ability.

More precisely, *sustainable value creation*, that is, developing long-run opportunities to invest above the cost of capital, is the ultimate test of competitive advantage.

Schendel and Hofer
This entrepreneurial choice is at the heart of the concept of strategy, and it is good strategy that insures the formation, renewal, and survival of the total enterprise, that in

Table 3.6. *(continued)*

turn leads to an integration of the functional areas of the business and not the other way around.

The second question [in the strategy evaluation task] seeks to determine whether the existing or proposed strategy will lead to accomplishment of the firm's objectives in the future given the changes that are anticipated in the firm's environment, its resources, or even its goals and objectives.

---

nization ("to remain effective and prosper over time"), a condition that they link to the degree of fit between decision-making about the outside world ("planning") and decision-making processes inside the organization ("integration of long- and short-run concerns").[184]

Lorange succinctly seeks institutionalization of the firm as a "self-corrective system" that decision-makers can fit to unfriendly external circumstances ("turbulent environments") by means of an internal "planning approach."[185]

Miles highlights the processes of strategy and character formation that decision-making specialists ("executive leaders") can fit together ("highly interactive") to produce "formal" and "informal" aspects of the organization en route to laying claim to an enduring position ("domains") for the organization that can become "institutionalized."[186]

Miles and Snow discuss how decision-making can be tailored ("internal pattern") to "perpetuate" a course of purposeful action at the organization. In particular, they match (" 'fit' ") internal attention ("technology . . . structures and processes") with external concerns ("product-market domain") in an iterative process ("constantly modify and refine") that can ensure perpetuation of the organization ("Organizational survival").[187]

Porter interprets competitive strategy in terms of the desirable match between decision-making processes ("search") and external fit ("favorable competitive position") that can be perpetuated for the firm ("sustainable position") amid potentially antagonistic influences ("against the forces"). Although Porter sets this story in the context of a relationship that he calls the "value chain," even going so far as to discuss creating value for others ("buyers"), he is clearly interested in preserving the firm and its strategy. He defines "value" in terms of a goal for the firm ("exceeds the firm's cost of creating it"), not the buyer. Moreover, he proposes "value" as the bone of contention between the firm ("can capture the value") and other contestants ("competed away to others").[188]

Quinn defines the "essence" of strategic decision-making as the creation of a lasting entity ("build a posture that is so strong") against the "unforeseeable ways external forces may actually interact" by means of an internal decision-making process ("formal strategic planning") that matches the firm with its environment of "all critical stakeholders."[189]

Quinn, Mintzberg, and James assign to the decision-making specialist ("the strategist") the task of intervening ("managing") in an evolving saga ("learning process") in search of a "cohesive" set of processes that can constitute a mechanism that facilitates the "emergence" of strategies that "will grow of their own accord." [190]

Rappaport offers a basic proposition for the sustenance of the corporate institution ("viable organization"; "going concern"; "sustainable value creation") as a "cash-generating" mechanism for shareholders. To sustain that kind of institution, he argues, decision-makers must take steps ("strive to enhance") to position the firm in a context of relationships with fickle partners ("simply withdraw their support"). [191]

Schendel and Hofer argue that "good strategy" arises from decisions ("choice") that can ensure institutionalization ("formation, renewal, and survival") of the "total enterprise." This can be accomplished through an internal fit ("integration") that can provide for the organization's problematic external fit ("changes that are anticipated") in pursuit of "the firm's objectives." [192]

This section justifies Strategy through Process in terms of three premises that deal explicitly with purposeful pursuits at the modern corporation. As such, the three premises can constitute an ethical genre about the Problem of Strategic Management. Central to this logic for STP is the act of diligently nurturing corporate purpose (Institution Premise) through undivided executive attention (Injunction Premise) and vigilant preparations for defending that purpose (Impediment Premise). The spirit of these premises can be integrated into a revised meaning for "strategy," compared with the one that I interpreted earlier at the juncture of Strategy through Process and the Problem of Strategic Management. The following reinterpretation of "strategy" summarizes my argument that Strategy through Process can be explained and justified as an ethical commentary about action at the modern corporation.

A Reinterpreted Reinterpretation of Strategy

A strategy is a set of decisions about the meaning of action taken at the corporation, meaning that senior decision-making specialists adopt as their own in commanding a structured decision-making process, where that process is intended to perpetuate corporate purpose through vigilant and wary interaction in relationships with other antagonists "outside" the corporation.

With this reinterpretation, I have fulfilled the purpose that I set for myself in writing this chapter. I now lay aside Strategy through Process until I return to critically analyze the Injunction, Impediment, and Institution Premises in Chapter 5. Before moving to complete my preparations for that critical showdown, a closing, self-critical comment about my storytelling efforts is appropriate.

A CLOSING SELF-CRITICAL COMMENT

In the epigraph to this chapter, Sinclair Lewis's character Frink calls for a new literary territory. I attempted here to respond by expanding our understanding of the corporate strategy concept in terms of the Strategy through Process genre. Along the way, I made a case for the durability of STP, first as a literary rendition and then as an ethical interpretation of the corporate strategy concept. I sought and received support for each of my interpretations—the Problem of Strategic Management, Strategy through Process, and Strategy through Process as an ethical genre—from a group of twelve diverse research stories about the corporate strategy concept. My creation then is a coherent logic for the corporate strategy concept that reaches into many corners of strategic management research. That creation also happens to challenge a prevalent commentary about the current state of strategic management research. I fully intended that challenge all along.

It has become fashionable to argue that strategic management research is still an infant enterprise. That claim is often expressed in the form of a hypothesis: strategic management research lacks any consensus about a distinct and distinguishing line of argument. Dan Schendel and Karel Cool note, in this spirit, "it can be said that there is still no central, organizing paradigm for the field."[193] James Fredrickson concurs: "Moreover, there remains the issue of a paradigm. Most scholars would agree that strategic management lacks an overarching paradigm, but they do not agree on the implications of that."[194] Clearly, my storytelling efforts in this chapter lead to a wholly different conclusion about the maturity of strategic management research.

I maintain that this difference suggests a reason for the absence of critical inquiry in mainstream strategic management research, as I noted in Chapter 1. Thus my point is not that this difference is particularly interesting per se.[195] Rather, if we take a pragmatist view on the matter, the divergence provides one more justification for this book. Recall that the pragmatist is concerned with the worldly usefulness of the stories that we choose to tell and share with one another. We can understand the absence of critical storytelling in terms of the kind of story that Schendel, Cool, and Fredrickson appear to value and the kind of story that I tell here.

If we want to assume that strategic management research is still in a state of foment, then we can readily justify "business as usual" in the

conduct of strategic management research. Schendel and Cool advocate just such an effort to intensify the tradition of scientific inquiry:
"We see a young, dynamic field, one with a sort of rough-and-tumble,
gold-rush character to it, one where anything goes, and only a few vigilantes are in evidence to keep out the most obvious violators of the
norms of scholarly, scientific research."[196] Schendel and Cool evidently
number themselves among the vigilantes, bemoaning "the inability or
unwillingness of workers to use scientific methodology as a basic way
of research life in strategic management."[197] Donald Hambrick concurs
as he nominates those researchers who gather data and test theories as
the heroes of strategic management research.[198]

The problem here is that closer adherence to "the norms of scholarly, scientific research" and the pursuit of more and more data and
more new theories have nothing to do with asking questions about the
meaningfulness of corporate strategy concepts in the first place. So the
"fragmentation" story can serve as a justification—and quite a coherent
one at that—for ignoring critical inquiry altogether.[199] For this reason,
there is no reason to expect that any critical tradition can emerge from
the corners of strategic management research where the "reduce-foment-
through-science" story holds popular appeal.

If, however, we seek knowledge about the meanings of the stories
that we tell and share in strategic management research, then we must
be willing to create clear and defensible means for examining those
meanings. A preference for the fragmentation story simply will not do.
In search of meanings, the issue is not *whether* or not a central paradigm is found, but *which* stories merit continued use and which do not.
Adena Rosmarin reminds us "that once genre is defined as pragmatic
rather than natural, as defined rather than found, and as used rather
than described, then there are precisely as many genres as we need,
genres whose shape is precisely determined by that need."[200] I have
arranged my argument in this book in terms of "precisely as many
genres" as I need to examine the worth of the corporate strategy concept in humanist terms. Thus far in this search, I have created both
the Problem of Strategic Management and the Strategy through Process genres. I now turn to interpreting another way to tell the Problem
of Strategic Management story.

4

A Genre About Persons, Strategy, and Justice

> If you listen to them long enough, you can start believing that your way in life is strewn with possibilities.
>
> TRACY KIDDER, *The Soul of a New Machine*

I tell a very different story about the Problem of Strategic Management in this chapter. It is a story that you will not read among the stories that mainstream strategic management researchers choose to tell. Nonetheless, I will argue that this different story is one that strategic management researchers could choose to tell.[1] My purpose in this chapter, then, is to articulate and defend a logic for this alternative story. In so doing, I make a case for the plausibility of that choice between research stories about the Problem of Strategic Management.

My different story, like my interpretation of Strategy through Process in ethical terms in Chapter 3, is a story about persons reflecting and acting purposefully at the corporation. I create this alternative story, in other words, as another ethical genre about the Problem of Strategic Management genre. The similarity between these two ethical genres ends, however, with their convergence on the Problem of Strategic Management.

I write this chapter to create a story in which each distinct man and woman acts on the belief that his or her own life is "strewn with possibilities," as Tracy Kidder phrases it.[2] As these persons act in search of their respective possibilities, they sooner or later turn a figurative street corner and run into others doing the same. At the intersections of their own evolving searches, in other words, these men and women jointly create the contexts for those searches. Accordingly, they must concern themselves with the conditions under which their interconnected lives can unfold. The story thus is told at the confluence of two kinds of ethical concerns.

First, my alternative story deals per se with the ethical concept of

118

purpose. The characters in this story understand "purpose" in terms of the possibilities to which Kidder refers. I infuse the story with an ethical concern for purpose by means of the concepts of strategy and corporate strategy, which I interpreted in Chapters 1 and 3 as concepts useful for interpreting purposeful action at the corporation.[3] Second, my alternative story deals with the connection between (1) a person's conception of her own purposes and (2) her concern with the context in which she acts on her purposes in association with others doing the same. In the study of ethics, or moral philosophy, this connection between (1) a person's purposes and (2) the terms by which many men and women associate in the course of their respective purposeful pursuits is the subject of the concept of *justice*.[4] In recognition of these two ethical concerns, then, I call my alternative story the *Strategy & Justice* genre.[5]

The chapter begins with an explanation of the "Strategy & Justice" designation in terms of the ethical concepts of *autonomy* and *person*. I then sketch four cases, or stories, in preparation for interpreting the Strategy & Justice genre. Two of these stories are set in an everyday context, and two are set in a corporate context. As I did in Chapter 3 with my Bell Atlantic case, I use these four stories as case evidence for three premises that will constitute Strategy & Justice: a Projects Premise, a Contracts Premise, and a Responsibility Premise. Since I create Strategy & Justice as a genre about the Problem of Strategic Management genre, each premise will correspond to an assumption from the latter genre. Taking these premises together, I culminate my creation of Strategy & Justice by interpreting an Alternative Conception of Strategy. The specific correspondence that I interpret between Strategy & Justice and the Problem of Strategic Management is seen in Figure 4.1.

The scope of this chapter is limited to my justification of Strategy & Justice as an alternative conception of the Problem of Strategic Management. Thus while I defend the plausibility of the Strategy & Justice story, I make no claim here about the worth of this story in comparison with Strategy through Process. Consideration of that issue, for which this chapter sets the stage, is the subject of Chapter 5.

AUTONOMY, PERSONS, AND JUSTICE

I choose to create my Strategy & Justice genre as an interpretation of arguments made among a community of modern philosophers who pay particular attention to autonomy, persons, and justice. For my purposes here, the most prominent stories in this community are those told by Hazel Barnes, David Gauthier, and John Rawls.[6] None of these scholars is commonly cited in strategic management research. Hence,

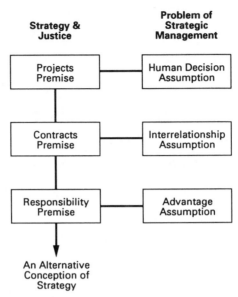

Figure 4.1. Strategy & Justice and the Problem of Strategic Management.

my choice to create a story to which they and their community colleagues could agree serves as that much more evidence for how different a story Strategy & Justice will be.

A distinguishing characteristic of the stories shared in this community is the general assumption that a person is capable of directing her
own ongoing efforts to construct a meaningful life plan. This capacity
to conduct a self-directed, self-interested search for meaning in one's
life is known, in the study of ethics, as *autonomy*.[7] The driving force in
the exercise of autonomy is an act of choice. In my Strategy & Justice
genre, a person's autonomy is manifest in three kinds of choices about
her life, choices that she continually confronts. Moreover, what she
chooses in these three regards gives substantive meaning to her personhood.[8] I provide for this meaning of "person," derived in the context
specific to each autonomous chooser, across the premises of the Strategy & Justice genre.

Autonomy, the Choice to Choose, and the Choice of Ends

Barnes argues that an autonomous person faces two basic choices over
and over again in her life. One is the choice to justify her life at all:
"Man is not what he is, for he is free to put everything into question—
his past, his present projects, the future which he envisions for himself."[9] We can usefully think of this as a choice to choose about the
course of one's life plans. In exercising the choice to call her life into

question, an autonomous person is continually willing to ask herself, "Do I choose to live a meaningful life?"[10]

An affirmative answer to this question gives rise, on Barnes's account, to a companion choice about the specific ends toward which an autonomous person chooses to commit her efforts. These ends can be understood as a person's purposes. This second choice thus enables an autonomous, or free, person to create a coherent story line by which she can conduct and justify her life. Barnes argues in this regard: "To justify one's life involves the belief that one's conduct is harmonious with the image which he has selected as the ideal pattern of a life he can admire or deem to be in itself a positive value."[11] In this way, Barnes creates a connection ("harmonious") between autonomous choice ("belief," "selected," and "admire or deem") and the usefulness of purpose as a crucial standard in a person's life ("ideal pattern of a life"). It is this connection between the choice to choose and the choice of purpose that can give meaning to "person" as one who exercises, in Barnes's terms, "the will to live the life which may be reflectively appraised as holding in truth the greatest value."[12] On this account, an autonomous person freely connects her "will to live" with her choice of ends that hold for her the "greatest value," or preferred meaning, for her life. I emphasize this pair of choices about the possibilities for personhood throughout my interpretation of Strategy & Justice. Furthermore, these two choices set the stage for a third choice that each autonomous person confronts in the Strategy & Justice genre.

Autonomy, Choice, and Association with Others

As the autonomous men and women in my Strategy & Justice story choose—and proceed with—courses of action in keeping with their aspirations, their lives can sooner or later become intertwined. They find it necessary to consider the significance of this state of affairs for two basic reasons. First, each autonomous person recognizes the likelihood that her interconnections with others can endure. After all, an autonomous person is one not easily swayed from her chosen path. As these characters meet while tenaciously pursuing their own ends, they jointly produce an evolving contingency among their pursuits. For each to act, therefore, she must consider the presence of others in the neighborhood of her actions.

Thomas Schelling describes this mutually contingent setting for autonomous action in terms of mutual responsiveness: "People are responding to an environment that consists of other people responding to *their* environment, which consists of people responding to an environment of people's responses."[13] The corporate context can be rife with contingencies of this kind. Supplier A and Supplier B meet and begin responding to each other in a rivalrous relationship. Supplier C and Buyer D encounter each other in a mutually contingent customer relationship. Executive E and Executive F cross paths and begin responding to each other in a political relationship involving resources and power. Union Leader G and Corporate Raider H meet and begin to shape an evolving governance relationship about reorganizing a corporation.[14] In each case, one autonomous person's pursuits become conditioned on the presence of another's pursuits and vice versa. But this is not all that can arise in the joint production of a relationship among autonomous men and women.

Second, each autonomous person in my Strategy & Justice story understands that her pursuits can intersect another's pursuits to produce a conflict for one of them, both of them, and/or "third parties" to their relationship. Conflict is significant for an autonomous person if it holds the potential for frustrating her chosen pursuits.[15] Once again, the corporate context can be fertile territory for such a concern. There are only so many customers to go around for Suppliers A and B in a given market. Buyer D places a premium on taking delivery soon after placing an order; Supplier C wants his customers to understand thoroughly how to use his product. Moreover, there is only so much production capacity with which Supplier C can satisfy the installation schedule that Buyer D prefers, and there are only so many training hours that D can devote to learning to operate C's product. There are only so many dollars for Executives E and F to divide. And Union Leader G and Corporate Raider H can entertain very different conceptions about what constitutes a "satisfactory" employment level at a restructured corporation.

At issue in my story in these two regards are the terms, or guiding principles, by which autonomous persons get along, or do not get along, in the evolving associations that they jointly create.[16] Certainly, these men and women could act according to terms of association that prove conducive for each party's pursuits. Certainly, too, they could adopt terms of association that can frustrate one or more parties' pursuits. Thus in recognition of her part in creating—through her pursuits—the conditions under which she seeks to fulfill her ends, each self-interested person has reason to make a third choice that provides explicitly for shaping those shared conditions.

In the Strategy & Justice story, each autonomous person chooses to include among her purposes a specific disposition to voluntarily coexist with those other persons who join her in creating the context for their pursuits. Furthermore, each chooses to coexist on terms that deny the legitimacy of any pursuits that undermine such coexistence.[17] We can thus understand this third choice as an ethical one, inasmuch as it makes provision for the effects of one's actions on the pursuits that others take seriously. Gauthier interprets such a choice in terms of a "moral dimension": "As rational persons understand the structure of their interactions, they recognize a place for mutual constraint, and so for a moral dimension in their affairs."[18] The characters in the Strategy & Justice story constrain themselves insofar as they temper their chosen ends with the choice of principles by which they prefer to get along with one another. In the course of making this choice, then, an autonomous person extends the meaning of her personhood to acknowledge a specific preference for the terms of her relationships with others. In this way, she makes a sophisticated choice. She chooses to integrate preferences for her own ends with preferences for dealing with the presence of others whose pursuits are intertwined with hers.

Autonomous Persons and Justice

My story about autonomous persons, and the choices that they can make, can be understood as a story about justice by the interpretation that Rawls gives to the concept of justice.[19] Central to Rawls's argument is his concern with each person's reasoned efforts at executing a satisfactory life plan. He refers to these efforts as the search for the "good" in one's life: "A person's good is determined by what is for him the most rational long-term plan of life given reasonably favorable circumstances."[20] Rawls cautions us that "reasonably favorable circumstances" are by no means assured. In particular, he argues that each person's pursuit of, or claims for, her good are necessarily conditioned by the claims made by others. At the intersection of these claims, Rawls proposes, the parties confront the "circumstances of justice" that can circumscribe each person's actions.[21] These circumstances come in two varieties.

One is the "moderate scarcity" of resources with which a person endeavors to advance her claims. The other is each person's greater interest in her own pursuits, relative to others' pursuits. Rawls refers to this disposition as "mutual disinterest."[22] Both circumstances can be understood as the products of persons' intersecting lives. I have chosen my examples of autonomy in a corporate context with this point clearly in mind.

Suppliers A and B and Executives E and F find that their respective claims raise scarcity issues. Scarcity becomes an issue because these persons' pursuits lead them into contention for resources that both covet.[23] Where the claims of Union Leader G and Corporate Raider H converge, they find themselves working through a conflict that Rawls would attribute to mutual disinterest. And Supplier C and Buyer D experience the circumstances of justice in both varieties. It is in keeping with Rawls's account of justice, then, that I situate my story about persons' self-directed ("rational long-term plan of life") pursuits of purposes amid the mutual contingencies ("circumstances of justice") that those pursuits create.

The good, justice, and mutual advantage. Rawls moves next to argue that the successful pursuit of a meaningful life turns, to a significant degree, on the choices that persons make toward enacting mutually advantageous terms for conducting their relationships. By "mutual advantage" Rawls refers to the general possibility that each person can flourish in her purposeful activities without denying others the same opportunity. In particular, he argues that it is in each person's interest to contribute directly to the determination of "the appropriate distribution of the benefits and burdens of social cooperation."[24] It is this "appropriate distribution" that gives substance to the concept of *social justice* in Rawls's argument.[25] Social interaction can be "well-ordered," or "just," on this account, if those who benefit from association with others also agree to share the burdens of their association in a manner that supports each party's pursuits.[26] Benefits and burdens pertain here to the efforts each person makes toward advancing her ends.

Rawls provides for this choice to act justly in terms of an ongoing self-critical practice that he calls "reflective equilibrium": "This state is one reached after a person has weighed various proposed conceptions and he has either revised his judgments to accord with one of them or held fast to his initial convictions (and the corresponding conception)."[27] With each person's choice to engage in such reflection, Rawls argues, she and others can jointly create a "conception" of principles to govern their claims on one another. Rawls refers to this conception of justice as the "right." In pursuit of the right, for example, men and women might come to general agreement about equal opportunity and respect for the anticipated pursuits of men and women in future generations.[28]

The right and the good. Rawls's argument culminates with his claim that in a just society the right must take priority over the good, if each person's search for her good is to be activated:

> The principles of right, and so of justice, put limits on which satisfactions have value; they impose restrictions on what are reasonable conceptions of one's good. . . . A just social system defines the scope within which individuals must develop their aims, and it provides a framework of rights and opportunities and the means of satisfaction within and by the use of which these ends may be equitably pursued.[29]

On this account, the terms of association that men and women can choose through reflective equilibrium about their claims and others' claims can improve the chances of a meaningful life: "The most stable conception of justice, therefore, is presumably one that is perspicuous to our reason, congruent with our good, and rooted not in abnegation but in affirmation of self."[30] Rawls concludes in this regard, from which

I interpret the third choice facing an autonomous person, that "an effective sense of justice belongs to a person's good."[31] In other words, persons acting with a sense of justice make "get along with others" one of their ends. Indeed, they value such coexistence.

In sum, Rawls's account of justice encompasses a person's choice to choose (1) a meaningful life in conjunction with others ("reflective equilibrium"), (2) a specific life plan that she values (the "good"), and (3) the terms by which she and others can each act on their claims (the "right").[32] It is where these purposeful pursuits converge at the corporation—and, hence, where the concept of strategy becomes useful—that a story about strategy *and* justice becomes plausible. I now turn to telling that kind of story.

Segue

Each character in the Strategy & Justice genre will be portrayed as an autonomous person. This means that each person can freely choose to live a meaningful life, can freely choose the ends that she considers meaningful, and can freely choose to include among her ends specific terms by which she and others can associate for mutual advantage. Each person is thus distinctly identifiable in terms of these three choices that she can make again and again in her life. Moreover, this distinctive identity can be understood in terms of her efforts, in connection with others who are similarly inclined, to create a just context within which each can flourish.[33] In this way, Strategy & Justice can be interpreted as a story about the Problem of Strategic Management that begins with, endures through, and can be continually reshaped by the actions of autonomous men and women who seek to contribute to justice through their pursuits. Before translating the concepts of autonomy, person, and justice into three premises of Strategy & Justice, I want to introduce a few of the characters who can be accommodated in this genre.

FOUR SHORT STORIES ABOUT AUTONOMY

I create four short stories in this section as prelude to interpreting the Projects, Contracts, and Responsibility Premises of Strategy & Justice.[34] The first story should be familiar to anyone who has driven on a controlled-access highway. The second is a revision to the basketball story that I told early in Chapter 3. The third and fourth stories are set in a corporate context. One involves a variety of characters in the modern telecommunications industry. The other involves a cast of characters who meet in the airline industry.[35]

Driving a Minnesota Freeway

Driver Smith heads south on Interstate 35W (I-35W) in Minneapolis, Minnesota.[36] She and her son are on their way to a Minnesota Twins baseball game in downtown Minneapolis. They both eagerly anticipate spending a leisurely Friday evening watching their favorite players, Kirby Puckett and Rick Lysander, in action. As Smith nears the University Avenue interchange and southbound access ramp, she is driving in the right-hand lane. Traffic coming onto I-35W is heavy this evening. Smith wants to take the Washington Avenue exit, approximately one-half mile ahead on the right. As she begins to look for an opening, she spies a bright-red sports car that appears to be moving rapidly down the ramp toward her.

In the red car, Driver Jones turns right from University Avenue onto the southbound ramp for I-35W. Jones is returning to his office in downtown St. Paul before catching a flight to Chicago. He spent all afternoon in sessions with his business associates and legal advisers. Tonight, he will present his corporate acquisition proposal to officials of the "target" company. As Jones hurries along the entrance ramp, he notices the silver sedan driven by Smith, who is flashing her right-turn signal. Jones wants to get into the left-hand lane as soon as he can, in order to exit one mile ahead onto I-94 East to St. Paul. He frets at the heavy traffic just as he notices a green van behind the silver car.

In the green van, Wilson and her husband, Anderson, are traveling to suburban Hopkins for a dinner meeting of a civic association that they co-chair. Tonight Wilson and Anderson will propose an action campaign that they have been preparing for months. As she passes under the University Avenue bridge, Wilson is driving in the passing lane, almost alongside the silver car driven by Smith. Wilson begins to look for an opening in the right-hand lane, since she wants to take I-94 West from the downtown area. Wilson sees Smith's turn signal. She also observes a red car, driven by Jones, moving along the entrance ramp at a high rate of speed. As she quickly observes the heavy traffic in her rear-view mirror, she grips the wheel and notes that the driver of the red car is flashing his left-turn signal.

Back to the Basketball Court

In the closing thirty seconds of a tightly contested basketball game between the Blue Rockets and the Red Devils, the score is tied. A Red Devil player deflects the ball out of bounds and promptly asks the referee for a timeout. While the players huddle around their respective coaches, the television commentator makes this observation: "It was a race between Rebound, the Red Devil coach, and Brick, the Blue Rockets coach, to see who would call the timeout first. Both have much to discuss with their players."

At the Red Devil bench, Rebound gets to the point quickly: "They will probably double-team Slim, what with the way he has been making his shots. I want you to look for West and East on the perimeter. Whatever you do, wait until the final five seconds. We don't want them to get a shot."

Then, while Brick is still talking with his players, Rebound dashes over to Stripes, the referee, and yells: "Can't you quiet this crowd? My players can hardly hear me. This is a travesty. It happens every time here." Stripes is not moved by the plea and lets Rebound know it: "They have been screaming since thirty minutes *before* the game began. Why do you come to me now? Can you imagine the ruckus if I tried to quiet them?! Look, they're as much a part of this game as the players, you, and me. Let's play the game."[37]

Meanwhile, at the Blue Rockets bench, Brick takes aside Airball, a veteran player who is quite talented and also quite erratic. Brick is his third coach in four seasons. It is also Brick's first year as a head coach anywhere. He says to Airball: "I know that you're going through a bad shooting streak and that Slim has been beating you all night. But I'm putting you back in the game. You've got thirty seconds to salvage your night." Brick then returns to the team: "They'll probably try to get the ball to Slim again, so we need some size inside. I'm substituting Airball and Feet for Ace and Hands. Remember that all we can hope for now is to send the game into overtime." As his team returns to the floor, Brick starts to ask Stripes what was bothering Rebound. Stripes waves Brick away and winks: "There's no problem. He's a little tense. I can't imagine why."

Once the game resumes, West passes to East. The player guarding East slips, whereupon East scores the winning basket with time expiring.[38] A disappointed Brick admits in an interview: "I simply wanted to get our best players matched up against their best in that situation. No, I do not like losing to the Red Devils. But there were no losers in this game. I would have paid to watch it."[39] He then turns to look for Airball.

The Telephone Lines Are Busy

The news hardly comes as a surprise. Still, each of them pauses to consider what the announcement could mean for him. They know that this is not the first time that an order has come from the Federal Communications Commission (FCC) about rolling back the access charges that long-distance carriers pay to the local telephone companies. This most recent decision would amount, if not reduced on appeal, to a $1.1 billion "refund."[40] It has become common practice for each of them to approve policies whereby these periodic refunds would be passed on to long-distance customers in the form of lower rates.[41] Each now has reason to ponder why it makes sense to continue with that practice. Each also knows that he has reason to diverge from that practice.

Robert Allen is one person in this group. He is consumed with the continuing task of redefining a composite of businesses for AT&T in the postdivestiture era. Chief among Allen's efforts is the redirection of the AT&T computer business. Although there were signs that that effort was paying off in terms of wider customer acceptance of AT&T products, Allen knows quite well that the AT&T long-distance cash flow is still subsidizing the computer turnaround.[42] Retention of the "refund" thus looks appealing from that angle. Allen knows, however, that the lower access costs are attractive in a different way for others at AT&T. Allen is chairman of AT&T. Allen and others at AT&T all have reason to be concerned about AT&T's dwindling share of the U.S. long-distance market.[43]

For Joseph Nacchio, lower rates would come in handy in the frenzied competition for multimillion-dollar corporate accounts. Over the past year, the FCC commissioners have granted Nacchio and his associates new latitude in discounting AT&T long-distance products.[44] It has become increasingly necessary to use this so-called Tariff 12, even if it does reduce AT&T profit margins, simply to retain long-time customers.[45] Nacchio heads AT&T marketing activities in the corporate long-distance marketplace.

Stan Lacks likewise has reason to welcome the lower access charges. Residential long-distance rates touch every telephone consumer. Lacks knows that this pervasive presence, coupled with AT&T's market share, keeps AT&T in the limelight as the dominant long-distance supplier in the United States. In particular, AT&T pricing policies are under continual scrutiny from federal and state regulators as well as from members of several congressional committees.[46] At the same time, Lacks wants very much to have customers subscribe to AT&T for reasons of AT&T product quality and diversity.[47] Here is an opportunity, by forgoing a further rate cut, to send that signal more clearly. Lacks is Nacchio's counterpart at AT&T in the residential marketplace.[48]

There is little doubt about the signals that William McGowan wants to send to long-distance users, competitors, and regulators. McGowan has long interpreted MCI as the "little upstart" in relation to AT&T, the dominant market player.[49] By continually pacing AT&T—price cut for price cut, aggressive advertisement for aggressive advertisement, and litigation for litigation—he has every reason to welcome the FCC order. This is one more opportunity for Allen, Nacchio, and Lacks to justify lower rates. Accordingly, it is one more opportunity for McGowan to harp on AT&T's dominant pricing role in the marketplace.[50] Yet McGowan—long-time chairman at MCI—has other opportunities to call attention to AT&T's dominance, and those opportunities require cash. Through a program of mergers and new product introductions, McGowan holds true to his belief that the MCI product line must grow and diversify simply to withstand AT&T's clout among customers.[51] Funding for that effort, McGowan knows, could be derived by retaining a portion of the access charge reduction.

McGowan is not alone in carefully studying the decisions made by Allen, Nacchio, and Lacks regarding the future role of AT&T in the U.S. long-distance marketplace. Alfred Sikes has gone so far as to throw open for public debate the whole question of AT&T's supposed market dominance.[52] Sikes has quickly demonstrated his willingness to encourage competitive initiatives, such as the Tariff 12 for AT&T.[53] Thus price cuts in the wake of the FCC order could serve as further evidence of his contention that the "market works." Nonetheless, Sikes, like McGowan, is increasingly aware of the growing trend toward consolidation in the industry as larger companies absorb smaller carriers. McGowan seeks to contribute to this trend by merging Telecom USA into MCI.[54] There is no ready indication, from Sikes's vantage point, that lower long-distance rates would appreciably help the hundreds of smaller long-distance players in the marketplace. Sikes has been FCC chairman since 1989.

William Esrey worries that the FCC order could put him into a bind that he does not need. On the one hand, there is reason for Esrey to welcome the opportunity to reduce long-distance rates charged by US Sprint, a subsidiary of United Telecommunications. Esrey is chairman at United Telecommunications. He and his predecessors carefully kept US Sprint on the sidelines as McGowan and Allen perpetuated the rancorous MCI–AT&T rivalry.[55] Esrey is now content with consolidating the recent improvements made in US Sprint customer service and network operations.[56] An opportunity to simply stay in step with others' pricing moves has a certain appeal at this point in the history of US Sprint.

The FCC order requires Esrey to stay in step in a less welcome way, on the other hand. The United Telephone subsidiaries of United Telecommunications are among the providers of local telephone service ordered to reduce access charges. Esrey thus faces the prospect of a future slowdown in cash flow precisely at a time when he is attempting to chart a course of modernization in these local operations and to create product possibilities from the US Sprint–United Telephone merger.[57] Access charges constitute almost 40 percent of the annual revenues at the United Telephone companies.[58]

Takeoffs and Holding Patterns

Frank Shrontz and Dean Thornton want United Airlines pilots to fly state-of-the-art widebodied aircraft. John McDonnell, Robert Hood, and Stephen Wolf want United Airlines pilots to fly state-of-the-art widebodied aircraft. So, too, do Gerald Greenwald, Frederick Dubinsky, and Samuel Skinner. Even Robert Crandall has reason to want this to come to pass.

Shrontz and Thornton, respectively chairman and head of the commercial aircraft division at Boeing, know that United pilots have for years flown a full range of Boeing jets, from the 727 to the widebodied 747.[59] McDonnell and Hood—CEO at McDonnell Douglas and president of Douglas Aircraft, respectively—know that United pilots have flown the DC-10 widebodied model for years.[60] All three know that Wolf and his counterparts at every other U.S. carrier are concerned with the skyrocketing costs of maintaining fleets of jet aircraft.[61] Moreover, Shrontz and McDonnell are busy guiding development efforts to replace the bellwether aircraft designs at their respective companies with the newer, more efficient Boeing 777 and MD-11, respectively.[62] Each would like nothing better than to see the orange and blue United logo painted on these new models. In Shrontz's case, it presents an opportunity to sustain Boeing's position as an industry innovator. From McDonnell's perspective, it is an opportunity to restore a long-lost credibility for McDonnell Douglas in the commercial aviation world.[63]

Greenwald and Dubinsky, chairman of the pilots' union, lead the latest attempt to reorganize the ownership of United.[64] Both know that United employees' jobs hinge on the wider availability of fuel-efficient airplanes to cover United's expanding worldwide route network. Secretary of transportation Skinner knows that prosperity for the two leading U.S. carriers, United and American Airlines, can forestall the growing trend toward foreign ownership of U.S. carriers.[65] Crandall—chairman at American and, by all rights, Wolf's fiercest rival—knows that in the high-technology business of aircraft operation and repair, prosperity among carriers can contribute to prosperity among manufacturers.[66] And Crandall, like all these persons, knows that airline safety, particularly in an era of aging aircraft, is in everyone's interest.[67]

The time is right to deliver airplanes to United. Still, getting new airplanes to United remains problematic.

Shrontz and McDonnell oversee marketing efforts that have produced record order backlogs at Boeing and McDonnell Douglas, respectively. Executives at airlines the world over have placed orders with these companies. Wolf is among them with regard to the smaller aircraft in the United fleet.[68] Yet deliveries from those backlogs have been slow. Only so many airplanes can be constructed in a month. Moreover, Thornton has had to contend with a strike, prolonged certification processes for jet engines, technical flaws in existing Boeing designs, and longer than expected training periods.[69] Hood has had to deal with cost overruns and a reduction in cash flow from the military side of the McDonnell Douglas product line.[70] Each is dividing resources between the current production schedules and the ongoing development efforts for the next-generation airplanes.

Greenwald wants Wolf's job, and Dubinsky wants Greenwald to get his wish. In the meantime, they search for ways to finance their plan for a "new," employee-owned, United. If successful, they could well saddle United—the corporation—with billions of dollars in new debt obligations. The cash for interest payments could be the cash used for buying airplanes.[71] Already, the expense and distraction of the buyout attempt are mounting.[72] Skinner finds himself under growing pressure to reconsider the federal policy of industry deregulation.[73] His critics complain about rising airfares, particularly at airports dominated by a single carrier, such as United at Chicago, and flight delays at congested airports. Still, he steadfastly resists reregulation of the industry and thus remains on the sidelines of the Wolf–Greenwald controversy.

Meanwhile, Crandall directs a campaign to extend American routes into South America, Europe, and Asia in one sweeping move.[74] He knows that American can afford to acquire new routes and aircraft. And after the failed takeover attempt by Donald Trump in 1989, Crandall does not have Wolf's worries about job security.[75] Still, what Crandall and his pilots do not have is a sufficient number of midsized and widebodied airplanes for the worldwide expansion. As a result, part of the swelling backlogs for MD-11s at McDonnell Douglas and 757s and 767s at Boeing is attributable to orders approved by Crandall.[76]

Wolf is still waiting in line for new airplanes.

Segue

I will now argue that we can read all four of these diverse stories as the same kind of story. My connecting device is the set of three premises that will constitute Strategy & Justice. By showing that the Strategy & Justice story line can be sustained across a pair of "everyday" cases and a pair of corporate cases, I make a claim for the plausibility of this genre by the test of breadth that I discussed in Chapter 1. By expressing these premises in terms of persons and their purposeful pursuits, moreover, I make the further claim that we can understand Strategy & Justice as a plausible ethical commentary about the three assumptions of the Problem of Strategic Management.

PERSONS AND PURPOSES

I begin the Strategy & Justice story by introducing each man and woman in terms of the pattern of ongoing activities in which each chooses to engage. These activities, or courses of action, are called *projects*.[77] A project carries significance for a person as a link between her present and some future state of affairs that she chooses to value. In this way, we can interpret a project as a means for activating what Loren Lomasky calls the "especially intimate relationship between a person and his ends."[78] Furthermore, we can understand projects as evolving courses of action with which a person seeks her ends, or purposes. Thus a person can survey the history of her projects as one way to account for the progress that she is making in her life. In all, the concept of project serves as a mark of distinction between persons and other entities.[79]

A First Premise for Strategy & Justice

I tell the Strategy & Justice story in terms of many men and women simultaneously pursuing projects that they call their own. In this way, I choose to act on the following premise:

> **Projects Premise:** *Purposeful action requires, in part, that each person take seriously not only the projects that she chooses to pursue, and the reasons for each project, but also the fact that her projects can intersect with the projects, and accompanying reasons, that other persons choose to pursue.*

With these words, I articulate the Projects Premise as one kind of commentary about the *Human Decision Assumption,* from the Problem of Strategic Management genre, which holds:

> *Purposeful action at the corporation requires, in part, that persons devote attention to questions about the purpose(s) for that action.*

With the Projects Premise I provide an account of the "devote attention" imperative through my assumption about men and women acting on their purposes through patterns of projects that they choose to value and enact. The Projects Premise corresponds further to the Human Decision Assumption with an expansive rendition of "attention to questions about the purpose(s) for that action." By the Projects Premise I provide for the prima facie legitimacy ("take seriously") of the project pursuits undertaken by any one character *and* by others.[80] Further still, the Projects Premise accounts for purposeful action through the explicit connection between each person and her reasons for acting.

In all these regards, we can understand this first premise of Strategy & Justice as a quite general commentary that transcends the "boundaries" of the corporation. Persons can pursue projects at the corporation just as easily as they can do so nowhere near the corporation. Thus, I deliberately interpret the Projects Premise without any reference to "corporation." I sketch the basic idea of the Projects Premise in Figure 4.2, in which the context for any one person's purposeful action is partially depicted as one where her projects intersect with another person's projects.

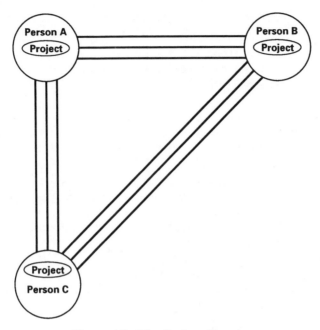

Figure 4.2. The Projects Premise.

The Projects Premise and Four Short Stories About Autonomy

I narrate each of my four short stories in such a way that each man and woman is introduced in terms of the projects that he and she pursues and the guiding reasons, or purposes, for those projects.

Driver Smith acts on the leisurely ends that she values through two projects: attending a Minnesota Twins game and driving on I-35W. I identify Driver Jones in terms of his aim of closing a big business deal, a purpose that he pursues through his travel projects first on I-35W and later on a flight to Chicago. Likewise, I introduce Driver Wilson as a person acting on a certain civic purpose by means, in part, of her driving on I-35W.

I introduce Brick in terms of his project to arrange a lineup that best matches what he anticipates Rebound will do and his ongoing project to understand and encourage Airball, his best player. We learn more about Brick as I connect those two projects to his purpose of establishing his standing, as a "rookie" coach who enters an unsettled situation, with his players.

In the telecommunications story, we become acquainted, for example, with McGowan as a person acting with a purpose of maintaining the hard-won acceptance of MCI by many customers.[81] Toward that end, I tell a story about two of McGowan's projects: (1) a recent merger and (2) a program of contentious responses to the projects that Allen, Nacchio, and Lacks are pursuing at AT&T.

Finally, I identify Shrontz at Boeing in terms of his purpose to reaffirm Boeing's technological leadership among Boeing's customers and competitors. One project through which he pursues this purpose is the Boeing 777 development.[82]

I narrated each of these stories to suggest also how commonplace it can be for one person's projects to lead her to an acquaintance with another person's projects. The story about the access charge presents numerous cases in point. Allen's project to find cash for financing the "turnaround" of the AT&T computer business, guided by his aim to redefine a composite of AT&T businesses, intersects with Nacchio's efforts to employ the FCC-approved Tariff 12 pricing, one project in keeping with his aim of retaining long-term corporate users of AT&T services. Likewise, Allen's project and purpose converge on Lacks's project to forgo rate cuts despite the access charge reductions. Lacks values retaining AT&T's residential customers for reasons other than pricing and, hence, sees forgoing a rate cut as one route to this end.

In pursuing his project, Nacchio converges on McGowan's pair of projects. McGowan's pursuits, in turn, become entangled with Sikes and his efforts to encourage greater competition in the long-distance marketplace, by means of projects such as looser controls on AT&T prices. Esrey pursues a project that we might call "quiet competition," in an effort to convince others that US Sprint will be around for a while.[83] In so doing, he runs into Lacks acting on his project of nonprice competition in the form of advertisements about service quality.[84]

Segue

I create the Projects Premise, in sum, as a first step in placing autonomous persons, and the choices that they choose to make, in the middle of a story about purposeful action at the corporation and elsewhere. Still, the mere fact of persons pursuing projects and the resulting fact of intersecting projects leaves open a question about the interpretations that persons can make about those intersections.[85] To address this question about the significance of men and women, through their projects, meeting other men and women, through their projects, I create a second assumption that complements the Projects Premise.

PERSONS, PROJECTS, AND ENDURING RELATIONSHIPS

My aim here is to enrich the Strategy & Justice genre with an account that connects intersecting projects and the autonomous persons whose identities can be interpreted in terms of their respective pursuits. Thus

I want to (1) maintain starring roles in Strategy & Justice for persons and their projects—that is, extend the Projects Premise—and I want to (2) say more about the context where they and their projects cross paths. I choose to address this pair of self-imposed requirements in terms of three salient features of this context.

At the Intersection of Projects

1. The connection between any two persons' projects is likely to endure with a history. This evolutionary characteristic of intersecting projects is understandable, in part, by each person's own temporal approach to her projects.[86] A project implies more than a fleeting and insignificant endeavor as a person tries to connect her present—and/or past—with the future. Even in the thirty seconds during which Drivers Smith and Jones interact, they have reason to think in terms of their unfolding relationship. This characteristic is also attributable, in part, to the determination of each person—as implied by "autonomy"—to see her efforts through to some outcome. In my telecommunications story, for instance, we have no reason to expect that McGowan will abandon his project to publicize the competitive moves of Nacchio and Lacks simply because Nacchio and Lacks pursue their respective projects in McGowan's "neighborhood." This tenacity squares with the "continuity" connotation of purpose that I developed in Chapter 1. Thus where two tenacious characters meet, we can reasonably expect their saga to unfold. That tenacity can give rise, as well, to a second feature of intersecting projects.

2. The enduring connection between men and women and their respective projects can be understood in terms of each person's moves and countermoves in response to another's moves and countermoves. In other words, as each autonomous party comes to recognize the connection, she has reason to choose interdependently. By this choice to choose in response to another, she factors others' likely actions into her own plans for conducting the projects in question. Once again, this choice is quite understandable in view of the crucial connection between a person's projects and her purposes.

In my basketball story, Rebound and Brick choose their respective lineups and their respective tactics partly in anticipation of what the other might do. On the freeway, Smith acts on her project, "reach the Washington Avenue exit," by flashing her turn signal in response to Jones acting on his project, "move into the left lane quickly," by speeding along the entrance ramp and flashing his left-turn signal. Wilson grips the wheel in response to the mutually responsive project pursuits of Smith and Jones. In these two cases, we can interpret project pursuit in terms of the conditional choices that each party chooses to make.

This practice of mutually conditioned action can spawn a third characteristic of intersecting projects.

3. The outcome of a conditioned and enduring connection between any two projects can be understood, at any given time, as the joint product of the two persons' actions. At the intersection of two autonomous persons' lives, in other words, no one person can, by virtue of her project alone, dictate the outcome of that relationship. Nor, on this account, can the men and women look to any central authority to dictate an outcome.[87] Once again, I have provided for this joint-product feature in my four stories.

Wolf, Greenwald, and Dubinsky would probably prefer that Crandall approve an order of planes from a supplier other than Boeing. They prefer, in other words, that Crandall not add to the backlog at Boeing. But they cannot compel Crandall to do so. Nor can they look to Skinner, an "authority figure," for automatic relief. Skinner has other projects to pursue in relation to his critics.[88] Esrey likely prefers that Nacchio, Lacks, and McGowan choose to "hold onto" a portion of the access charge reduction. Yet he cannot expect to dictate that outcome simply by pursuing a project of retaining the "refund" for US Sprint. Nor can he expect Sikes to ordain a solution, inasmuch as Sikes is occupied with projects aimed at encouraging "market solutions" for pricing matters. Rebound, Brick, and Stripes might all prefer a quieter arena for playing the final thirty seconds of the game. But even Stripes—in his authority role as referee—cannot hope to attain such an outcome exclusively through his act, say, of issuing an order for quiet. At the very least, Brick, as the "home" coach, might play a part in encouraging that outcome.[89] Stripes could halt the game unilaterally. But such a project, and the likely ruckus that it would create among the fans, runs counter to his purpose of playing the game under the present circumstances, a preference that he expressed to Rebound. In all these cases, then, men and women choose to condition their actions on others' actions. In so doing, they create an outcome that is contingent on their mutually conditioned choices. No one can "wish away" another's lasting presence.

A Second Premise for Strategy & Justice

In the study of ethics, a situation such as this where persons, through their voluntary actions, create an enduring interdependent context is commonly known as a *contract*.[90] We can interpret each character in my stories as a party to multiple concurrent contracts. Moreover, we can shine the brightest spotlight on persons and their projects if we interpret in bilateral terms the contracts that they jointly create. Smith and Jones and Smith and Wilson are parties to bilateral contracts at the freeway interchange, for instance.[91] I integrate this conception of contract into the Strategy & Justice story as follows:

Contracts Premise: *Purposeful action requires, in part, that any two persons whose respective projects intersect in an enduring relationship—or contract—take seriously the meaning of that contract by choosing to act interdependently en route to a jointly produced outcome for the contract and, hence, their projects.*

I thus interpret the Contracts Premise as one kind of commentary about the *Interrelationship Assumption*, from the Problem of Strategic Management, which holds:

Purposeful action at the corporation requires, in part, acknowledgment of the influences that relationships with others "outside" the corporation can bring to bear on that action.

I create the Contracts Premise by specifying "acknowledgment of the influences" in terms of each person's choice to condition her actions on the actions of others. Interdependent choice constitutes one kind of acknowledgment in this regard. As in the case of the Projects Premise, I make this interpretation a general one. I create the Contracts Premise in a language that effectively erases the distinction between contexts "inside" and "outside" the corporation.[92] This general conception of interdependence among persons and their projects is depicted in Figure 4.3.

The Contracts Premise provides an interpretation of the context within which the Projects Premise can hold. In this complementary sense, then, the Contracts Premise also provides for a more sophisticated identification of each person in the Strategy & Justice genre. Each person accommodated by Strategy & Justice is now known not only for her search for a meaningful life through her projects (Projects Premise) but also for the jointly produced situations (Contracts Premise) in which she can meaningfully act out her projects.

I wrote my four short stories to account for this link between the Projects and Contracts Premises. In particular, I make it possible to identify each person in terms of her contribution to what I call an *issue of interdependence* that she and others hold in common. Each such issue can serve as a focus for acting interdependently. That issue, in other words, gives meaning to each contract for the persons involved.[93]

Issues, Contracts, and Four Short Stories About Autonomy

At the confluence of their projects, Smith, Jones, and Wilson create—and interact about—one issue: Where do we accommodate three drivers safely on a given stretch of I-35W? We can just as readily narrow our focus to a pair of bilateral issues that give meaning to this accommodation issue. For example, the contract created by Smith and Jones

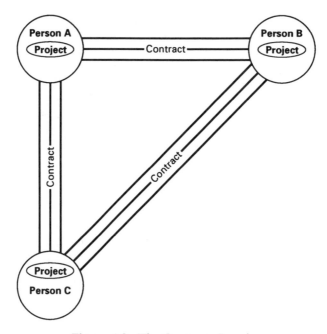

Figure 4.3. The Contracts Premise.

could be interpreted in terms of the issue Where do we accommodate both drivers safely at the end of the University Avenue entrance ramp? Note that I express these issues in a language that clearly makes room for both parties to choose interdependently.[94]

In the basketball story, Rebound, Brick, and Stripes are all parties to one issue: With what actions will we conduct the closing thirty seconds of a tied game? Rebound and Brick, in turn, can be understood as parties to the issue With what lineup matches will our teams play the closing thirty seconds of a tied game? Likewise, Rebound and Stripes interact on an issue regarding what to do about noise created by the home team's fans. Note that my interpretation for each bilateral issue here would likely change if, in the final thirty seconds, the Red Devils led the Blue Rockets by forty points. In that case, for example, both Rebound and Brick might pursue a project of permitting their less talented players to gain some game experience under less stressful conditions.

In the telecommunications story, I portray each person as a party to one issue: What do we do about the access charge reduction? Note that this expression provides for each person and his project amid their contracts with one another. Under this rubric, for instance, Esrey and McGowan might mutually condition their projects around the issue What do we do to keep Nacchio and Lacks at bay? Simultaneously, they could act interdependently on the issue Through what medium do we continue to inform Sikes, Congress, and the world about the dominant market status of AT&T?

Finally, I narrated the United Airlines story in terms of persons converging on one issue: From where will widebodied airplanes be delivered to United? In that context, I portrayed Shrontz and McDonnell as parties to the issue When do we put new designs into production, given the current order backlog? Likewise, Crandall and Wolf have a common interest in the issue What can be done to lessen airport congestion and flight delays through our selection of airplane models and routes? In this story, as in the other three, I illustrate the Contracts Premise in terms of mutually conditioned issues in order to connect my account of autonomous persons with my account of the context that they help create.

Segue

I have, to this point in the Strategy & Justice story, joined considerations about persons, their projects, and the contexts—expressed as issues of interdependence—that they jointly create through their pursuits. In this way, I have constructed an account of an environment within which autonomous men and women can choose to act. In that environment, a person's projects take on meaning, first, in terms of the connection between her own projects and purposes and, second, in terms of the enduring setting within which she enacts her projects in interdependence with others doing the same.

I have not, however, said anything about whether that environment can be conducive, or discouraging, for each person's projects and guiding purposes. Mere recognition of a contractual relationship leaves open a question about the worth of that contract for the men and women involved. Clearly, this question can prove to be crucial for an autonomous person, whose sense of self and good turns on her projects and purposes. I now turn to this matter as the culmination of my Strategy & Justice genre.

PERSONS, PROJECTS, CONTRACTS, AND SELF-CONSTRAINT

The very idea of an autonomous person seeking meaning through her projects makes sense only if she is able to act on those projects in contractual relations with others. It follows, then, that there must be something about those contractual conditions that can empower one's meaningful project pursuits. I locate my interpretation of such *enabling* conditions in a contractual setting in order, once again, to sustain the emphasis in Strategy & Justice on distinct persons and their purposeful activities. Since I have already given meaning to each person's part in Strategy & Justice in terms of her projects and the contractual relations that she helps create, it follows further that the terms by which those relationships can be conducted hold the key to empowering or not empowering a person's pursuits.

This matter has a broader temporal significance for each autonomous person, because she cannot predict when and with whom her future projects will become interconnected.[95] Hence, each has reason to prefer that any conditions that enable her project pursuits must hold over a host of contracts, current and future. With this search in mind for the conditions that enable men and women to fulfill generally their purposes through their projects, I must create a premise that complements the Projects and Contracts Premises.

A Third Premise for Strategy & Justice

Each autonomous person, whose projects hold meaning in contractual terms, has an interest in shaping the terms of her association with others in a way that is favorable for her. This follows from the self-interest connotation of autonomy. Moreover, this preference for favorable contractual terms can hold quite generally across a web of contractual relationships. Each person acts in the same kind of contractual context by the Contracts Premise. Given her self-interest, each person thus prefers that other persons choose to entertain this same perspective on shaping their contracts in favorable terms.

The upshot is that autonomous men and women have a common interest in creating, by means of their chosen and interconnected projects, a sense of community across their contracts.[96] In the absence of community, their project pursuits are very much at risk. Put somewhat differently, none of them values contractual relations where their lists of projects are dominated by projects designed to defend their purposes against others' actions. Each autonomous person has much better things to do.[97]

Chief among these "better things" is a self-directed commitment to create a condition of community by pursuing their projects with the specific aim of empowering persons generally. In the study of ethics, such a voluntary act of setting constraints on one's own pursuits in relation to others is known as an act of *responsibility*.[98] In my Strategy & Justice genre, each person has reason to conduct her projects in accordance with a specific comprehensive term, or principle, by which she prefers to deal with others: *act so as to empower persons and their projects generally*.[99] There are, of course, many specific meanings that parties can agree to interpret for this comprehensive principle. They can, for example, confirm through their respective actions their aim to uphold their promises to one another.[100] Each such ethical principle follows from the parties' agreement to exercise self-constraint in the first place.

This guiding principle for acting with self-constraint in contractual association with others can be formally interpreted in the following third premise of Strategy & Justice:

> **Responsibility Premise:** *Purposeful action requires, in part, that any two persons whose respective projects and purposes become interconnected in contractual relationships take seriously the possibility that they can voluntarily constrain the mutually conditioned conduct of their respective projects to create a conducive context for their projects and the projects of "third parties" to their contract.*

I express the Responsibility Premise as one interpretation of the *Advantage Assumption*, from the Problem of Strategic Management, which holds:

> *Purposeful action at the corporation requires, in part, that persons choose and actively seek a position of lasting benefit in relation to influential "outside" forces.*

The Responsibility Premise gives meaning to the "lasting benefit" concept in terms of each person's successful search for meaning in her life through her chosen projects. If that search is frustrated by others' refusals to exercise self-constraint, the "lasting benefit" condition is violated. The Responsibility Premise also specifies that a man or woman can "choose and actively seek" such benefits by means of the voluntary, self-constrained actions that he or she chooses to take. In this way, the premise makes room for the possibility that each person's projects can be enabled in a contractual context.[101] We can thus think of the Responsibility Premise as a complement to the Projects and Contracts Premises. I depict this liberating value of self-constrained action in Figure 4.4, where the exercise of responsibility through self-constraint is shown as a buttress for each contract and, therefore, each person and her projects.

As I did in interpreting the Projects and Contractual Premises, I create the Responsibility Premise in terms that can apply generally to persons and their associations. By omitting any reference to corporations in the Responsibility Premise, I provide for the general possibility of human interaction for mutual advantage. All four short stories about autonomy illustrate this general possibility that persons can pursue meaningful lives by explicitly incorporating self-constraint into their mutually conditioned projects.

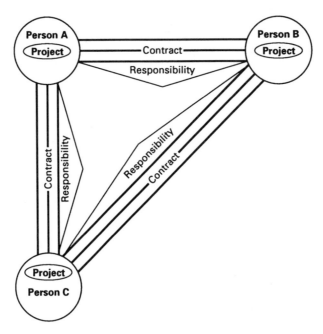

Figure 4.4. The Responsibility Premise.

Projects, Purpose, and the Looming Freeway Collision

There is no guarantee in any of my four stories that the pursuit of projects through contractual relations will produce an outcome favorable to anyone. We can understand just how fragile the search for meaning can be when we revisit Drivers Smith, Jones, and Wilson at the University Avenue freeway interchange. I maintain that their contracts, and the possibilities for mutual advantage, can serve as a model case of the need for a premise that highlights the value of responsible action in any story about the Problem of Strategic Management.

Drivers Smith, Jones, and Wilson can clearly mutually temper, or coordinate, their projects so that each receives a satisfactory outcome according to the standards of their respective purposes.[102] For instance, Smith can maintain her speed in the right-hand lane, Jones can wait his turn on the entrance ramp, and Wilson can reduce her speed to give Smith sufficient room to maneuver if she needs to do so. Across this pattern of choices about enacting projects, each person honors the Responsibility Premise by voluntarily conducting her or his project in a manner anticipated to benefit each party to the contracts in question. Each sets a constraint on her or his own action.

These drivers can also clearly coordinate their contracts in a manner that proves disastrous for all, and perhaps for other parties as well. For instance, Smith can stay in her lane, Wilson can pull alongside Smith, and Jones can continue speeding down the ramp in an attempt to force his way onto I-35W. It goes without saying that, in view of their reasons for driving on the freeway, a collision between Smith and Jones that sends the two cars careening into Wilson's car serves everyone's interests badly. It is precisely this possibility, framed by the Projects and Contracts Premises, that necessitates my interpretation of the Responsibility Premise in the first place if we are to take seriously any person's search for meaning in her life. I set the stage for a freeway collision in each of my other three stories about autonomy.

Rebound, Brick, and Stripes can get involved in an argument about crowd noise such that each distracts the others from acting on their respective purposes. Recall that each, in his own fashion, seeks to be thoroughly prepared for the final thirty seconds of the game. Stripes, for example, wants to have the game determined on the playing floor. Brick, for example, seeks to further his relationship with Airball, and needs the timeout to arrange his project of putting Airball back into the game. At worst, the very argument among the two coaches and the referee can incite members of the crowd to make even more noise than ever.

Allen, Nacchio, Lacks, McGowan, Esrey, and Sikes can jointly create a pattern of responses to lower access charges in the form of a price war. In view of their efforts to fund their respective projects, this contractual scenario hardly seems attractive to Allen, Nacchio, Lacks, McGowan, and Esrey. The last thing that Sikes needs, in his effort to build confidence in the FCC as a watchdog for and champion of open competition, is an out-of-control pricing scenario that "invites" greater scrutiny from other would-be regulators.

The huge order backlogs at Boeing and McDonnell Douglas can be interpreted as a kind of broadly disadvantageous freeway collision. We might explain the backlog in terms of the apparently unconstrained project pursuits of Crandall and Wolf—each wanting to add to their aircraft fleet—and the apparently unconstrained project pursuits of Thornton and Hood—each valuing more orders to fewer orders and each valuing the unabated development of new aircraft. All four appear to be stymied in pursuit of their respective aims. With the slow delivery of newer aircraft, Wolf's hopes for lower maintainence costs are dashed. Additionally, his standing with key stockholders—whose support Greenwald and Dubinsky are seeking—could suffer if United profitability is hindered by a lack of suitable aircraft. With the slow delivery of newer aircraft, Crandall's expansion aspirations are crimped. With the slow delivery of newer aircraft, Thornton's aims for cash-generating operations are impeded, as are Shrontz's hopes for a wider worldwide presence for Boeing jets. With the slow delivery of newer aircraft, McDonnell's vision of a rejuvenated McDonnell Douglas commercial airplane business is clouded for want of cash. Moreover, Skinner, as a third party to these contracts, likely comes under increasing pressure from his congressional critics as older planes, carrying fewer passengers per plane, contribute to longer delays at major airports. Even Greenwald and Dubinsky can be stalled in their efforts. Bankers might be less willing to lend funds to a company facing a delayed program of fleet modernization.

I tell these four stories about freeway collisions in order to enhance my justification for the Responsibility Premise as a complement to the Projects and Contracts Premises. That justification follows from the relative ease with which any two men and women choosing in the context of each other—much less, many persons—can create their own version of the freeway collisions. The damage that a freeway collision can impose is good reason for the Responsibility Premise.

Reprise About Responsibility, Persons, and Projects

I articulated the Responsibility Premise in terms that continue to give prominence to autonomous persons and their pursuits. This connection among men and women, their projects, and their voluntary acts of self-constraint is prominent in three regards. First, each person has a responsibility *to* another distinct person. This follows from both the Projects Premise, whereby persons are identified through their projects, and the Contracts Premise, whereby persons are identified through their linkage with other persons.[103] Next, a responsibility pertains to a specific project undertaken by a distinct man or woman. By the Responsibility Premise, a statement about responsibility takes the following form: Person A is responsible to Person B to pursue her chosen project Z with self-constraint.[104] Third, a responsibility holds meaning in a specific contractual context. By this interpretation of responsibility, we cannot justify Jones contributing to Smith's favorite charity as a tradeoff for Jones's reckless driving that results in a dented fender on Smith's car.[105] Although we might praise Jones for his generosity, we must do so in the context of perhaps *another* contract. The fact remains that he has a contractual relationship with Smith at the freeway interchange.[106] In all three regards, the Responsibility Premise provides hope that autonomous men and women can work through their respective unique life plans.

THE CONCEPT OF STRATEGY ACCORDING TO STRATEGY & JUSTICE

I can now connect the meanings that I have interpreted for the Projects, Contracts, and Responsibility Premises to articulate an alternative conception of strategy that is supported by my Strategy & Justice genre.

An Alternative Conception of Strategy

A strategy is a plan of action whereby any one person ac-
commodates (1) multiple, diverse purposes and corresponding projects—including her own—that become interconnected; (2) the resulting contractual relationships that hold
meaning for the persons who pursue their projects interdependently around issues that they jointly create; and (3) the
choices available to those persons to conduct their pursuits
voluntarily in a manner that creates a context conducive to
their ends and the ends of others whose projects are affected
in that context.

By Strategy & Justice, a strategy can be understood as a jointly created
meaning held among persons who, through their joint project pursuits,
could beneficially coexist in a community.[107] In this regard, I draw on
Jerome Bruner's account of the search for meaning in a discourse among
diverse persons: "Meaning is what we can agree upon or at least accept
as a working basis for seeking agreement about the concept at hand. If
one is arguing about social 'realities' . . . the reality is not the thing,
not in the head, but in the act of arguing and negotiating about the
meaning of such concepts."[108] We could certainly characterize that
"concept at hand" as a "corporate purpose" if we choose, as long as we
interpret this concept as merely the result of the "arguing and negotiating" to which Bruner refers.[109] My emphasis on persons—those who
argue and negotiate through their project pursuits—throughout this
alternative definition of strategy underscores my aim of providing a
humanist account of the Problem of Strategic Management. In this regard, the concept of corporate purpose is not necessary. Hence, it is
conspicuously absent from my alternative conception of strategy.

CONCLUSION

My purpose for this chapter has been to interpret and defend a logic,
using an ethical language, for an alternative story about the Problem
of Strategic Management. The Strategy & Justice genre is the product
of this effort. We can understand Strategy & Justice as an ethical genre
in the sense that each of its premises is stated in a language of autonomous persons and their enduring connections with one another. In
the Strategy & Justice story, men and women pursue their projects with
a sense of purpose for their lives (Projects Premise). In the course of
those project pursuits, these men and women come to recognize and
act on the enduring relationships that they jointly create through their
individual efforts (Contracts Premise). In that interdependent context,

each person has reason to conduct her projects with a disposition of voluntary self-constraint in search of conditions conducive to each person's pursuits (Responsibility Premise). Throughout this story line, we meet persons acting autonomously in their joint search for justice in their relationships. In this regard, then, I offer Strategy & Justice as a genre about purposeful action that can be narrated in a language of ethics.

Along the way, I made three claims for the plausibility of the Strategy & Justice genre. First, I interpreted the genre as a commentary about the Problem of Strategic Management. To the extent that the Problem of Strategic Management holds wide appeal—as I showed across my group of twelve in Chapter 3—the logical appeal of Strategy & Justice follows. Second, I articulated the premises of Strategy & Justice as an expression of arguments shared by members in a community of moral philosophers. A person who subscribes to those arguments could subscribe to my logic for Strategy & Justice. Finally, I made a pragmatist case for Strategy & Justice by showing how the genre can hold across a diverse set of four cases, some corporate and some of an everyday variety. In this way, I begin to connect Strategy & Justice with the stories that you and I can choose to tell in our lives.

Strategy & Justice is a story that strategic management researchers *could* choose to use as justification for their projects. Whether or not they choose to do so is, of course, another matter. I now move to argue that they have good reason to prefer the Strategy & Justice genre over the Strategy through Process story to which they have become accustomed.

5

Twilight for Strategy Through Process

Had he ever noticed that living in Clyde was like walking through spiderwebs without any spiders?

JOHN MARQUAND, *Point of No Return*

A sanitized kind of language in which all emotion, all opinion, all the feel, taste, and smell of human experience had been removed.

GEORGE LEE WALKER, *The Chronicles of Doodah*

The time has come to place the corporate strategy concept in twilight. I have two meanings in mind as I make this statement. Each follows from Nietzsche's conception of twilight as a period when the worldly worth of an idea is open to critical assessment. That assessment is "critical" insofar as the meaning of a concept about human endeavor is thrown open to question. I write this chapter by weaving the two meanings that I give to "twilight of corporate strategy" into the critical climax to my argument for this book.

First, I put the corporate strategy concept in Nietzschean twilight by critically analyzing the hopeful promise, which I interpreted in Chapter 1, of that concept. By that hopeful prospect, the corporate strategy concept can prove useful for men and women who seek to understand the possibilities for their purposeful pursuits in the context of the modern corporation. The centerpiece of this chapter is my articulation, in such a worldly context, of a response to the research question that I posed in Chapter 1:

> Of what value is strategic management research as a humanist perspective on the modern corporation?

I will develop an answer to this question by means of a comparative showdown set against the backdrop of the Problem of Strategic Management, which I interpreted in Chapter 3 as a widely used conception

147

of the corporate strategy concept.[1] In particular, I will assess—premise for premise—the comparative humanist promise of the two different interpretations of the Problem of Strategic Management that I created in Chapters 3 and 4, the Strategy through Process genre and the Strategy & Justice genre.

I interpreted each of these two genres as a kind of human story set at the corporation. Moreover, I justified both as ethical stories. That is, each kind of story can be read as a commentary about persons, their respective purposeful pursuits, and their relationships. For this reason, my effort to put the corporate strategy concept in the twilight of criticism can be construed as an act of ethical criticism. This kind of criticism is informed by the restated research question that I also defended in Chapter 1:

> Of what relative value is strategic management research as
> an ethical interpretation of the modern corporation?

My particular answer to this question gives impetus to a second meaning of "twilight of corporate strategy."

Second, I conclude from my comparative critical analysis that we must abandon the logic of Strategy through Process as a usable language about the modern corporation.[2] In other words, I answer both versions of my research question as follows:

> Not much, as long as the corporate strategy concept is interpreted with the Strategy through Process genre.

My thesis for this chapter is straightforward. *If we value the corporate strategy concept as a kind of commentary about men and women acting on matters of purpose in the context of the modern corporation, then we must condemn Strategy through Process to the end, or "twilight," of its popular usage, and then move on.*[3] This second kind of Nietzschean twilight is always a possible consequence of the first kind of twilight. I travel two paths to reach this conclusion about Strategy through Process.

In one regard, I will argue that the logic of Strategy through Process is beset with an idiosyncratic emphasis on the structure of human action absent the men and women who inhabit that structure. It is this focus that inspires my choice of Marquand's reference to "spiderwebs without spiders" for the epigraph to this chapter.[4] I will show that, like the spiderwebs in Marquand's story, the logic of Strategy through Process serves to diminish a hopeful outlook on human activity by severing the connection between persons and purpose.

In the other regard, I will argue that hope for persons and their purposes in a corporate context is undermined irreparably by the very logic of the Strategy through Process genre. Indeed, I argue that hope for persons and their purposes is necessarily driven out of the Strategy through Process story. It is this disparagement of persons throughout the Strategy through Process story that inspires my quotation, in the epigraph, of a passage from Walker's nightmarish tale of life at the modern corporation. I will show that the language of Strategy through Process, like the language in that corporate setting, is too "sanitized" of "the taste, feel, and smell of human experience" to be salvaged as a humanist story.[5]

The upshot of the chapter is that I put corporate strategy in twilight in the first Nietzschean sense and thereby give strategic management researchers—and anyone else who chooses to use the corporate strategy concept—good reason to cast Strategy through Process into the oblivion of Nietzsche's second sense of twilight. Still, I write this chapter with a hopeful purpose as well.

At the same time that I justify the demise of Strategy through Process as a meaningful story about the corporation, I begin to make the case that we can enhance the corporate strategy concept in humanist terms. Since I reach my conclusions by a comparative analysis, and since the logic of Strategy & Justice serves as the standard for that critical comparison, one byproduct of my critique is a companion justification for the relative usefulness of Strategy & Justice. Thus I give reason to believe that the Strategy & Justice genre is a better way to tell stories about the corporate strategy concept.[6] In so doing, I clearly argue on the assumption that the corporate strategy concept per se is well worth saving. The potential for connecting that concept and Strategy & Justice is the subject of the Epilogue. In the meantime, I turn to explain and then to apply the criteria by which I interpret Strategy & Justice as a "better" humanist account of the Problem of Strategic Management than Strategy through Process.

TERMS OF COMPARISON IN TWILIGHT

The point of my comparative critical analysis is to determine which of the two ethical genres about the Problem of Strategic Management— and thus the corporate strategy concept—supports a better account of men and women and their purposeful pursuits at the corporation. For my purposes here, I interpret "better" with criteria that are favorable to persons and their chosen activities. After all, as I argued in Chapter 1, to adopt a humanist point of view is to give priority, at the very least, to persons and their pursuits. In particular, I employ two criteria of favorability for making an assessment of the relative worth of the Strategy through Process and Strategy & Justice genres. Each criterion follows from the humanist perspective with which I choose to put corporate strategy in twilight.[7]

First, an account about the Problem of Strategic Management can be favorable if it *celebrates the possibility that a person can grow* through her chosen purposeful actions at the corporation.[8] The "better" account, in other words, is one written with a hopefulness that a person can successfully create and sustain a search for meaning in her life. It is a story line that is thoroughly biased toward the potential for a person's worldly progress.[9] Certainly, none of this presumes that persons are infallible, omniscient, or immune to accidents.[10] Self-doubt, rash judgment, and serendipity can clearly attend one's search for meaning. These complications notwithstanding, however, an account that champions the potential for a person's growth is preferable, by this first criterion, to an account that subordinates, or even impugns, a person's search for meaning. My second criterion extends this celebratory theme.

Second, an account about the Problem of Strategic Management can be favorable in a humanist sense if it *celebrates the distinctions among persons* who seek to enact lives that they prefer.[11] This criterion complements my first criterion with a generalized story line that encompasses many diverse men and women searching for avenues of growth in their own lives. The "better" human story, in other words, provides for the widespread prima facie legitimacy of purposeful human endeavor.[12] By this criterion as well, persons are accorded equal status as purposeful actors, regardless of how different their ends might be.[13] Certainly, none of this presumes that each person has the same ability or temperament or ambition to carry out a meaningful plan for living. Rather, the criterion admits men and women to a worldly story on the basis of their preference for acting purposefully. Thus an account that celebrates the distinctions among, and hence the generalizability of, persons seeking their own meanings is preferable, by my criterion, to an account that sorts, or even excludes, men and women on the basis of their cognitive status.[14]

I apply these two criteria in three pairwise critical comparisons. Each comparison is set in the context of the Problem of Strategic Management. I begin by comparing critically the Injunction Premise of Strategy through Process and the Projects Premise of Strategy & Justice— both expressions of the Human Decision Assumption of the Problem of Strategic Management—in terms of their favorability toward a humanist perspective. Subsequently, I compare the Impediment Premise of Strategy through Process and the Contracts Premise of Strategy & Justice—both expressions of the Interrelationship Assumption of the Problem of Strategic Management—and the Institution Premise of Strategy through Process and the Responsibility Premise of Strategy & Justice—both expressions of the Advantage Assumption of the Problem of Strategic Management—on the same critical terms. I depict this plan of critical analysis in Figure 5.1.

I now turn to defend my claim that Strategy through Process, as an

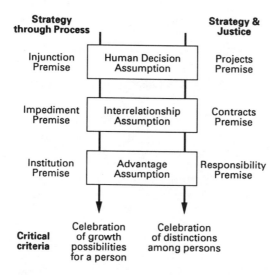

Figure 5.1. A comparative critical showdown.

ethical genre, fails all three comparative humanist tests and does so irreparably.

A COMPARATIVE CRITIQUE ABOUT THE HUMAN DECISION ASSUMPTION

The Human Decision Assumption of the Problem of Strategic Management holds:

> *Purposeful action at the corporation requires, in part, that persons devote attention to questions about the purpose(s) for that action.*

According to the Projects Premise of Strategy & Justice, this assumption is meaningful in terms of many persons deciding to pursue projects for reasons (purposes) of their own:

> **Projects Premise:** *Purposeful action requires, in part, that each person take seriously not only the projects that she chooses to pursue, and the reasons for each project, but also the fact that her projects can intersect with the projects, and accompanying reasons, that other persons choose to pursue.*

According to the Injunction Premise of Strategy through Process, on the contrary, the pertinent human activities at the corporation are those that guide a structured decision-making process with which a purpose is acquired for the corporation:

> **Injunction Premise:** *Purposeful action at the corporation requires, in part, that senior decision-making specialists be enjoined, as they command a structured decision-making process, by that process from distinguishing between the corporate purpose(s) derived from that process and their own respective purposes.*

The men and women covered by the Injunction Premise must interpret the reasons for their decision-making activities as "corporate" reasons, not their own. This is the reason why I call this the Injunction Premise. Hence, for persons to act meaningfully at the corporation, they must—by the Injunction Premise—subordinate their own reasons for acting to the "corporate" reasons that emanate from the process that they guide.

The contrast in meanings here is as unmistakable as it is telling. *The Injunction Premise justifies placing restrictions on the very phenomenon that the Projects Premise highlights generally: men and women pursuing their own projects for reasons that they choose to value.* In no small way, persons and their own projects pose a fundamental threat to organized decision-making in the Strategy through Process story.[15] For that process to successfully yield a purposeful plan of corporate action, the Injunction Premise holds that men and women must suppress their urge to think about their own pursuits. This is the key message of a premise that enjoins, in the name of preserving a structure of decision-making activities, each person from taking action because she values that action. The Injunction Premise, in short, supports a story about "spiderwebs" with the "spiders" enjoined from reasoning about why they, as spiders, are spinning the web in the first place.

A First Critical Comparison

The upshot is this: to adopt the Injunction Premise of Strategy through Process is to adopt a less favorable account, relative to the Projects Premise of Strategy & Justice, by my two humanist criteria. I attribute this shortcoming of Strategy through Process to the idiosyncratic interpretation of human purpose conveyed by the Injunction Premise. In particular, this premise clearly narrows purposeful action to a person's participation in the strategy-acquisition process.

As a result, the Injunction Premise celebrates neither the possibility for a person's growth through her pursuits at the corporation nor the distinctions among persons who seek meaning in that context. On the first count, the premise specifically deters a person from paying attention to her own purposes, unless those aims happen to coincide with the corporate purpose. This condition severely restricts the very celebration of personal growth to which the Projects Premise gives priority. On the second count, the Injunction Premise denies the importance of diversity among persons with the requirement that corporate decision-making be directed by the singular beacon of corporate purpose. More-over, the Injunction Premise applies only to those senior managers who are specialized in operating a strategic decision-making process. This near-total exclusion of men and women from the Strategy through Process story serves to downplay, far from generally supporting, the value of human diversity.[16] By contrast, the Projects Premise opens the door on human diversity by explicitly placing one person's projects in the context of others' projects, by the broad imperative to "take seri-ously" the presence of other men and women.

The Injunction Premise Beyond Humanist Repair

I thus conclude that Strategy through Process fails in comparison with Strategy & Justice on this first count about persons engaged in deci-sion-making activities at the corporation. In two key respects, the In-junction Premise supports a story that is largely "sanitized" of persons acting in search of meaningful lives. First, by the Injunction Premise, the Strategy through Process story is open only to those persons who formally guide the strategic decision-making process. Second, those men and women are required by the Injunction Premise to adopt, as their own, the purpose that emerges from that process. Indeed, the Injunc-tion Premise *must* remain sanitized in these ways if Strategy through Process is to remain a coherent story about the act of acquiring a strat-egy for the corporation.

Both "sanitizing" assumptions confirm just how much the Injunction Premise, and the Specialization Proviso from which it follows, empha-size the importance of controlling the behavior of persons engaged in the strategy-acquisition process at the corporation. To add more men and women, especially those who are unspecialized in the practice of strategy acquisition, is to complicate the process and lose a measure of control over the course that it might take. Likewise, the injunction un-der which senior managers act is necessary to quell in advance any aims and pursuits that might divert the process.

My point is that both kinds of control are necessary for the logic of Strategy through Process. At the same time, these kinds of control en-sure that Strategy through Process cannot be interpreted in any less sanitized terms. If a strategic management researcher wants to improve on the logic of Strategy through Process, he can begin by creating new forms of injunction on senior managers' actions. That improvement is not, however, the product of a humanist interpretation.[17] Hence, the very importance of the Injunction Premise for the coherence of Strategy through Process renders this genre, focused as it is on the strategy-acquisition processes, beyond conceptual repair in humanist terms.

Reprise on a First Critical Comparison

According to the Projects Premise, each person has a prima facie claim to have her interests, expressed through her chosen projects, taken into account.[18] This specific attention to a person and his or her projects applies to Allen, Nacchio, and Lacks and everyone else "inside" AT&T. This applies as well to McGowan, Esrey, Sikes, and every other project pursuer acting "outside" AT&T. At the same time, the Projects Premise makes provision for the possibility that Shrontz, McDonnell, Wolf, Skinner, and every other project pursuer in my story about the airline industry in Chapter 4 will choose to value different ends and pursue different projects accordingly. In short, I interpret the Projects Premise as a widely applicable commentary on persons making decisions and taking action at the corporation or elsewhere. On that account, I create the premise to support a rich story that celebrates what men and women can choose to do with their lives.

By contrast, the Injunction Premise implies that persons and their own projects pose a significant problem for the corporate decision-making structure. For men and women to act meaningfully at the corporation, they must act as agents for that structure. For them to act as agents, they are enjoined from interpreting their activities in terms other than the corporate purpose that they act to nurture. Moreover, these conditions apply to only a handful of persons, all of whom are employed in operating the decision-making process at a single corporation.

One clear manifestation of this logic is the narrow account that the Injunction Premise supports with regard to human activity at the corporation.[19] I narrated my story in Chapter 3 about Bell Atlantic with this in mind. We meet only Raymond Smith and his unnamed associates at Bell Atlantic in that story. True to the Strategy through Process genre, I portray Smith's purposeful action in terms of his stewardship of the strategy-acquisition process at that corporation. With his purposes trained on the acquisition process, Smith assumes a role in the story that renders him interchangeable with others who are specialized in conducting such a process.[20] Across this narrative, the Injunction Premise dampens the very celebration of human progress that the Projects Premise supports.

In sum, a critical comparison between the Injunction Premise and the Projects Premise offers evidence that Strategy & Justice is a better story than Strategy through Process, by the humanist criteria that I set for this analysis. But there is still stronger evidence against the proposition that Strategy through Process can be useful in a worldly sense.

A COMPARATIVE CRITIQUE ABOUT THE
INTERRELATIONSHIP ASSUMPTION

The Interrelationship Assumption of the Problem of Strategic Management holds:

> *Purposeful action at the corporation requires, in part, acknowledgment of the influences that relationships with others "outside" the corporation can bring to bear on that action.*

According to the Contracts Premise of Strategy & Justice, the influences of others are meaningful in terms of enduring and evolving relationships, called contracts, through which each person seeks to fulfill her ends in the presence of others doing the same. Each person "acknowledges" the relationship with the other party by choosing her actions in anticipation of the steps that others might take. Each reasons and acts interdependently.

> **Contracts Premise:** *Purposeful action requires, in part, that any two persons whose respective projects intersect in an enduring relationship—or contract—take seriously the meaning of that contract by choosing to act interdependently en route to a jointly shaped outcome for the contract and, hence, their projects.*

According to the Impediment Premise of Strategy through Process, on the contrary, relationships with others must be interpreted as threats to the enactment of a plan of purposeful action at the corporation. The proper purposeful response, on this logic, is to prevent each relationship—and, hence, the other parties to each relationship—from interfering with the decision-making process that yields this plan of action.

> **Impediment Premise:** *Purposeful action at the corporation requires, in part, that senior decision-making specialists command a systematic decision-making process to impede the potential constraining influences that relationships with others "outside" the corporation can bring to bear on that action.*

To act meaningfully as an agent in this process of decision-making, in short, a person must take it upon herself to impede the pursuits of others if the latter encroach on that process. Hence, meaningful action turns, in part, on the disposition to impede others' attempts to seek meaning.

Once again, the contrast in meanings here is unmistakable from a humanist point of view. *The Impediment Premise justifies acting unilaterally with great suspicion toward the very relationships that the Contracts Premise promotes as jointly shaped avenues for mutual growth.* Relationships portend difficulties for the corporation, according to the Impediment Premise. They are venues in which agents of the corporation must struggle to keep the strategy-acquisition process on track. In this sense, the Impediment Premise complements the Injunction Premise by explaining the influence of a relationship in terms of what senior managers do alone— acting at one end of the relationship—at a single corporation. We meet no outside parties in the Injunction Premise. Nor should we expect to do so in the Impediment Premise. As a consequence, the Strategy through Process genre provides little usable guidance about working out relationships with others for the men and women for whom the genre is ostensibly useful.

By contrast, relationships are conduits for purposeful action for each party addressed by the Contracts Premise. Given the likelihood that their projects can intersect in a lasting way, any two persons have good reason to act in specific recognition of each other. In this regard, the Contracts Premise complements the Projects Premise by enriching the context within which projects can be meaningfully pursued.[21]

A Second Critical Comparison

The upshot of this comparative critique once again confirms the deficiency of the Strategy through Process genre. To adopt the Impediment Premise of Strategy through Process is to adopt a less favorable account, relative to the Contracts Premise of Strategy & Justice, by my two humanist criteria. Once again, I attribute this shortcoming of Strategy through Process to the idiosyncratic interpretation of purposeful action that is conveyed by the Impediment Premise. By virtue of the emphasis on shielding the strategy-acquisition process in a world of unfriendly relationships, the Impediment Premise legitimizes only those actions that serve such a defensive purpose. As a result, neither the celebration of human growth nor the celebration of diversity among persons is advanced by this premise from Strategy through Process.

On the first count, the Impediment Premise compounds the aversion to human growth that I attributed to the Injunction Premise. Not only is legitimate human activity at the corporation confined to the senior managers who specialize in faithfully shepherding the strategy-acquisition process, but that legitimacy is denied to others "outside" that process. When senior managers' strategy-acquisition activity evolves into relationships with others, the Impediment Premise accounts for those relationships in a language of defiance and fear. Specifically, the Impediment Premise empowers senior managers to interfere with others' activities when those others stray too closely to the corporation. A person's growth prospects, already heavily conditioned for senior managers by the Injunction Premise, are thus dealt another blow. The preservation of the acquisition process must come at the expense of others' pursuits, on this logic. What thus results from this logic is a most confining and idiosyncratic story about men and women coping with their worlds.

The Impediment Premise, in short, supports a story that sanctions struggling with, and even fighting, other men and women in the name of preserving the process of strategic decision-making at the corporation. On this view, relationships become battlegrounds.[22] We hardly need to read very widely in human history to suspect that such an approach to human relationships does not bode well for the idea of personal development.

On the subject of human diversity, the Impediment Premise expressly devalues the pursuits of others who take action from a position "outside" the strategy-acquisition process. Indeed, the reference to "outside" is significant here. The Impediment Premise turns on a two-tiered interpretation of the legitimacy of a person's purposeful activities. Those pursuits are legitimate, on this view, if they coincide with the formulation and implementation of a plan of purposeful action at Bell Atlantic, for example. Those pursuits are immediately suspect and subject to resistance—and hence are less legitimate—if they are pursued in a relationship that links the outsider—say, a person acting at AT&T or the Federal Communications Commission—in a relationship with Smith at Bell Atlantic. Nothing in this logic appears to place a value on the diversity of activities in these relationships. Once again, the usefulness of this story for a discourse with managers and students—who are ostensibly presented a story in which they can take their place—is doubtful.

The Impediment Premise Beyond Humanist Repair

I thus conclude that Strategy through Process fails in comparison with Strategy & Justice on this second count about the context of relationships within which men and women can act purposefully at the corporation. The Impediment Premise bolsters the Strategy through Process genre with the clear implication that spiderwebs of relationships are meaningful as potential traps. Moreover, the premise further "sanitizes" Strategy through Process by denying the possibility that a particular relationship can have meaning for *both* parties at the same time. But this flight from a humanist perspective should not surprise us.[23] It is in truth quite necessary for the coherence of Strategy through Process.

The Impediment Premise, and the Struggle Proviso from which it follows logically, sustains the emphasis on control over the actions of persons at the corporation.[24] In particular, the Impediment Premise supplements the Injunction Premise with a deterrent against admitting outsiders to the strategy-acquisition process. If senior managers were to relax their vigilance against the troubles that relationships with outsiders can transmit, they would seriously weaken their expert control over the process. As a consequence, they would also likely cede control over the outcome of that process. It is more preferable, by the logic of the Impediment Premise, to deny the legitimacy of outsiders' pursuits in advance than it is to admit them to the discourse about purposeful action at that corporation.

I work through the foregoing line of argument to make the point, one more time, that the Impediment Premise extends the kind of control over certain persons' actions that is necessary for the Strategy through Process genre to make sense. Both the Injunction and Impediment Premises are quite useful if we choose to tell a story about strategy-acquisition processes at an organization. Yet that very need for an imperative designed to impede others' endeavors ensures further that Strategy through Process cannot be reformulated in humanist terms. If a strategic management researcher seeks to improve on the logic of Strategy through Process in a relational context, he has reason to create new defensive mechanisms for the corporation and new postures vis-à-vis outside parties.[25] Such improvements, however, have the effect of pitting persons against persons. This act of widening the separation among persons clearly runs counter to the notion of persons coexisting with a sense of community. Hence, the very importance of the Impediment Premise for the coherence of Strategy through Process continues to disqualify this genre from conceptual rehabilitation in humanist terms.

Reprise on a Second Critical Comparison

With the Contracts Premise, I articulate an account that celebrates the possibility that men and women can make headway in their lives, yet remain distinct, through their mutually shaped relationships. The Contracts Premise thus complements the Projects Premise by creating a context within which persons can jointly act on their own projects. By the Contracts Premise, we can tell a story about Allen, Nacchio, Lacks, McGowan, Sikes, and Esrey pursuing their chosen ends simultaneously and in enduring conjunction with one another. For them, their lasting relationships take on meaning because each contract provides an avenue for them to act on their chosen ends.

With the Impediment Premise, I provide an account that extends the skeptical and highly restrictive perspective on human action that I attributed earlier to the Injunction Premise. For persons to act meaningfully according to the Impediment Premise, they must take steps to deter the progress that persons acting "outside" the corporation hope to make. Accordingly, they must concentrate on defensive, not creative, efforts. Throughout my story at Bell Atlantic, Smith and his unnamed associates are on constant guard against the encroachment of others.

Moreover, the few human agents in the Strategy through Process narrative do not meet their potential adversaries. I make this point in my Bell Atlantic story by omitting any reference to specific persons taking action at AT&T, the Federal Communications Commission, or the labor unions at Bell Atlantic. Nor do the few human agents at Bell Atlantic interact, move for move, with these unnamed outsiders.[26] Instead, Smith and his associates are required to read the signals coming from relationships with these parties and then, more likely than not, "circle the decision-making wagons" to fend off these unidentified forces.[27]

With the Impediment Premise, then, I interpret a story about human relationships that gives priority to putting distance between persons.[28] Accordingly, this kind of story severs a meaningful connection between persons and the concept of purpose as a joint pursuit in a context of relationships. By contrast to the connection between persons that the Contracts Premise affords, the Impediment Premise supports a discouraging, if not sterile, conception of persons dealing with one another.[29] Accordingly, a critical comparison between the Impediment Premise and the Contracts Premise bolsters my claim that Strategy & Justice is better than Strategy through Process as a humanist interpretation of the modern corporation. But I do not stop here. There is even more evidence to deliver against the ostensible worldly usefulness of Strategy through Process.

A COMPARATIVE CRITIQUE ABOUT THE ADVANTAGE ASSUMPTION

The Advantage Assumption of the Problem of Strategic Management holds:

> *Purposeful action at the corporation requires, in part, that persons choose and actively seek a position of lasting benefit in relation to influential "outside" forces.*

According to the Responsibility Premise of Strategy & Justice, the search for advantage is a mutual concern among the persons who find their lives interconnected in lasting ways.

> ***Responsibility Premise:*** *Purposeful action requires, in part, that any two persons whose respective projects and purposes become interconnected in contractual relationships take seriously the possibility that they can voluntarily constrain the mutually conditioned conduct of their respective proj-*

*ects to create a conducive context for their projects and the projects of
"third parties" to their contract.*

This search for advantage is mutual, first of all, in that the Responsibility Premise expressly provides for the possibility that *each* party to a
contract, including third parties, can gain a lasting benefit—hence, an
"advantage"—relative to her own standards of purpose.[30] By this premise, "lasting benefit" is interpeted in terms of a context conducive to
many diverse pursuits. Furthermore, persons can "actively seek" that
prospect for lasting advantage through their choices to constrain voluntarily their respective actions in interdependence with one another.
By the logic of the Responsibility Premise, mutual self-constraint im-
proves the prospects for mutual advantage.

The Institution Premise of Strategy through Process, on the contrary, confines the meaningful context for "advantage" to the single
corporation in question:

> **Institution Premise:** *Purposeful action at the corporation requires, in
> part, that senior decision-making specialists, by means of an internally
> coherent decision-making process, seek a fit between the corporation and
> potentially antagonistic "outside" relationships such that the corporate purpose
> can become institutionalized.*

At this single corporation, a "lasting benefit" is achieved if the plan of
purposeful corporate action becomes widely adopted, or institutionalized, at that corporation. Whether or not this state of permanence is
realized depends on how well senior managers "actively seek" that end
by acting in accordance with the Injunction and Impediment Premises.

There is nothing in this logic, however, that interprets the costs and
benefits that men and women receive as a consequence of this drive to
institutionalize a corporate purpose. What happens to these persons,
inside and outside the corporation, is irrelevant by the Institution
Premise. The silence on this matter extends from the senior managers
most closely tied to the strategy-acquisition process to the third parties
affected, for better or worse, by that process. In short, the logic of the
Institution Premise disconnects the concept of advantage from the men
and women whose purposeful endeavors are influenced by the strategy-
acquisition process and the institutionalized purpose that emerges from
that process.[31]

This contrast in meanings clinches my case about the literary and
ethical shortcomings of the Strategy through Process genre. *The Institution Premise justifies removing consideration of the benefits of purposeful action from the very worldly context in which the Responsibility Premise situates
the possibilities for mutual advantage among the men and women whose contracts give meaning to that context.* The strategic management researcher

who advocates the Institution Premise clearly sets a standard of advantage that is meaningful only "beyond mankind."[32] The premise supports a story about spiderwebs where there is no place for consideration of what advantages are available for the spiders and at what cost. By contrast, the Responsibility Premise gives prominence to the meaning of advantage relative to the purposes that each person chooses to entertain. At the same time, the premise gives prominence to the self-constrained actions that can contribute to a general incidence of persons growing in their lives. This premise of Strategy & Justice thus is a thoroughly worldly commentary.

In short, the Institution Premise caps the progressive expulsion of human concerns from the Strategy through Process genre. The cast of characters is reduced first to include only the heavily restricted senior managers who act as specialized agents in the acquisition of a strategy (Injunction Premise). The cast is reduced further with the exclusion of troublesome outsiders who can impinge on the strategy-acquisition process (Impediment Premise). It is not surprising, then, that the Institution Premise, as a logical sequel to these two exclusionary premises, is silent about what happens to men and women at the corporation.[33]

A Third Critical Comparison

My conclusion here should sound familiar. To adopt the Institution Premise of Strategy through Process is to adopt a less favorable account, relative to the Responsibility Premise of Strategy & Justice, by my two humanist criteria. I attribute this failing of Strategy through Process to the idiosyncratic conception of purposeful action on which the Institution Premise turns. The premise compels senior managers to ensure that their own purposes will remain secondary by ensuring that the corporate purpose will endure in institutional form. This purposeful act serves to perpetuate the disconnection between persons and their own ends at the corporation. We can understand this further sanitization of life at the corporation in two respects.

First, the celebration of human growth is denied by the Institution Premise inasmuch as the standard for assessing the "advantage" of purposeful action is a corporate one. There is no room for assessing a person's development, in the context of her chosen ends, in a story that heralds the institutionalization of a corporate purpose. The Institution Premise defines advantage in terms that wholly transcend a person's pursuits, now and in the future.

Second, the very notion of institutionalization implies an aversion to dissent, and even more so diversity, about the direction of corporate activity. The entire thrust of the Institution Premise is to have persons adopt the corporate purpose as the relevant and lasting source of meaning for their actions at the corporation.[34] The value of such en-

during homogeneity is communicated, first of all, in the imperative that
senior decision-making specialists operate an internally consistent decision process. It is extended by the imperative that senior managers seek
an external fit that helps perpetuate the corporate purpose. The drive
to homogenize is bolstered still further with the ever-present distinction
between those who are governed by the institutionalized purpose and
those outsiders who are not. Finally, the silence of the Institution Premise about the effects of the institutionalization process on any one man
or woman clearly rules out the value of dissent about the corporate
purpose. Such silence closes the door on any consideration about a person's claim to distinction through her projects. In all, there is little reason for a person to take comfort that her distinctive identity has any
value in the Strategy through Process story.

The Institution Premise Beyond Humanist Repair

I thus conclude that Strategy through Process fails in comparison to
Strategy & Justice on this third count about the benefits and costs of
purposeful action at the corporation. In particular, I have shown how
the emphasis on transforming a plan for purposeful action into an institution denies any meaningful consideration about whether men and
women gain or lose from that process. Indeed, the Institution Premise
must be sanitized in this respect if the Strategy through Process story
is to reach a meaningful conclusion.

Once more, the Institution Premise, and the Fitness Proviso from
which it logically follows, stresses the need to control what persons seek
and do in the context of the strategy-acquisition process. In particular,
for senior managers to worry about the effects of corporate purpose
on particular persons is to prolong the process with a potentially limit-
less set of claims on the corporation. Moreover, such a compromise of
the process lends legitimacy to men and women who likely have no
reason to otherwise affiliate with that plan of purposeful action. It is
far preferable, then, if the Strategy through Process story is to unfold,
to shield senior managers from profound questions about the consequences of their decisions.[35]

My point here is that the Institution Premise is essential if senior
managers' specialized control over the strategy-acquisition process is to
be perpetuated. Yet this institutionalizing focus for Strategy through
Process further ensures that this genre cannot be reinterpreted in humanist terms. If a strategic management researcher seeks to improve
on the Institution Premise, he can begin by proposing new kinds of
external fit for the corporation and new mechanisms of long-term institutional control over persons' behavior.[36] That effort at conceptual
improvement, however, casts the Strategy through Process story further adrift from a humanist perspective. If better institutionalization is

the key, then the Institution Premise helps make Strategy through Process the very kind of story that, bereft of men and women as protagonists, once aroused Nietzsche's ire and now extinguishes any hope that Strategy through Process can be repaired.

Reprise on a Third Critical Comparison

With the Responsibility Premise, I incorporate a concern for others directly into the actions that persons can take in contractual ties with one another. On this account, to act purposefully includes the imperative that one acts with self-constraint of some kind.[37] I thus create the Responsibility Premise as a complement to the Projects and Contracts Premises. Each person's preference for self-constraint provides a key condition that can enable each, even as her project becomes intertwined with those of other persons, to have hope that she can move forward in her life. By using this third premise of Strategy & Justice, we can tell a story about the hopes that Shrontz, Thornton, McDonnell, Hood, Wolf, Greenwald, Dubinsky, Skinner, and Crandall can simultaneously entertain about benefiting from their relationships with one another. Put somewhat differently, the meaningfulness of their search for their respective advantages turns on the inclusion of a basic sense of justice in their projects.

With the Institution Premise, I provide one more account that serves to diminish the "feel, taste, and smell" of persons whose lives meet at the corporation. By the time we reach the Institution Premise in the logical flow of Strategy through Process, the few remaining persons are required to establish a corporate purpose to which they, and other unnamed actors at the corporation, must look for enduring inspiration. To act purposefully in this sense is to voluntarily surrender one's own projects at the corporate doorway. Moreover, these survivors of the ethical logic that I attribute to Strategy through Process are permitted to operate under a lesser ethical standard than applies to the characters in my Strategy & Justice story. In particular, these senior decision-making specialists are absolved from worrying about anything more than doing what it takes to institutionalize a plan for action that advances a corporate purpose. Nothing in the Institution Premise requires that senior managers at Bell Atlantic, for example, concern themselves with one another, much less with what happens to the "strangers" whose lives those managers can touch.[38]

With the addition of the Institution Premise, then, I interpret Strategy through Process as a story that serves to entrench the separation of persons from one another. With the concept of advantage separated from the lives of men and women whose endeavors interconnect at the corporation, I am left to conclude that Strategy through Process is not *about* persons in any convincing and usable way. In sum, a critical comparison between the Institution Premise and the Responsibility Premise confirms my thesis that Strategy & Justice is a better kind of literature and ethical commentary than Strategy through Process.

DOUBLE ENTENDRE FOR STRATEGY THROUGH PROCESS

I have concluded my critical assessment of the Strategy through Process genre as an ethical story about the modern corporation. I have presented a case that thoroughly discredits Strategy through Process as a usable account of human activity in that context. At the heart of my argument is a double entendre that I fully intend. That is, I interpret each of the three premises that constitute Strategy through Process with a double meaning clearly in mind.

In an affirmative sense, each of the Strategy through Process premises provides a coherent account about the process of deciding about the purpose(s) for action at a corporation. *If we value a story about the acquisition of a strategy that can be attributed to the corporation, then we have good reason to write research stories that direct senior decision-making specialists' attention (Injunction Premise) toward the threatening complexities of the corporate environment (Impediment Premise) within which a plan of purposeful action can take root (Institution Premise).* We can readily weave these premises into a kind of literature about purposeful human activity at the corporation. Many strategic management researchers—most prominently, those responsible for my "group of twelve" arguments—have in fact spun variations of such a tale.

The problem is that such a story line generally disparages the pursuits of men and women for whom the story is written and ostensibly worthwhile. I have designated the Injunction, Impediment, and Institution Premises to underscore precisely this point. Neither "injunction" nor "impediment" suggests much encouragement for human endeavor in a story about human endeavor. Both terms clearly connote restrictions on, if not a distaste for, a person's search for meaning in her activities.[39] Moreover, the word "institution" does not readily suggest a place for men and women acting as autonomous characters in a story about the corporation. It makes little sense to talk about a person "interacting with an institution" if we value contact with others.[40] If anything, "institution" implies a permanence that transcends what any one person hopes to accomplish in her lifetime.

I have designated all three premises—eminently useful as they are for Strategy through Process—to communicate a Nietzschean warning that Strategy through Process is a story that celebrates the corporation at the expense of autonomous men and women. I make this point, in short, by interpreting a double meaning for each of the Strategy through Process premises. One kind of meaning lends coherence to the Strategy through Process genre. The other kind of meaning renders Strategy through Process ineligible and wholly unfit as a useful worldly commentary about the modern corporation.

In sum, I create the premises of Strategy & Justice in order to interpret the double entendre that dooms Strategy through Process from a humanist point of view. It is time to begin to translate the relative humanist strengths of the Strategy & Justice genre into a richer story about the corporate strategy concept. In particular, it is time to move ahead with the business of reinterpreting a worldly meaning for the concept. The Strategy through Process genre simply does not work, nor will it ever work, if we value strategic management research as a commentary created by men and women for a discourse with men and women about the modern corporation.[41]

Epilogue
Toward Dawn for Strategy, Management, and the Humanities

> . . . a world that coheres through human connection rather than through systems of rules.
>
> CAROL GILLIGAN, *In a Different Voice: Psychological Theory and Women's Development*

> Differences are a source of strength for each of us—so long as they are not used against us. We all have a long history of learning to fear difference.
>
> JEAN BAKER MILLER, *Toward a New Psychology of Women*

I wrote this book to make the point that we can ask new questions and craft unconventional interpretations with those questions if we are willing to adopt a humanist perspective on corporate strategy and strategic management research. By interpreting the promise of the corporate strategy concept in literary and ethical terms that highlight persons' purposeful endeavors, I justify posing such new questions for strategic management inquiry as

Of what value is strategic management research as a humanist perspective on the modern corporation?

Of what relative value is strategic management research as an ethical interpretation of the modern corporation?

Moreover, by creating two different literary, ethical interpretations of persons' actions at the corporation, I answer both questions with the conclusion that Strategy through Process, an enduring and popular story about corporate strategy, offers scant hope that we can understand the corporation in terms that celebrate personhood. In short, I attempted to upset the contemporary complacency about the meaningfulness of strategic management research.[1] I committed this act first by interpreting the possible humanist worth of that enterprise (Chapter 1) and subsequently by arguing that Strategy through Process is relatively useless as a story that men and women can apply to their pursuits at the corporation.[2] The twilight of corporate strategy is not meant to be a comforting story.

At the same time, I told my story about corporate strategy in twilight to open a vista on a "dawn" of meanings with which we can choose to talk about corporate strategy and the modern corporation. By the first faint rays of that dawn, we can choose to accord men and women and their own chosen pursuits—and not processes, structures, and other entities "beyond" persons—a lasting and dignified place in the research stories that we tell.[3] I wrote this epilogue to outline one specific interpretive venture beyond corporate strategy in twilight. In this pursuit, I acted on Richard Rorty's pragmatist cue to think "horizontally" about the search for truth as an effort to connect one useful worldly interpretation—here, corporate strategy in twilight—with other potentially useful worldly interpretations.[4]

AN INTERPRETIVE VENTURE TOWARD DAWN

I extend my suggestion, from Chapter 5, that we can tell a new story about the corporate strategy concept, and thus the Problem of Strategic Management, by means of the very Strategy & Justice genre that has "trumped" Strategy through Process in a humanist comparison.[5] In particular, I will sketch an interpretation of Strategy & Justice in terms that highlight the search for "human connection" among a cast of characters who bring "differences" to their relationships. For this reason, I chose comments by Carol Gilligan and Jean Baker Miller for the epigraph to this chapter.[6] At the heart of this interpretation, I introduce the concept of *convention* to the discussion. A convention can be usefully construed as a jointly shaped kind of human association that holds promise for men and women seeking to advance their ends in the context of one another's pursuits.[7] I show how we can employ this interpretation of Strategy & Justice—which I call *Strategy through Convention* (STC)—to ask new questions about persons and their purposeful actions at the corporation.[8] In short, I introduce Strategy through Convention as one kind of "horizontal" search for truths about what we can do with the corporate strategy concept as a worldly idea.

I depict this horizontal search in Figure E.1. Clearly, there are many other questions that I could choose to pursue in the aftermath of cor-

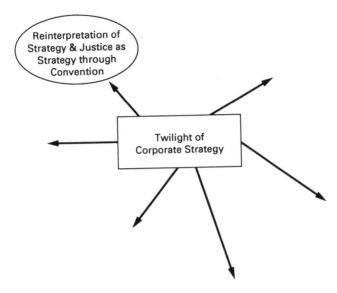

Figure E.1. Pragmatist consequences of the twilight of corporate strategy.

porate strategy in twilight; I suggest one such pursuit at the conclusion of this chapter. I indicate these interpretive efforts by the smaller arrows in the figure.[9] What is important for now is my intent on arguing that corporate strategy in twilight is one stop en route to a dawn whereby we can connect a long and varied tradition of inquiry about human concerns—that is, the "humanities"—with inquiry about corporate strategy and the modern corporation.[10] I thus write this Epilogue to share my thoughts about one destination that we can seek if we connect the language of strategy and management and the language of the humanities. In so doing, I voluntarily begin to put my own argument into twilight as I begin to critically appraise the pragmatist value of my own efforts in this book.

REPRISE ON STRATEGY & JUSTICE AS A HUMANIST COMMENTARY

My Strategy & Justice genre about the Problem of Strategic Management culminates in the joint search conducted by autonomous men and women for a context that can prove conducive for their quests for meaning. On this account of purposeful action, we can explain each person's interest in, and contribution to, this search (1) partially in terms of her purposes and associated activities (Projects Premise), (2) partially in terms of her enduring relationships whereby she and her projects become intertwined with others and their projects (Contracts Premise), and (3) partially in terms of the self-constraint that she and others can choose to incorporate into their respective projects (Responsibility Premise). Throughout this kind of story, men and women and their chosen activities enjoy "top billing."

I emphasized such centrality for personhood in the Alternative Conception of Strategy that I interpreted from Strategy & Justice in Chapter 4:

> A strategy is a plan of action whereby any one person accommodates (1) multiple, diverse purposes and corresponding projects—including her own—that become interconnected; (2) the resulting contractual relationships that hold meaning for the persons who pursue their projects interdependently around issues that they jointly create; and (3) the choices available to those persons to conduct their pursuits voluntarily in a manner that creates a context conducive to their ends and the ends of others whose projects are affected in that context.

I offer this conception of purposeful action—commonly taken in the name of "strategy" in a corporate setting—as a point of departure for thinking about corporate strategy in a thoroughly humanist way. In my Alternative Conception of Strategy, I interpret strategy from the standpoint of "any one person" whose life is interconnected with others' lives in a joint pursuit for conditions by which each can gain. My claim is that we can use this story line to begin to talk about corporate strategy in a worldly manner that the creators of Strategy through Process have continually sought to avoid or devalue. I now turn to extend the Strategy & Justice genre further still into the world of autonomous persons. More specifically, I will consider more closely what it might mean to create a "conducive context" for human interaction.

STRATEGY & JUSTICE AND THE CONCEPT OF CONVENTION

Each character in the Strategy & Justice story chooses purposes as standards by which she can value her life. She chooses, as well, a set of projects that, at one and the same time, she hopes will enable her to advance her purposes and help create relationships between her and other project pursuers. Since her purposeful activities are thus necessarily conditioned by others' pursuits, she also has reason to make choices about the kinds of contractual contexts that she prefers for her search for meaning. And her contractual partners have the same kind of reason to prefer certain contextual conditions to others.

We can readily understand just how crucial this concern about the substantive terms of human associations can become. In Chapter 4, I told my stories about freeway collisions to underscore the possibility that contractual relationships are not automatically conducive to all, some, or even any of the parties to those relationships. The point is that we, as storytellers, have good reason to extend our conception of purposeful action to take account of the possible terms by which men and women can fulfill their search for conditions in which they can each flourish.[11]

Continuing this line of reasoning, I propose that we can choose to reinterpret purposeful action as *a search conducted by and among a particular group of distinct autonomous men and women for enduring agreement A, which they can create, sustain, and revise as they agree necessary, that is tailored to promote mutual gain in their own pattern of relationships B.*[12] With such an agreement, each party to a given pattern of contracts can act with confidence that her pursuits will not be overrun by other parties to those relationships.[13] What I suggest, in short, is that each person can be interpreted as a searcher for a kind of social regularity by which each can act to contribute to the governance of his contracts.[14] On this view, we can move from a general conception of "conducive context" for autonomy to consider the kind of specific agreements that give meaning to "conducive" in my Strategy & Justice genre. It turns out that this horizontal interpretive effort is well under way beyond the territory of management research.

Conventions and Strategy Through Convention

Among a far-flung community of scholars—including philosophers of language, moral philosophers, institutional economists, anthropologists, and decision theorists—such a mutually conditioned social agreement is known as a convention.[15] The central idea in this first part of the chapter is that we can enrich our interpretations of the corporate strategy concept with a story line about persons acting in accordance with conventions as a means for advancing their respective ends at the modern corporation.[16] Since my account will depict each person in a pattern of contractual relationships pursuing a strategy through the means of a convention, I call this new conception of strategic management Strategy through Convention.

Strategy through Convention is my creation using concepts that should by now be familiar: autonomous persons and their projects (Projects Premise) linked in enduring relationships (Contracts Premise) that are shaped by the self-constrained actions of those men and women (Responsibility Premise). What I now add to tell a story about corporate strategy in terms of Strategy & Justice is the notion of each person's search for a shared understanding, in a corporate context, that enables each to grow as the person she wants to be.[17] In this way, I create Strategy through Convention as a horizontal reinterpretation of the

Strategy & Justice genre that is already more useful than Strategy through Process in literary and ethical terms.

My justification of this connection between Strategy & Justice and the concept of convention has three parts. I consider first the concept of convention as a humanist interpretation and, hence, as a valuable addition to my search for a humanist interpretation of the modern corporation. Then I narrate four cases about the part that conventions can play in everyday life, which many readers will find familiar. I tell these stories to defend the pragmatist worth of conventions. I conclude this discussion by sketching the kind of story that Strategy through Convention enables us to tell about purposeful action at the corporation. In that regard, I interpret a set of questions with which we can begin to reinterpret—and thereby salvage—the corporate strategy concept as a humanist idea. Throughout the next section, my intent is to introduce a new language for making sense of persons and their pursuits at the corporation.

CONVENTIONS, AUTONOMY, AND PURPOSEFUL ACTION

David Lewis defines a convention as a stable regularity of behavior among some group of autonomous persons involved in an ongoing interdependent relationship, where those persons prefer that regularity in a conditional way.[18] On this account, a convention is stable when no one person prefers to take an alternative action, given the behaviors of the others involved, and she prefers that the others think about their joint agreement—either explicitly or tacitly—to this regularity in this very same way.[19] A convention is thus conditionally preferred in the sense that each person conditions her preference for a given regularity—that preference made commonly known through her conforming actions— on the actions of those with whom she is interdependent. In such a pattern of conditional preferences, Lewis argues, (1) all persons conform to a particular regularity, (2) each expects everyone else to conform, and (3) each prefers to conform to the regularity on the condition that everyone else does.[20]

We can thus understand a convention as a concept that enables us to tell stories about men and women trying to make sense of their lasting associations. Few of us regularly use the word "convention" in our daily lives. And when we do, we typically refer to some large-scale meeting held at some exotic resort. Yet if we choose to interpret our own lives in terms of projects, contracts, and self-constraint, then we can conclude that each of us does rely, and indeed must rely, on conventions as a means for advancing our ends. Moreover, we need not stop and verify our joint faithfulness to the conditional pattern of reasoning, to which Lewis refers, each time we act conventionally. All we need to do is accept a truth that our lives would be so much the poorer if not for our willing participation in conventions and our willingness to periodically put any given convention in twilight.[21] Conventions are all around us, if we choose to think in such terms.

Cases of Connection Between Conventions and Purposeful Action

Language is perhaps the most common example of a convention in our daily lives. A particular convention exists, for example, such that we refer to the concept under study here by the word "convention." From a pragmatist perspective, there is no reason why this word applies— and why "baseball" and "xbcjzczaj" do not—other than the fact that many persons have agreed, without central direction, on this specific meaning for the word in this context.[22] The case of language follows from Lewis's illustration of a convention as an "achievement of coordination by means of shared acquaintance with a *regularity* governing the achievement of coordination in a class of past cases which bear some conspicuous analogy to one another and to our present coordination problem."[23] Lewis clearly suggests here that conformity to a particular convention occurs in the context of some community of men and women who, acknowledging the history of a given regularity, look to, prefer to, and hence continue to trade in that convention. Just as clearly, we can understand convention as a humanist concept that provides explicitly for persons and their evolving purposeful activities. Consider now four short cases of everyday experience that I will subsequently defend as further evidence of the worldly, humanist promise of the concept of convention.

Disconnected telephones with a Minnesota variation. It is a typical springtime week in Minnesota. One week after the ice disappeared from the lakes, a series of thunderstorms moves across the state, enlivened here and there with tornadoes. Through all this, Person A and Person B have reasons to communicate throughout the week. On Monday, Person A initiates a call to Person B and, several hours after a gusty storm disrupts the conversation, takes it upon herself to call back. On Wednesday, Person B calls Person A from an airport pay telephone. But when the tornado sirens begin to wail, he quickly hangs up without discussing with Person A how they will resume their conversation. An hour later, he calls Person A again. On Thursday, Person A pages Person B at a conference session in another state. After a torrential downpour in Minnesota floods the telephone cables carrying the call, she reinitiates the page later that day. Through wind, rain, and gloom of night, they are able to stay in contact with each other.

Driving a Minnesota freeway again. When we last left Drivers Smith, Jones, and Wilson, Driver Jones had appeared on the freeway entrance ramp and Driver Wilson had moved alongside Driver Smith. Now Driver Jones, seeing both other drivers, decides to proceed down the ramp at a slow, steady speed. Driver Smith, seeing this action, remains in her lane of the freeway. Driver Wilson, seeing how Drivers Smith and Jones respond to each other's actions, remains in her lane and—with no cars behind hers—reduces her speed slightly. Driver Jones, interpreting what Drivers Smith and Wilson are doing, continues to drive down the ramp at the same slow and steady rate. Driver Smith interprets this action as an indication that Driver Jones will wait his turn to enter the freeway. Driver Smith continues on her present course, accordingly. Driver Wilson observes all this and remains in her lane, now somewhat behind Driver Smith in order to provide her some maneuvering room should she require it. After each driver takes note of the others' actions several more times, Driver Smith moves past the ramp, while staying in her lane. Driver Wilson also moves past the ramp, while staying in her lane. Driver Jones waits his turn and easily enters the freeway after the two others have passed ahead.

To send or not to send. Every December, millions of Americans send greeting cards prior to several major religious and secular holidays. While every sender probably receives some cards in return, it is unlikely that every sender receives exactly the number of cards that he sends. Nor is it likely that every card sent will prompt a response. In fact, the custom is fraught with uncertainty on the very subject of exchange.

Suppose that LaFleur is deciding on her list of recipients. Does she send a card to everyone who sent her one last year?[24] The answer is not obvious, since she may not want to send greetings to someone anymore. What does LaFleur do about a past recipient who sends her a card once every three years? Suppose that this particular intermittent stream of cards comes from someone LaFleur would like to get to know better and that LaFleur sent him a card each of the two years following her receipt of a card from him. How does LaFleur send greetings to a corporation "who" sends her a card? How early in the season should LaFleur send the cards? If she waits until receiving a card—certainly an efficient custom—she may offend friends who have come to expect an unsolicited card from her. To ensure that no one beats her to the mailbox, LaFleur might send her cards in September. But her recipients might then wonder how to interpret that practice! Still, millions like LaFleur and her friends try to make some sense of this situation and flood the mails every December.[25]

Turning the tables. Wisdom is the chairman at a U.S.–based corporation. He has spent many months attempting to persuade his counterparts in the industry and a number of influential U.S. senators that a trade bill will seriously harm those participants in the industry. At long last, the chairman of the pertinent Senate committee calls to say, "Wis, you will be pleased to know that the legislation has been tabled for this session." After calling several fellow chairpersons with the news, and now satisfied that the storm has passed for the time being, Wisdom travels to Toronto, Ontario. There he addresses an audience that includes a number of senior managers from the Canadian segment of the industry. Wisdom proudly announces that the noxious bill has been tabled in the U.S. Senate. He is shocked to find many in his audience indignant at his victory claim. Wisdom is almost hooted off the podium until Mapleleaf, realizing what is happening, intervenes to restore order.[26]

What happened? It is "simply" a matter of semantics.[27] The verb "table" can have two meanings among North American versions of the English language. In the British tradition, many Canadians interpret "table" to mean that a legislative or another important matter has been placed *on* an agenda. In the United States, "table" is commonly understood to carry precisely the opposite meaning.[28]

Convention as Pragmatist Agreement

I wrote each of these short stories to call attention to a question to which the autonomous characters in each case seek an answer:

> By what specific agreements can we shape a joint understanding about our relationships such that we can pursue our purposes in mutually beneficial association with one another?

In search of answers to this question, each person participates in a search for conventions. Three particular aspects of this search deserve further explanation. I discuss each aspect as testimony to the worldly usefulness of the concept of convention.

First, the parties in each story could agree to multiple terms in search of mutually beneficial relationships. This is why I refer to agreements in the plural in the preceding question.

In the telephone case, Persons A and B can be interpreted as adopting this convention: the original caller reinitiates a disconnected conversation. They act by that convention three times in the story. Other conventions could prove useful to them, as we have likely learned in our own experiences. The older of the two, for example, could have reinitiated the call. Or, in certain settings, the person with "more junior" status could reinitiate the call to the "more senior" person.[29]

In the Minnesota freeway example, Drivers Smith, Jones, and Wilson observe a convention whereby a driver on the freeway entrance ramp waits his turn to enter the flow of traffic. The three drivers could also have created mutual benefit—that is, safe travel on that section of the freeway—through self-constraint by acting in accordance with a convention commonly taught in driver education classes: Driver Wilson drops back while Driver Smith moves to her left to make room for Driver Jones.

In the same spirit, we might explain the confusion encountered by LaFleur and her correspondents in terms of multiple conventions. LaFleur and her friends could decide to adopt a "tit for tat" criterion from one year to the next.[30] Or each could send two cards in the year following a "cardless" year, in order to convey a willingness to continue with the practice. LaFleur and company could even decide to exchange summertime postcards to determine in advance whether the other party is likely to respond during the holiday season. Each such agreement could serve to keep the parties in touch.

Likewise, the multiplicity of conventions regarding the verb "table" can be interpreted as a cause of the confusion experienced among Wisdom and the members of his Canadian audience. On this account, Wisdom encounters difficulties when he moves between two communities of persons who find it in their respective mutual interests to adopt different conventions about the meaning of the verb "table."[31]

In all these regards, the concept of convention provides continuing opportunities for autonomous men and women to exercise choices about their lives. In this way, the many possibilities for each person's efforts to advance her ends offer an element of hope to a story about purposeful action.

Second, no sovereign authority is present in any of these cases to compel the characters to abide by a particular convention.[32] Each character, in other words, confronts a self-governance problem in association with others. It is this opportunity for self-governance by means of conventions that heightens the humanist promise of the concept of convention. It takes a considerable stretch of the imagination to argue that a sovereign, or central, authority is present to dictate the alternative agreements that are available to the men and women involved in the telephone case, the greeting cards case, and the case of the "turned" tables.[33] Yet these cases are no less problems of interdependent choice wherein conventions can prove useful. In each situation, each person has an autonomous incentive to produce with the other a stable, satisfactory basis for interdependence.

Even in the event that we add an "authority figure" to this kind of story, we can still create a story about persons making choices about the terms of their relationships. Take a variation on the freeway story as a case in point. Suppose that a Minnesota highway patrol officer, named Stern, has placed his clearly marked patrol car squarely at the junction of the freeway and entrance ramp, in plain view of Drivers

Smith, Jones, and Wilson. It is reasonable to assume that one or two or all three drivers take the presence of Stern, as "the law," into account. In other words, assume that all three consider a citation from Stern to be costly. In that context, Driver Smith understands that she could be cited for reckless driving if she maintains her position while Driver Jones accelerates down the ramp or if she chooses to change lanes while Driver Wilson holds her position. But this is merely to say that Stern's presence is factored by Driver Smith into her interpretation of her payoffs. Stated somewhat differently, Stern's presence gives Driver Smith one more independent reason to take the actions of the others into account.[34] Whether Stern is there or not, the three drivers have an interdependence problem to solve, and the opportunity to interact by means of a mutually beneficial convention.[35]

Third, the concept of convention can be applied as flexibly as we choose in order to accommodate the pattern of relationships among autonomous persons that interests us. We can apply the concept of convention quite "locally" to one or several bilateral contracts. I have done this with my telephone and freeway cases. Alternatively, we can tell stories about conventions to which many persons willingly contribute. Such a "global" applicability of the concept of convention is the case in my greeting-card and cross-border-language stories. The pragmatist value of this flexibility is that the storyteller who focuses on conventions can tailor the concept to deal with problems of interdependence while simultaneously keeping the spotlight on distinct men and women and their ends.[36]

The upshot here is that the concept of convention is available for our efforts to create thoroughly humanist accounts about purposeful action. In each of my diverse stories, autonomous persons, acting for reasons that they value as their own, have reason to exercise self-constraint to help shape an agreement from which each can benefit. I now make the straightforward move from the everyday usefulness of conventions to the usefulness of conventions in stories about life at the corporation.

STRATEGY THROUGH CONVENTION

I have already set the stage, with my stories about the telecommunications and airline industries in Chapter 4, for reinterpreting purposeful action at the corporation—that is, actions informed by "strategy"—in terms of persons, projects, and conventions. I now begin to frame the Strategy through Convention genre by putting myself in the shoes of any one person—say, Allen at AT&T or Shrontz at Boeing—and posing a set of questions in accordance with Strategy & Justice and the search for conventions. What follow are four sets of questions with which

I begin to interpret Strategy through Convention. Each question is posed vicariously as a manifestation of respect for any one person's auton-omy.[37]

1. Whose projects intersect with my choice to pursue project P?

This question follows from the Projects Premise of Strategy & Justice. It is a humanist query in that I place it on the "turf" of persons ("whose"; "my") and the matters that are important to them ("projects"). We can supplement this question with such further inquiries as

> Why (for what chosen reasons) am I pursuing P, and why (for what chosen reasons) are persons J, K, and others, pur-suing their respective projects M, N, and so on?

> Of what importance to me is P relative to my pursuit of proj-ects Q, R, and so on, and of what relative importance is M to person J, N to person K, and so on?

With this line of questioning, a storyteller using Strategy through Con-vention quickly puts "names and faces" on the men and women about whom he will write.[38] This patent attention to distinct persons is sus-tained across the following set of questions that I interpret for Strategy through Convention.

2. What issue emerges at the conjunction of my project P and the proj-ect M pursued by person J (and project N pursued by person K, etc.) with which P becomes entwined such that I and person J (and person K, etc.) become parties to enduring relationships?

This question about what I have called an "issue of interdependence" (Chapter 4) follows from the Contracts Premise of Strategy & Justice. It can likewise be understood as a humanist query by virtue of the focus on purposeful pursuits ("projects") and the connection among persons ("enduring relationships") whose projects intersect. We can en-rich this line of questioning with such queries as

> What alternative approaches are available to me for pursu-ing project P, and what alternative approaches are available to person J to pursue M (and person K to pursue N, etc.) in our relationship(s)?

> What historical pattern of interdependent actions have I helped create, through P, in conjunction with person J doing M (and person K doing N, etc.)?

In both preceding cases, I pose questions about projects ("approaches"; "actions") and their continuation.[39]

3. What pattern of self-constrained actions is available and suitable to me—in view of my purpose(s) for acting on project P—and to person J (and person K, etc.)—in view of person J's reasons for pursuing M (and N, etc.) that become entwined with P—in order to sustain our contract for mutual benefit?

This question follows from the Responsibility Premise of Strategy & Justice. The humanist appeal of this question is the patent implication that the desirable end for joint purposeful action is the possibility that distinct men and women ("me"; "person J"; "person K") can flourish in association with one another ("mutual benefit").[40] Moreover, the explicit focus on a "pattern of self-constrained actions"—for example, "I do P and person J does M and . . ."—keeps human connection prominently on the storytelling agenda of Strategy through Convention. We can extend this line of inquiry in such directions as

> What are the effects of a given pattern of self-constrained actions on my purpose for pursuing P and on person J's purpose for pursuing project M (and person K's purpose for pursuing N, etc.)?

> What is the history of the relationship connecting me and person J (and person K, etc.), through my pursuit of P and J's pursuit of M (and N, etc.), with regard to the stability of our actions and counteractions?[41]

4. What specific agreement can I reach and sustain in collaboration with person J (and person K, etc.), through my pursuing P and person J pursuing M (and N, etc.), for creating a context that can be jointly conducive to our purposeful endeavors?

This question can be answered in terms of conventions that these parties can jointly create and sustain and revise as they deem necessary. Thus the question follows from the three premises of Strategy & Justice. I pose this question, once again, in a humanist language with special attention accorded to men and women and their hopes ("conducive") for deriving meaning from their chosen pursuits ("projects"). This line of inquiry can be extended with such questions as

> What specific alternative agreements are available to me and my contractual partners, person J, person K, and so on, in our joint search for mutually beneficial contexts?

> What are the effects of this specific agreement, which pertains to the context created by my pursuing P and person J's pursuit of M (and person K's pursuit of N, etc.), on (1) my pursuit of projects Q, R, and so on; (2) person J's pursuit of

B, C, and so on (and person K's pursuit of L, etc.); and (3) "third" parties (persons X, Y, etc.) not involved in the contract partially created by my doing P, but involved instead in a contract created at the intersection of my doing P and person X's pursuit of XX (and person Y's pursuit of YY, etc.)?

The latter question is crucial as I choose to broaden the Strategy through Convention story from any one contractual relationship to a web of such relationships.[42] Such an extension can clearly prove useful for stories about corporate strategy, where any one autonomous actor's pursuits can be interpreted in terms of his multiple simultaneous projects that help create multiple, simultaneous contracts with other pursuers of multiple projects.[43]

Segue

The vast difference between stories that can be written about the corporate strategy concept with Strategy through Process and with Strategy through Convention deserves comment. In particular, the story about corporate strategy at Bell Atlantic (Chapter 3) would need to be radically revised if we want to create a story about Raymond Smith and his purposeful pursuits in the humanist terms of Strategy through Convention.[44] We would need to "erase" the corporate boundaries of Bell Atlantic, as I do for any corporation with my four sets of Strategy through Convention questions. We would need to admit other distinct men and women, as project pursuers themselves, to the story as I do with my STC questions about not only my "star character," but also persons J, K, and so on.

We would need, in short, to ask an altogether different kind of question about what these persons are doing in the first place. By Strategy through Process, we would ask: *How* do a select few persons go about the specialized decision-making process of attributing a plan of purposeful action to the corporation? By Strategy through Convention, we would need to ask: *What* are the terms to which autonomous men and women, creators of relationships among themselves, can agree for the conduct of their respective projects in search of lasting and beneficial association with one another at the corporation?[45] In short, we would need to rewrite the entire story about corporate strategy at Bell Atlantic.

I offer Strategy through Convention as an avenue for telling humanist tales about the corporate strategy concept. In so doing, I introduced STC as a radical departure from the limited human account—and decidedly nonhumanist account—that has become conventionally popular in contemporary strategic management research. And I did so by means of ethical criticism, one genre of the humanities. I now draw my argument to a close by considering briefly the possibilities for other lines of critical inquiry regarding management concepts more generally.

THE TWILIGHT OF OTHER MANAGEMENT CONCEPTS

One way to read this book is to interpret it as a commentary about corporate strategy as a concept that is "loaded" with multiple meanings. Thus rather than dealing with "How many meanings?" as an interesting question, I concentrated on the humanist issue: What meanings serve our purposes well and what meanings do not?[46] I intend a general coverage of "our" in posing this question, in order to call attention to a second connotation of "loaded" meanings. That is, we can each interpret our respective research efforts as *purposeful endeavors to employ meanings that we prefer to use.* Put somewhat differently, we can interpret research as a conscious attempt to tell "biased" stories and to ask questions about which biases deserve replication and which do not.[47] This has been my critical agenda in this book. And it is an agenda that occupies many humanities researchers.

I have shown a diverse cast of storytellers—those in my "group of twelve"—who merge meanings for "strategy" and "purpose" into a genre that emphasizes the process of acquiring a strategy as a useful attribute for some nonhuman entity called "the corporation." I have interpreted this as their "loaded" approach to the corporate strategy concept.[48] In parallel, I have offered a loaded story of my own. In that story, I deliberately connect "strategy" and "purpose" in the context of a search by distinct and self-directed men and women for coordinated agreements through which each can prosper on her own terms. Moreover, I have told this Strategy & Justice story as part of my loaded effort to question whether the corporate strategy concept can serve as a humanist interpretation of the modern corporation. In that pursuit, I have concluded that the widely preferred Strategy through Process story is quite coherent and quite unsuited for persons—managers, students, and so on— for whom it is offered as ostensibly useful. In sum, I have argued that Strategy through Process is loaded with a comparatively unhelpful meaning when it comes to interpreting human endeavor at the modern corporation.

This focus on the worthiness of a particular concept need not be confined to matters involving strategy, corporate strategy, and purposeful action at the corporation. I simply want to suggest here the value of critical conversation about other management concepts that could be interpreted as "loaded" with meanings that are inhospitable to humanist concerns. These other concepts are, in short, candidates for interpretation in the lengthened twilight of critical analysis. Such an effort to apply the humanities in a critical way could constitute another arrow in Figure E.1.

The suggestion here, as I have shown with my project to place Strategy through Process in the twilight of ethical criticism and the twilight of obsolescence, is that the humanist worth of a story is assured by neither merely making reference to "human" action nor merely making the story available to other persons. To adopt a humanist disposition is to voluntarily celebrate personhood in increasingly wider and more diverse contexts. The Strategy through Process genre does little to encourage such a celebration. Nor are other management concepts necessarily immune to the conclusions that I have drawn about STP.[49]

A CLOSING COMMENT

I wrote *The Twilight of Corporate Strategy* to defend a thesis that, with regard to the corporate strategy concept, there is a long and arduous road to travel before the human practice of telling research stories about strategy and the modern corporation can become even a modestly humanist project. In a humanist discourse about the corporate strategy concept, men and women share stories with men and women in an ongoing search for meanings that celebrate what it means to be a man or a woman. I have created Strategy & Justice and Strategy through Convention on the premise that corporate strategy is an idea that still can hold great promise for the men and women who jointly shape that search.

Notes

Chapter 1

1. This discussion draws on the interpretation of purpose developed in R. E. Freeman, and D. Gilbert, Jr., *Corporate Strategy and the Search for Ethics* (Englewood Cliffs, N.J.: Prentice-Hall, 1988), 13–20. For my purposes in this introductory section, I draw on the propositions on page 14 that purposes are personal, purposes guide action, and purposes denote a "bottom line" for performance. Throughout this book, I rely on the other two propositions that we discuss on page 14. They are not, however, needed at this point in the argument.

2. A. Chandler, Jr., *Strategy and Structure: Chapters in the History of American Industrial Enterprise* (Cambridge, Mass.: MIT Press, 1962), 13.

3. On this basis, I draw a distinction throughout the book between human action and humanist action, whereby the latter is one possibility for the former. Clearly, not all human activities turn on humanist premises. Apartheid is one case in point. My conception of humanism is a liberal one, adapted primarily from the arguments made by Richard Rorty. See, in particular, R. Rorty, *Contingency, Irony, and Solidarity* (Cambridge: Cambridge University Press, 1989). I sketch this conception of humanism in the Preface.

4. F. Nietzsche, *Twilight of the Idols (Or How to Philosophize with a Hammer)*, trans. R. J. Hollingdale (Harmondsworth: Penguin Books, 1986), 110. The premise that persons can exercise meaningful control over the direction of their lives, surprises notwithstanding, pervades Nietzsche's arguments in *Twilight of the Idols* and in F. Nietzsche, *Thus Spoke Zarathustra*, trans. R. J. Hollingdale (London: Penguin Books, 1987); and F. Nietzsche, *Beyond Good and Evil*, trans. W. Kaufmann (New York: Vintage Books, 1966). Among other places, Nietzsche articulates the humanist—rather than merely human—theme in the following terms: "But may the will to truth mean this to you: that everything shall be transformed into the humanly-conceivable, the humanly-evident, the humanly-palpable! You should follow your own senses to the end!" (*Thus Spoke Zarathustra*, 110). And: "The noble type of man experiences *itself* as determining values; it does not need approval; it judges 'what is harmful to me is harmful in itself'; it knows itself to be that which first accords honor to things; it is *value-creating*"

(*Beyond Good and Evil*, 205). For several vivid portrayals of this obsession with self-directed human growth, see Ayn Rand's characterizations of Howard Roark and Dominique Francon in A. Rand, *The Fountainhead* (New York: Bobbs-Merrill, 1943); and Dagny Taggart and John Galt in A. Rand, *Atlas Shrugged* (New York: Random House, 1957).

5. The notion that the corporation can serve an instrumental function for reasoning persons, rather than assume a transcendent existence, is a hallmark of the stakeholder conception of the modern corporation. See R. E. Freeman, *Strategic Management: A Stakeholder Approach* (Cambridge, Mass.: Ballinger, 1984), 22–27; W. Evan and R. E. Freeman, "A Stakeholder Theory of the Modern Corporation: Kantian Capitalism," in T. Beauchamp and N. Bowie, eds., *Ethical Theory and Business*, 3rd ed. (Englewood Cliffs, N.J.: Prentice-Hall, 1988), 97–106; and Freeman and Gilbert, *Corporate Strategy*, 164–165. Among many aims, I intend that this book provide one more justification for the stakeholder conception of the corporation. In particular, I show how we can give a reasoned account of the corporation that supplements Nietzsche's "instinct," insofar as human endeavor at the corporation is concerned. My references to interaction among persons is chosen carefully here. While I give a great deal of attention to purpose at an individual level of action, I connect (1) purpose as an individual human being's concern with (2) purposeful pursuits as inevitably joint pursuits among persons who are guided by their respective purposes. In short, we can construct an account where the *level* of meaningful action is with the person and the *unit* of meaningful action is something jointly created by persons, such as a contract or bargain or a mess for them all. I say all this in response to a common and naive criticism to the effect that inquiry about persons is necessarily an act of solipsism. Thomas Schelling dispels such a complaint with his entertaining account of individual and joint actions. See T. Schelling, *Micromotives and Macrobehavior* (New York: Norton, 1978), 11–24. Schelling simply shows how purposeful individual acts and joint products of those acts are not necessarily reducible in either direction. Indeed, Rorty argues in *Contingency, Irony, and Solidarity* that there is no need for such an attempt at reduction.

6. The concept of enterprise strategy holds promise as one vehicle for keeping such questions continually on the agendas of corporate managers. See Freeman *Strategic Management* 89–110; and Freeman and Gilbert, *Corporate Strategy*, 64–86. For a comprehensive, and largely forgotten, account of the connection between purpose and management, see C. Barnard, *The Functions of the Executive*, Thirtieth Anniversary Edition (Cambridge, Mass.: Harvard University Press, 1968), 86–89, 231–234. Barnard's argument can apply extensively to strategic management, as we show in D. Gilbert, Jr., E. Hartman, J. Mauriel, and R. E. Freeman, *A Logic for Strategy* (Cambridge, Mass.: Ballinger, 1988), 10–13. There are, of course, few women to be found in Chandler's story. Still, gender differences notwithstanding, Chandler provides us with a story about corporate strategy that men and women can begin to adapt to their respective lives.

7. Oftentimes, these instructive efforts are conducted under the rubric of "business policy." For a discussion tracing the evolution of strategic management research from business policy, see D. Schendel and C. Hofer, "Introduction," in D. Schendel and C. Hofer, eds., *Strategic Management: A New View of*

Business Policy and Planning (Boston: Little, Brown, 1979), 5–13; and K. Andrews, *The Concept of Corporate Strategy*, rev. ed. (Homewood, Ill.: Irwin, 1980), iii–x.

8. E. Greenberg, *The Celebrant* (New York: Penguin Books, 1986), 91. Hundreds of Bucknell students have joined me in interpreting and reinterpreting this captivating narrative about, in part, the life and times of Mathewson, a Bucknellian at the turn of the century.

9. I use the archaeological metaphor deliberately, for reasons that I explain in Chapter 2. See A. Rosmarin, *The Power of Genre* (Minneapolis: University of Minnesota Press, 1985), 8–10. It is telling that the *Strategic Management Journal*, where many strategic management researchers look for insights, contains no book review section and therefore no forum for acknowledging that there might be reason for scholarly debate about the value of corporate strategy.

10. A characteristic defense of strategic management research is mounted in terms of scope: for example, more researchers attending more conferences and submitting more articles and books for reviews that reject more articles and books for publication. This is hardly surprising in two respects. First, the rhetoric of business activity in general is dominated by a fascination with scale and achieving greater scale. Since strategic management research focuses on business practice, the "scale" emphasis should be understandable. On this view, a line of research, like a corporation, that stops expanding becomes suspect. Second, strategic management researchers commonly think of themselves as scientists engaged in the yeoman pursuit of what Thomas Kuhn terms "normal science." This period of confirmation of existing theories and models proceeds "normally" when more and more studies are conducted under the rubric of known idols. Scope in this regard thus indicates researchers' commitment to familiar questions, theories, and methods. See T. Kuhn, *The Structure of Scientific Revolutions*, 2nd ed. (Chicago: University of Chicago Press, 1970). As I show in Chapter 2, these researchers act on an abridged interpretation of Kuhn's argument. On that view, normal science becomes detached from the context in which it is practiced and the distinct persons who engage in that practice. For reason of this kind of selective reading of Kuhn, the practice of mainstream strategic management research needs to be critically examined. I take up this task in Chapter 2. For a discussion of the "arrival" of strategic management research, see J. Fredrickson, "Introduction: The Need for Perspectives," in J. Fredrickson, ed., *Perspectives on Strategic Management* (New York: Harper & Row, 1990), 1.

11. This discussion—and, for that matter, the heart of this book—relies on the explanations of purpose, language, and human community given by Richard Rorty. See, in particular, R. Rorty, *Consequences of Pragmatism* (Minneapolis: University of Minnesota Press, 1982). Among social scientists, the proposition that research destinations can be chosen can be quite unsettling, as I discuss in Chapter 2. My only concern for the time being is that the customary defense of strategic management research in terms of scope and scale has nothing whatsoever to do with the corporate strategy idea per se. So perhaps a more sensible destination can be selected.

12. Throughout Nietzsche's arguments, we confront the deliberate contrast between the creation and sustenance of truths and the willful destruction of

those ideas. As Hollingdale notes, this dialectic tension is necessary in Nietzsche's logic (*Thus Spoke Zarathustra*, 12–13). My line of argument in this book is similarly Hegelian.

13. Ibid., 60.

14. Nietzsche refers to the repetition in our struggles for meaning as "eternal recurrence," a theme that pervades *Thus Spoke Zarathustra*. Ibid., 237.

15. Nietzsche, *Twilight of the Idols*, 21–22.

16. Nietzsche, *Beyond Good and Evil*, 217.

17. Nietzsche, *Thus Spoke Zarathustra*, 58.

18. The epitome of mass self-entrapment is the sheep—it is the same word singular and plural. Nietzsche, *Beyond Good and Evil*, 114. I thank R. Edward Freeman and Roger Hudson for bringing this to my attention.

19. In this regard, Hollingdale interprets Nietzsche to argue that truth is "a concept belonging to the human mind and will" (*Thus Spoke Zarathustra*, 25). I have read few accounts more vivid on this score than the novels by Rand and Jean-Paul Sartre. Once again, I am grateful to R. Edward Freeman for acquainting me with this intellectual progression.

20. Nietzsche, *Thus Spoke Zarathustra*, 213.

21. Indeed, a logical consequence of this part of the argument is that the notion "real world"—a beacon for twentieth-century social scientists—becomes optional: "The 'real world'—an idea no longer of any use . . . let us abolish it!" (Nietzsche, *Twilight of the Idols*, 40).

22. Ibid., 110. Jean Baker Miller makes a similar point, in terms of a person's voluntary engagement with differences: "Our ability to engage with that new thought and feeling is the source of our growth and the growth of the relationship between us" (*Toward a New Psychology of Women*, 2nd ed. [Boston: Beacon Press, 1986], 140). For a discussion about Nietzsche's emphasis on "difference" as an impetus for human growth, and just how different an emphasis on difference can be, see M. Taylor, "Descartes, Nietzsche, and the Search for the Unsayable," *New York Times Book Review*, 1 February 1987, 3, 34.

23. In the preface to his autobiography and in reference to his "fans," Lee Iacocca provides a lucid expression of the worldly claim that a writer can choose to make: "I discovered that the secret to the book was simple: Most people who wrote had lived parts of my life themselves. I wasn't writing about a strange place like the bottom of the ocean or the surface of the moon; I was writing about somewhere they'd all been" (L. Iacocca, with W. Novak, *Iacocca: An Autobiography* [New York: Bantam, 1986], ix–x).

24. I make this point, for now, in general *human* terms.

25. One exception is P. Shrivastava, "Is Strategic Management Ideological?," *Journal of Management* 12, no. 3 (1986): 363–377. After answering "yes," Shrivastava apparently argues for *less* normative emphasis, given the dominant "managerial" ideology that he attributes to strategic management research. I take precisely the opposite approach toward normative interpretation, as will become clear in Chapter 2.

26. Curiously, it is not unusual for strategic management researchers to create models and theories that incorporate some degree of debate among executives in the course of strategic decision-making. Kenneth Andrews argues, for example, that "a critic of strategy must be at heart enough of a nonconformist to raise questions about generally accepted modes of thought and the conven-

tional thinking which serves as a substitute for original analysis" (*Concept of Corporate Strategy,* 44). Still, when it comes to conducting a parallel debate among themselves, mainstream strategic management researchers tend to retreat to the cloak of positivist science that smothers such direct contact with concepts and "modes of thought." For a contrasting view, see Kuhn, *Structure of Scientific Revolutions,* regarding how scientists might interpret their work as conscious and joint efforts to maintain commitments to certain central beliefs, which he calls paradigms.

27. Liam Fahey and Kurt Christensen provide an illustrative example. Their "evaluation" is confined to observing that certain areas of so-called strategy content research remain unexamined, or examined by means of relatively simple models—those with few independent variables. Their emphasis on "fine-tuning" is unmistakable in such claims as "no strategy content issue has been studied to the point where the marginal returns from an additional well-conceived study would be trivial" (L. Fahey and H. K. Christensen, "Evaluating the Research on Strategy Content," *Journal of Management* 12, no. 2 [1986]: 177). My point is that their evaluative effort, although quite informative, is not predicated on an assumption that challenging corporate strategy and related concepts is worthwhile. They confirm the status quo, and nothing more. Fredrickson searches, in the same spirit, for "appropriate 'course corrections' " ("Introduction," 8).

28. It is rare to come across an argument in the strategic management research literature that examines managerial application of that research. It is instructive to note that, in an ostensibly critical analysis of the state of strategic management research, Fredrickson commissioned a study conducted by "insiders"—notwithstanding his claim to the contrary—who approach the corporate strategy concept from the "insider" standpoints of management science, industrial organization economics, organization theory, and business policy ("Introduction," 3). Where are the poets here, for example? For a rare and refreshing alternative to the kind of "in-house" discourse that Fredrickson leads, see L. Smircich and C. Stubbart, "Strategic Management in an Enacted World," *Academy of Management Review* 10, no. 4 (1985): 724–736. The essay by Smircich and Stubbart has been a prime source of encouragement for my effort here, as have been their respective expressions of support.

29. The key criterion that distinguishes my study from other, ostensibly critical commentaries by strategic management researchers is my willingness to put the very idea of strategic management "up for grabs." *Geistesgeschichte* is the term that Richard Rorty applies to this kind of inquiry. See R. Rorty, "The Historiography of Philosophy: Four Genres," in R. Rorty, J. Schneewind, and Q. Skinner, eds., *Philosophy in History* (Cambridge: Cambridge University Press, 1984), 56–61. Rorty argues that this genre of philosophical inquiry is applicable "at the level of problematics rather than of solutions to problems. It spends more of its time asking 'Why should anyone have made the question of _____ central to his thought?' or 'Why did anyone take the problem of _____ seriously?' " (57). One who practices this inquiry does so by "assembling a cast of historical characters, and a dramatic narrative, which shows how we have come to ask the questions we now think inescapable and profound" (61). In one elegant and succinct passage, Rorty describes what I intend to do with this study. The particular "dramatic narrative" that occupies my attention is the

study of corporate strategy. I am indebted to R. Edward Freeman for not only introducing me to Rorty's arguments, but also for one day pointing out that "you're doing *Geistesgeschichte*."

30. Richard Daft and Victoria Buenger criticize strategic management research for becoming idol-bound: "Our premise is that in the race to embrace its own paradigm, strategic management research has been ensnared by the rituals and paraphernalia of normal science" ("Hitching a Ride on a Fast Train to Nowhere: The Past and Future of Strategic Management Research," in Fredrickson, *Perspectives on Strategic Management*, 82). Curiously, Daft and Buenger then proceed to recommend a solution that is bound to the familiar idol of "theory building" in strategic management research. The likely effect is to preserve the idolatry of that research enterprise.

31. My Nietzschean justification for the major league baseball program of "rehabilitation assignment" follows Nietzsche's maxim to "live dangerously" when it comes to defending one's truths. What is "dangerous" is the uncertainty about the outcome of that assignment. See Hollingdale's commentary in Nietzsche, *Thus Spoke Zarathustra*, 18.

32. This discussion is adapted from Gilbert, Hartman, Mauriel, and Freeman, *Logic for Strategy*, 13–16.

33. See, for example, "The Best B-Schools," *Business Week*, 28 November 1988, 76–80; "Where the Schools Aren't Doing Their Homework," *Business Week*, 28 November 1988, 84–85, 88; and J. Main, "B-Schools Get a Global Vision," *Fortune*, 17 July 1989, 78–80, 85–86.

34. See R. Reich, *The Next American Frontier* (New York: New York Times Books, 1983), 140–172. This point probably marks the only intersection between Reich's thesis and mine.

35. The debate about whether ethics belongs in a business school curriculum can be rendered a nondebate if we understand "get mine first and always" as an ethical principle—the credo of an ethical egoist. See T. Beauchamp, "Ethical Theory and Its Application to Business," in Beauchamp and Bowie, eds., *Ethical Theory and Business*, 16–21. Once we interpret managerial activities as thoroughly ethical actions—that is, having ethical implications, as opposed to economic implications—we can finally begin considering acceptable and unacceptable approaches to human interaction at the modern corporation. Researchers' willingness to cross this interpretive divide is by no means just around the corner. For an important commentary in this regard, see T. Mulligan, "The Two Cultures in Business Education," *Academy of Management Review* 12, no. 4 (1987): 593–599. Particularly popular, and resistant to reassessment, is the economist's premise that markets are morally neutral. Robert Heilbroner argues, for example, "It is part of the nature of capitalism that the circuit of capital has no intrinsic moral dimension, no vision of art or idea aside from the commodity in which it is embodied" (*The Nature and Logic of Capitalism* [New York: Norton, 1985], 140). As a result of the unquestioned constancy of market efficiency as an end, Peter Koslowski notes: "Through the acceptance of given, constant goals, the moral problem is reduced to an economic one, and ethics is replaced by economics" ("The Ethics of Capitalism," in S. Pejovich, ed., *Philosophical and Economic Foundations of Capitalism* [Lexington, Mass.: Lexington Books, 1983], 42). For an argument that contrasts with Heilbroner's, and argues for a way to

overcome the reduction that Koslowski laments, see D. Gilbert, Jr., "Corporate Strategy and Ethics," *Journal of Business Ethics* 5, no. 2 (1986): 137–150.

36. D. Halberstam, *The Reckoning* (New York: Avon, 1986), 99–101.

37. A well-known expression of this criticism can be found in T. Peters and R. Waterman, Jr., *In Search of Excellence: Lessons from America's Best Run Companies* (New York: Harper & Row, 1982). Nietzsche refers to the need for persons to "overcome" themselves in terms of resisting the temptation to become a follower in the herd. Only when such a "common" instinct is consciously counteracted, Nietzsche argues, can persons realize "the theme of joy in existence, of the self-sufficiency-in-joy of the sovereign individual" (*Thus Spoke Zarathustra*, 29, 32). If a person's liberation from the routine course of organizational activity can be understood in terms of voluntary choice and action, then such notions as "managing innovation" can be exposed as possible non sequiturs if they turn on coercion.

38. An instructive introduction to the property rights defense of the corporation is provided in C. Stone, *Where the Law Ends: The Social Control of Corporate Behavior* (New York: Harper & Row, 1975), 8–29. For one version of this criticism, as applied to corporate strategy, see Gilbert, Hartman, Mauriel, and Freeman, *Logic for Strategy*, 55–79. Our point is that those inclined to assert a theory of the firm based on financial theory must specifically defend the exclusion of non–property rights claimants from their story. It does not appear that conventional financial theory can help with that defense, however.

39. Ethical considerations can be separated from the context of persons' daily lives in at least two ways. One is for researchers to interpret ethics as a transcendent kind of aura that necessarily eludes the grasp of mere mortals, but not researchers. A modern version of this claim to special expertise is S. Srivastva and Associates, *Executive Integrity: The Search for High Human Values in Organizational Life* (San Francisco: Jossey-Bass, 1988). For arguments about the unacceptability, from a humanist point of view, of this approach to business ethics, see R. E. Freeman, *"Executive Integrity: The Search for High Human Values in Organizational Life*, by Suresh Srivastva and Associates" (book review), *Academy of Management Executive* 3, no. 1 (1989): 78–80; and D. Gilbert, Jr., *"Executive Integrity: The Search for High Human Values in Organizational Life* by Suresh Srivastva and Associates" (book review), *Business Horizons*, July–August 1989, 80–81. A second approach, which is common to a great deal of business ethics research, is to treat ethics as simply another "natural" force available for scientific measurement and subsequent lawlike generalization. Once again, matters of ethics are removed from the everyday, problem-solving context of persons' lives and elevated "beyond mankind" to a status of "collective property," in the parlance of management research. A prime example of this activity is cross-cultural measurement of managers' beliefs. See, for example, H. Becker and D. Fritzsche, "Business Ethics: A Cross-Cultural Comparison of Managers' Attitudes," *Journal of Business Ethics* 6, no. 4 (1987): 289–295. Nothing in this kind of study suggests a meaningful connection between what distinct persons do at the corporation and how ethical arguments, principles, and so on, can help those persons direct their own pursuits. For such a study to make sense, in short, distinctions among persons must be ignored.

40. An earlier version of this line of argument was developed in D. Gilbert,

Jr., and R. E. Freeman, "The Flight from Meaning: A Critical Interpretation of the Management Classics" (Paper presented at the Critical Perspectives in Organizational Analysis Conference, Baruch College–CUNY, New York, September 1985). We are particularly grateful to Linda Smircich and William Frederick for their early encouragement along this line of reasoning. I repeatedly stress hopefulness in my argument, on the assumption that persons will continue to find reason to pursue their purposes in a complex pattern of interrelationships among themselves. Whether we call that activity "corporate" or not, the connection between human interactions and distinct human purposes remains. This premise distinguishes my analysis from more radical Marxist approaches to the same kind of questions that I pose.

41. P. Drucker, *Concept of the Corporation*, 2nd rev. ed. (New York: New American Library, 1983), 42.

42. Ibid., 36.

43. D. Katz and R. Kahn, *The Social Psychology of Organizations* (New York: Wiley, 1966), 51.

44. K. Goodpaster and J. Matthews, Jr., "Can a Corporation Have a Conscience?," *Harvard Business Review*, January–February 1982, 132–141. What Goodpaster and Matthews choose not to consider—notwithstanding their unconvincing argument (140)—is the reason *why* it is useful at all to think about a corporate conscience. Their response to this objection, in keeping with the modern fascination with organizations, is more or less "that's the way the world is." For a critique on this point, see M. Velasquez, "Why Corporations Are Not Morally Responsible for Anything They Do," *Business & Professional Ethics* 2 (1983): 1–4, 6–17.

45. H. Simon, *Administrative Behavior*, 3rd ed. (New York: Free Press, 1976), 102.

46. Katz and Kahn, *Social Psychology of Organizations*, 34. Such a formula for managing organizations turns on a premise that, in Nietzsche's terms, necessitates "this degeneration and diminution of man into the perfect herd animal" (*Beyond Good and Evil*, 118).

47. I use the phrase "organization science" here, rather than "organization theory," to emphasize the great distance that mainstream organization theorists place between themselves—using a positivist science—and human beings as purposeful actors. For an introduction to this chasm, see A. Van de Ven and W. Joyce, eds., *Perspectives on Organization Design and Behavior* (New York: Wiley, 1981). An insightful critique of organization theory and organization science is offered in E. Hartman, *Conceptual Foundations of Organization Theory* (Cambridge, Mass.: Ballinger, 1988). A recent discussion of the criteria for "good" theory building in organization science is presented without any reference whatsoever to persons who might read and act on that kind of theory. See, for example, S. Bacharach, "Organizational Theories: Some Criteria for Evaluation," *Academy of Management Review* 14, no. 4 (1989): 501. See also the "alternative strategy for theory building" in M. Poole and A. Van de Ven, "Using Paradox to Build Management and Organization Theories," *Academy of Management Review* 14, no. 4 (1989): 563. One would never know, from that passage, that the theory builders are dealing with anything remotely concerned with persons acting at the corporation.

48. J. Pfeffer, *Organizations and Organization Theory* (Cambridge, Mass.: Bal-

linger, 1982), 294. Pfeffer confirms the drift of organization science by arguing that organization theorists' attempts to link research with managerial practice are a source of problems for organization theory (3).

49. G. Morgan, "Rethinking Corporate Strategy: A Cybernetic Perspective," *Human Relations* 36, no. 4 (1983): 345–360.

50. G. Astley, "Toward an Appreciation of Collective Strategy," *Academy of Management Review* 9, no. 3 (1984): 526–535; A. Van de Ven and G. Astley, "Mapping the Field to Create a Dynamic Perspective on Organization Design and Behavior," in Van de Ven and Joyce, *Perspectives*, 427–468. Van de Ven and Astley suggest that a perspective on organizations is not "complete" if voluntary, purposeful action is adopted as a guiding premise (464).

51. Writing a century earlier, Nietzsche anticipated this deliberate effort to hold persons' idiosyncrasies and fallibility against them in a permanent, theoretical way, such that "the highest and strongest drives . . . are branded and slandered most. High and independent spirituality, the will to stand alone, even a powerful reason are experienced as dangers; everything that elevates an individual above the herd and intimidates the neighbor is henceforth called *evil.*" (*Beyond Good and Evil*, 113–114). Pfeffer argues that an assumption about the primacy of human autonomy is tautological and, hence, suspect as a basis for organization theory (*Organizations*, 77). What he misses is that his assumption about the primacy of organizations is open to an analogous challenge: organization theory can be understood to turn on a tautology about the intrinsic worth of organizations. His appeal to tautology as a basis for justifying his argument appears rather futile.

52. Unlike mainstream organization science research, however, the accounts provided by these writers examine the problems of the business world in human terms, that is, at a personal level of analysis. If management researchers generally are to make progress in developing humanist perspectives on the modern corporation, working at this level of analysis is a minimum condition. Studying *organizations* as the least aggregated level of analysis simply denies that organized activity can have harmful effects on persons, since persons are not central to those studies. Thus for a sampler of a different approach to management, organizations, and the corporation, see S. Terkel, *The Great Divide: Second Thoughts on the American Dream* (New York: Pantheon, 1988); J. Dos Passos, *The Big Money* (New York: New American Library, 1969); A. Miller, *Death of a Salesman* (New York: Penguin Books, 1976); T. Dreiser, *The Financier* (New York: New American Library, 1967); and S. Lewis *Babbitt* (New York: New American Library, 1961).

53. Each of these writers, regarding the individual level of analysis, can be understood as contrasting a preferred notion of personhood with a host of collectivizing forces that threaten the integrity of personhood. See J. Marquand, *Point of No Return* (Chicago: Academy Chicago, 1985); S. Wilson, *The Man in the Gray Flannel Suit* (New York: Arbor House, 1955); J. Kubicki, *Breaker Boys* (New York: Warner, 1986); U. Sinclair, *The Jungle* (New York: New American Library, 1960); G. Walker, *The Chronicles of Doodah* (Boston: Houghton Mifflin, 1985); and G. Orwell, *1984* (New York: New American Library, 1981). One implication here is that management educators could provide a more believable account of the modern corporation by using literary works, as opposed to social scientific research materials, for instructional and discussion purposes.

See R. Coles, "Gatsby at the B School," *New York Times Book Review*, 25 October 1987, 1, 40–41; and E. Fowler, "Refreshing Literature for MBA's," *New York Times*, 4 October 1988, D25.

54. More specifically, I use this line of argument as occasion to extend the premise that "purpose is personal" into several hopeful directions (Freeman and Gilbert, *Corporate Strategy*).

55. Put somewhat differently, my argument here provides one challenge to the widespread belief that corporation boundaries serve a meaningful explanatory purpose.

56. H. Barnes, *An Existentialist Ethics* (Chicago: University of Chicago Press, 1985), ix.

57. Contrast this to the hopeless sense of entrapment portrayed through such characters as Tom Rath in Wilson, *Man in the Gray Flannel Suit;* Ona and Jurgis Rudkus in Sinclair, *Jungle;* and the Native American young adults in L. Erdrich, *Love Medicine* (New York: Bantam, 1985). Nothing that I argue here about freedom to choose precludes the importance of commitments with others. I concentrate on the connection between purpose and commitment in relationships in Chapter 4.

58. For a readable account about when these alternatives first became available, and the reasons why AT&T executives such as Charles Brown embraced them vigorously, see S. Coll, *The Deal of the Century: The Breakup of AT&T* (New York: Atheneum, 1986).

59. M. Pastin, *The Hard Problems of Management: Gaining the Ethics Edge* (San Francisco: Jossey-Bass, 1986), 213.

60. Barnes, *Existentialist Ethics*, 27.

61. For a captivating, albeit sobering, narrative about purpose and self-assessment, see R. Ford, *The Sportswriter* (New York: Vintage Books, 1986). My thinking about purpose in this specific regard has been influenced by the characterizations of Howard Roark in Rand, *Fountainhead*, and Mathieu Delarue in J. P. Sartre, *The Age of Reason* (New York: Vintage Books, 1973).

62. A brief overview of these developments can be gleaned from B. Feder, "MCI Struggles to Ward Off Deregulation's Sting," *New York Times*, 3 August 1986, sec. 3, 12–13; "MCI's Fight for a Future in the World It Helped Create," *Business Week*, 27 May 1987, 114–115; J. Guyon, "MCI, US Sprint Should Be Able to Shine, Even in Long-Distance Shadow of AT&T," *Wall Street Journal*, 21 October 1988, A2, A10; C. Sims, "AT&T's New Call to Arms," *New York Times*, 22 January 1989, sec. 3, 1, 11; C. Sims, "Sprint Picks Up Steam at Last," *New York Times*, 11 June 1989, sec. 3, 4; and A. Kupfer, "Bob Allen Rattles the Cages at AT&T," *Fortune*, 19 June 1989, 58–61, 64, 66.

63. The point is that by throwing open considerations of purpose to evaluation and debate, these executives could convince themselves that the pursuit of market share is (1) optional, (2) subordinate to the pursuit of greater regulatory latitude, and (3) even a mere resultant of other pursuits. Hence, thinking about purpose in evaluative terms enables—and even prods—executives and nonexecutives alike to think in terms of possibilities. In this way, these two connotations of purpose are connected.

64. Such a sense of connectedness helps establish purpose as a concept very much germane to our daily activities. A common tendency in business dis-

course is to separate "long-term" considerations of purpose from "short-term" operational matters. If executives (and researchers) succumb to that temptation, then they can always find reasons either to defer reflection about purpose or to relegate responsibility for such analysis to some staff department. Purpose, in short, must be placed in a day-to-day context, lest those everyday actions lose meaning.

65. Pastin, *Hard Problems of Management*, 151. On this basis, Pastin draws a distinction between purposes and an exhaustible derivative called goals.

66. Sinclair Lewis's character George Babbitt is a classic reminder of the line between a stable self-awareness and self-deception. Babbitt is all the more tragic a figure because he knows the difference but cannot find the will to help himself. So he takes the fateful and hopeless steps toward permitting others to define his purposes for him. It is important to note that I say "stable," not "permanent," to suggest clearly the possibility of that which Rorty in *Contingency, Irony, and Solidarity* calls the "contingency of self."

67. R. Coles, *The Call of Stories: Teaching and the Moral Imagination* (Boston: Houghton Mifflin, 1989), 11.

68. Alvin von Auw raised concerns before the AT&T divestiture about such a diversion from the time-honored credo of "universal service." A. von Auw, *Heritage & Destiny: Reflections on the Bell System in Transition* (New York: Praeger, 1983), 137–237. See also P. Temin, with L. Galambos, *The Fall of the Bell System: A Study in Prices and Politics* (Cambridge: Cambridge University Press, 1987), 277–366, and M. Carnevale, "Phone Service Shows Only Minor Advances 5 Years After Breakup," *Wall Street Journal*, 6 January 1989, A1, A4.

69. Hence, a stable sense of self-worth can serve as a springboard toward growing into a more autonomous person. Accordingly, a sense of continuity need not be synonymous with a stifling sense of conservatism about ourselves. Contrast this provisional and instrumental perspective on self-identity with the once-and-for-all argument in D. Seibert and W. Proctor, *The Ethical Executive: A Top C.E.O.'s Program for Success with Integrity in the Corporate World* (New York: Simon and Schuster, 1984), and the confinement of continuity experienced by Charles Gray in Marquand, *Point of No Return*.

70. For an overview of Greene's pattern of willingness to grant latitude to the RHCs, even before the divestiture took effect in 1984, see H. Shooshan III, "The Bell Breakup: Putting It in Perspective," in H. Shooshan III, ed., *Disconnecting Bell: The Impact of the AT&T Divestiture* (New York: Pergamon Press, 1984), 18–20; C. Sims, "Most Regulatory Curbs on 7 'Baby Bells' Kept," *New York Times*, 11 September 1987, D1–D2; C. Sims, "Judge Lets 'Baby Bells' Offer Some Information Services," *New York Times*, 8 March 1988, D1–D2; "How Bell South Is Plugging into the Information Age," *Business Week*, 31 October 1988, 148, 150; and J. Lopez, "Pacific Telesis Gets Overseas Rights; Nynex Effort Fails," *Wall Street Journal*, 14 February 1989, A4. With regard to regulatory changes at the state level, see B. Davis, "Many States Deregulate Telephone Rates, Hurting Residential User in Short Run," *Wall Street Journal*, 19 September 1986, 21.

71. Andrews, *Concept of Corporate Strategy*, 11–15.

72. Ibid., 10–11. For a more extensive analysis of Andrews's arguments in this regard, see R. E. Freeman, D. Gilbert, Jr., and E. Hartman, "Values and

the Foundations of Strategic Management," *Journal of Business Ethics* 7, no. 11 (1988): 821–834.

73. This issue could also be discussed in terms of strategic management researchers acting in good faith with respect to what they convey to their students as knowledge. I take up this issue in Chapter 2, where I connect the corporate strategy concept with the act of strategic management research.

74. Prominent across literature and philosophy (e.g., Nietzsche's discussion of "eternal recurrence") is the metaphor of a person's life as a journey. Coles quotes William Carlos Williams in this regard: "Their story, yours, mine—it's what we all carry with us on this trip we take, and we owe it to each other to respect our stories and learn from them" (*Call of Stories*, 30).

75. Coles draws on this piece of Eliot's commentary (ibid., 67). Compare this sense of time with the attempt to make time a "variable" in organization science research. See, for example, G. Hermes, "Structural Change in Social Processes," *American Journal of Sociology* 82, no. 3 (1976): 513–545. Eliot's commentary seems to doom survey research as having no usable meaning for understanding actions taken by distinct human beings, who have histories of their own.

76. Coles, *Call of Stories*, 129.

77. Ibid., 159.

78. See Coles's discussion of memory (ibid., 183) and stories (189). This suggests that the reader plays a key role in the conception of strategic management research as literature. I take up this issue, along with the companion issue mentioned in note 73, in Chapter 2.

79. Even as I build a corollary case against orthodox organization science for humanist reasons, I readily acknowledge that we can talk about organization science in interpretive terms. For a prominent example, see G. Morgan, *Images of Organization* (Beverly Hills, Calif.: Sage, 1986). Morgan invites organization scientists to use interpretations quite differently than I use them, however. Specifically, I am not interested in interpretation as a "better" way to uncover the natural foundations of truth, as I discuss in Chapter 2.

80. I do not mean to suggest, however, that the literary potential of corporate strategy and strategic management research will be obvious in rhetorical terms. In other words, the ponderous prose of strategic management research journals and books certainly seems different from what novelists, poets, and playwrights deliver. The possibility for a meaningful literary rhetoric about corporate strategy is a principal theme in D. Gilbert, Jr., "*The Deal of the Century: The Breakup of AT&T*, by Steven Coll; *Chronicles of Corporate Change: Management Lessons from AT&T and Its Offspring*, by Leonard A. Schlesinger, Davis Dyer, Thomas N. Clough, and Diane Landau; *The Fall of the Bell System: A Study in Prices and Politics*, by Peter Temin, with Louis Galambos; *Disconnecting Parties: Managing the Bell System Break-Up: An Inside View*, by W. Brooke Tunstall" (book review), *Academy of Management Review* 14, no. 1 (1989): 107–110.

81. See, for example, P. Gethers, *Getting Blue* (New York: Dell, 1987); Greenberg, *Celebrant;* and J. Hough, Jr. *The Conduct of the Game* (San Diego: Harcourt Brace Jovanovich, 1986).

82. Note that the arguments made by Simon and Barnes, for example, can both be extended to support interpretations of the modern corporation as a "human institution." Yet these are two sharply contrasting conceptions of "hu-

man," which leads me to distinguish between "human" and "humanist" interpretations (see note 3). Simon's "human" corporation can readily become, ironically, a hostile context for meaningful human reasoning, given Simon's worry about persons' limited reasoning skills. This point about the precision of language is a principal theme in Chapter 2.

83. I do not mean to imply that the corporate strategy concept is some fixed and "natural" origin from which stories flow like lava from a volcanic fissure. Rather, I simply choose corporate strategy—as opposed to other rallying points such as marketing, transaction costs, and population ecology—as a point of analytical departure.

84. Rosmarin draws the distinction, which I follow here, between a "class" and a "classifying statement" (*Power of Genre*, 46). She argues that it is useful to think of genre in the latter terms. This frees us to analyze lines of argument for their worldly pertinence, by freeing us from worry about the foundational, or "bedrock," basis for some class of argument. See also pages 3–22.

85. Iacocca, by contrast, presents in *Iacocca* a different genre about the immigrants' lot in "corporate" America. His account is not better, or worse, in some transcendent sense. It simply differs from that provided by, say, Upton Sinclair, in *The Jungle*. Kubicki offers a third genre in this regard, in *Breaker Boys*, with an account that places coal miners and coal barons alike on the same troublesome "turf" of human striving.

86. T. Kidder, *The Soul of a New Machine* (New York: Avon, 1981). A shocking update on the detachment of a speechwriter from his speech—and hence his sense of creative self-worth (Wilson, *Man in the Gray Flannel Suit*)—can be read in Walker, *Chronicles of Doodah*.

87. Chandler, *Strategy and Structure*, 13–17. The contemporary fascination with strategy implementation is a case in point.

88. This genre is more succinctly known as strategic planning. See Gilbert, Hartman, Mauriel, and Freeman, *Logic for Strategy*, 127–143.

89. This conclusion turns on my choice of human reasoning as a persistent analytical emphasis, or genre. By contrast, neither Morgan, *Images of the Organization,* nor Pfeffer, *Organizations*, writes in this genre. In fact, they appear to reject its value. Accordingly, their accounts become ineligible for pertinence to corporate strategy by the conditions that I am developing here.

90. This is simply to say that, with economists, sociologists, would-be biologists, and philosophers all converging on strategic management research from the standpoints of the genres with which they are familiar, multiple genres about corporate strategy are likely. That is impressive, as long as we do not confuse proliferation with worth.

91. The tendency in management research generally is to idolize new genres *because* they are new and then to search for ways to synthesize new and already idolized genres. We can liken this to approaching the question of conceptual worth with a dispenser of adhesive tape, as opposed to a scalpel or, as included in the subtitle to Nietzsche's *Twilight of the Idols*, a hammer. For an introductory discussion of the difference between tape and hammer in strategic management research, see Gilbert, Hartman, Mauriel, and Freeman, *Logic for Strategy*, 153–159. For a contrasting, hammerless view, see Van de Ven and Astley, "Mapping the Field."

92. R. Rorty, "Texts and Lumps," *New Literary History* 17, no. 1 (1985): 3.

93. Rorty, "Historiography of Philosophy," 61. For a readable introduction to pragmatism, see Rorty, ibid., and Rorty, *Consequences of Pragmatism*. I am indebted to R. Edward Freeman for introducing me to the pragmatist argument from Rorty to Stanley Fish to John Dewey to Nietzsche. I am grateful as well to Thelma Lavine and James Buchanan for their patient encouragement as I wrestled with my arguments in this genre.

94. Once again, I am not searching for, nor am I about to pull out of my hat à la Bullwinkle the Moose, some magical solution. Rather, I seek one more reason with which to defend the corporate strategy concept in humanist terms. Thus "deficiency" carries a contingent connotation here.

95. A graduate school colleague of mine, in faithful deference to Simon's argument (*Administrative Behavior*, 102), was prone to bemoaning some "truth" to the effect that human beings could process only five to nine bits of information at one time. If we want to talk in terms of this "fact," why not, I argue, see how we can make the *most* of five to nine bits of information? I thank Hal Angle, who is not the colleague in question here, for his patient conversation on this point.

96. J. Rawls, *A Theory of Justice* (Cambridge, Mass.: Harvard University Press, 1971), 3. There are, of course, multiple genres of ethical analysis, some of which accord greater priority to persons than do others. Rawls's argument is aimed at utilitarianism, one well-known version in the latter kind of genre. Thus by "priority" I simply refer to the preference for persons—as opposed to collectives—as objects of inquiry in ethical analysis.

97. This is simply to say that those engaged in any line of inquiry must willingly and wholeheartedly embrace some starting assumptions as being thoroughly worthwhile.

98. See Freeman and Gilbert, *Corporate Strategy*, 2–8.

99. For an analysis and justification of this kind, see Gilbert, "Corporate Strategy."

100. Andrews, *Concept of Corporate Strategy*, 18.

101. M. Porter, *Competitive Strategy: Techniques for Analyzing Industries and Competitors* (New York: Free Press, 1980), 3.

102. Ibid., 4.

103. Nothing in my approach suggests that Strategy & Justice is the only genre about corporate strategy that might be derived from the study of ethics. If I were to make such a claim, I would clearly be guilty of abandoning my pragmatist inclinations. It might well turn out that Strategy & Justice can, upon further reflection and pragmatist analysis, be reinterpreted in several derivative genres. Hence, I offer Strategy & Justice as one among many possible genres that can support better explanations of the modern corporation than can Strategy through Process. In fact, as I learned to respond in the course of defending my doctoral dissertation on this point, the more genres that can outperform Strategy through Process, the better. Robert Solomon helped me understand this point.

104. By "critical" I refer only to inquiry about meanings (see note 40).

105. See D. Gilbert, Jr. "Diane Vaughan, *Unlawful Organizational Behavior: Social Structure and Corporate Misconduct*" (book review), *Journal of Business Ethics* 7, no. 10 (1989): 800–802.

Chapter 2

1. This is why an article such as S. Lubove, "In the Computer Age, Certain Workers Are Still Vital to Success," *Wall Street Journal*, 3 August 1987, 1, 14, makes news at all. Recent futurist sketches in the *Wall Street Journal* and *Fortune* pay scant attention to persons as meaning-seeking beings. See, in this regard, C. Hymowitz, "Day in the Life of Tomorrow's Manager," *Wall Street Journal*, 20 March 1989, B1, and "Managing Now for the 1990s," *Fortune*, 26 September 1988, 44–47, 50–52, 56, 60. More often than not, suppressing that search for meaning is reported as a necessary principle for management. See, for example, "Catch a Falling Star System," *U.S. News & World Report*, 5 June 1989, 43–44.

2. Put somewhat differently, it makes no sense to say that we value an idea, such as a humanist corporate strategy concept, unless we are also able to act on that idea. For a discussion about values in this regard, see R. E. Freeman, D. Gilbert, Jr., and E. Hartman, "Values and the Foundations of Strategic Management," *Journal of Business Ethics* 7 (1988): 825–827.

3. I make this point regarding the tendency among business ethics researchers to commit this very logical separation in D. Gilbert, Jr., "Business Ethics and Three Genres of Stakeholder Research" (Paper presented at the Quality-of-Life/Marketing Conference, Blacksburg, Virginia, November 1989). Throughout the book, I refer to corporate strategy as the guiding concept of strategic management research.

4. See R. Rorty, "Texts and Lumps," *New Literary History* 17, no. 1 (1985): 1–2, and A. Rosmarin, *The Power of Genre* (Minneapolis: University of Minnesota Press, 1985), 3–22. Rorty prefers to give credit to literary critics as the bellwethers of modern pragmatism ("Texts and Lumps," 1–2), partly out of concern that persons can be prone to taking philosophers' commentaries as determinative. This has led me, with the assistance of R. Edward Freeman, to Rosmarin's defense of pragmatism, which I follow throughout my study.

5. In other words, I defend my approach as one replication of a widespread pragmatist practice that can include, among other pursuits, strategic management research.

6. To connect my argument to discourse about the worldly relevance of literary texts, I use "pragmatism" as an umbrella concept that subsumes the liberal humanism that I propose as a possible attribute for the corporate strategy concept. In this regard, I follow the arguments in R. Rorty, *Contingency, Irony, and Solidarity* (Cambridge: Cambridge University Press, 1989). Rorty delineates humanist concern with self-creation and solidarity. It is possible to entertain a conservative notion of pragmatism as well, whereby human progress plays a less central role than I accord that idea. Throughout, I use "pragmatist" and "ethical" as separate modifiers at certain times to call attention to finer points in the argument. I thank R. Edward Freeman for helping me clarify these distinctions.

7. For a classic rendition of this kind of opposition, see J. Kirk and M. Miller, *Reliability and Validity in Qualitative Research* (Beverly Hills, Calif.: Sage, 1986). My account of pragmatist research, by contrast, shares kinship with that found in T. Kuhn, *The Structure of Scientific Revolutions*, 2nd ed. (Chicago: University of Chicago Press, 1970). I use the phrase "management science" here to

encompass those organizational and management theorists who adopt a positivist perspective for their trade. My use of "management science" is intended to be generic, by contrast to the more specialized realm of management science. Hence, I include organization behavior research in this generic category, for example.

8. This interpretation is my own evolving rendition of John Rawls's account regarding what we might call the "problem of justice." See J. Rawls, *A Theory of Justice* (Cambridge, Mass.: Harvard University Press, 1971), 3–16, 126–161. Rawls sets what I call "humanist practice" against a backdrop of what he terms "the circumstances of justice."

9. I say "prima facie" because we clearly need to leave room in our dealings with others for rejecting their purposes if their aims are intended to impede, if not destroy, even one person's life without compelling justification. This is why we need Rawls's "theory of the right," or something like it, to accompany his "theory of the good."

10. I adopt this from David Gauthier's discussion of rational action by a "constrained maximizer" who expects to encounter "straightforward maximizers" who are willing to loot her projects. See D. Gauthier, *Morals by Agreement* (Oxford: Clarendon Press, 1986), 157–189.

11. Both Jean Baker Miller and Carol Gilligan warn us about the propensity for persons to ignore the prospects for kinship when those persons use a familiar, male-created language of modern social exchange. Miller argues that kinship necessarily turns on conflict as a healthy kind of interchange among persons holding different perspectives. A male language of "domination," as she terms it, denies this possibility: "Within a framework of inequality, the existence of conflict is denied and the means to engage openly in conflict are excluded" (J. B. Miller, *Toward a New Psychology of Women*, 2nd ed. [Boston: Beacon Press, 1986], 13). See also C. Gilligan, *In a Different Voice: Psychological Theory and Women's Development* (Cambridge, Mass.: Harvard University Press, 1982), 29.

12. R. Coles, *The Call of Stories: Teaching and the Moral Imagination* (Boston: Houghton Mifflin, 1989), 30.

13. Ibid., 22.

14. See Rosmarin, *Power of Genre*, 19. Ayn Rand expresses this same point through her character Howard Roark, in A. Rand, *The Fountainhead* (New York: New American Library, 1971), 681.

15. Rorty, "Texts and Lumps," 7.

16. This particular orthodoxy has been broached only three times since 1958, by Dale Long (1958), Mike Squires (1980), and Benny DiStefano (1989). See J. Reichler, ed., *The Baseball Encyclopedia*, 6th ed. (New York: Macmillan, 1985). Developments by certain feminists, literary critics, philosophers, and management researchers give cause for hope that it might not take thirty-two seasons for the connection to be drawn in strategic management research. Certainly, contemporary legal scholars know about these developments in the "critical legal studies" debate.

17. Management researchers routinely refer to Herbert Simon in defense of this denial of choice. Herbert Simon urges that "an administrative science, like any science, is concerned purely with factual statements. There is no place for ethical assertions in the body of a science" (*Administrative Behavior*, 3rd ed. [New

York: Free Press, 1976], 253). For a readable narrative about how one literary critic made the long intellectual passage from a foundationalist perspective to a pragmatist interpretation of literature, see S. Fish, *Is There a Text in This Class? The Authority of Interpretive Communities* (Cambridge, Mass.: Harvard University Press, 1980). I note only the possibility of research-as-choosing, because a foundationalist approach to literature, akin to Simon's view of the world, persists. Conversations with Max Clarkson have helped me understand this point.

18. Rosmarin notes the irony in this obsession with bias and "hard truth" (*Power of Genre*, 4). I encountered this kind of charge early in my doctoral studies in the course of writing a case study. Admonished by one critic in particular for doing too much "editorializing," I quickly came to see that my critic could not clarify the guidelines by which I should practice "self-erasure" (Rorty, "Texts and Lumps," 15). That would involve making a choice, of course.

19. F. Nietzsche, *Thus Spoke Zarathustra*, trans. R. J. Hollingdale (London: Penguin Books, 1987), 147.

20. For a pair of accessible introductions to this coherent account about truth, see Rosmarin, *Power of Genre*, 8–10; and R. Rorty, *Consequences of Pragmatism* (Minneapolis: University of Minnesota Press, 1982), 90–95.

21. K. R. Harrigan, *Strategic Flexibility: A Management Guide for Changing Times* (Lexington, Mass.: Lexington Books, 1985), 6.

22. D. Schendel and K. Cool, "Development of the Strategic Management Field: Some Accomplishments and Challenges," in J. Grant, ed., *Strategic Management Frontiers* (Greenwich, Conn.: JAI Press, 1988), 31.

23. F. Nietzsche, *Beyond Good and Evil*, trans. W. Kaufmann (New York: Vintage Books, 1966), 205.

24. Wayne Booth argues that these various rhetorical forms can never be meaningfully detached from the writer who uses them: "The author's judgment is always present, always evident to anyone who knows how to look for it" (*The Rhetoric of Fiction*, 2nd ed. [Chicago: University of Chicago Press, 1983], 20). Jerome Bruner, on the contrary, expresses doubt about just how far an interpreter can proceed in choosing genres. Bruner wants to argue that a finite collection of genres—"something altogether too universal"—is found in the structure of writing and interpretation. J. Bruner, *Actual Minds, Possible Worlds* (Cambridge, Mass.: Harvard University Press, 1986), 7. I thank Carol Jacobson and Paul Johnson for bringing Bruner's work to my attention.

25. We can understand Miller, *Toward a New Psychology of Women*, and Gilligan, *In a Different Voice*, to argue that a genre about power as a means of social interaction can be optional, if such a language impairs human growth in a community. A context ripe for a critical reading in this regard is T. Dreiser, *The Financier* (New York: New American Library, 1967).

26. For a recent expression of this orthodoxy, see the October 1989 issue of *Academy of Management Review*. The orthodoxy is plainly advocated in, for example, S. Bacharach, "Organizational Theories: Some Criteria for Evaluation," *Academy of Management Review* 14, no. 4 (1989): 496–515; and M. S. Poole and A. Van de Ven, "Using Paradox to Build Management and Organization Theories," *Academy of Management Review* 14, no. 4 (1989): 562–578. Neither essay refers to Kuhn. What I do here is place the discussion on the Popperian scientist's turf and then move toward a Popperian strategic management research tradition as one case example.

27. As a pragmatist, I approach these four lines of comparison as separate genres, and not some rigid typology of successively "deeper" levels. These are simply four different, albeit logically connected, variations on the same general theme. See Rorty, "Texts and Lumps," 7–12. I work in the spirit of Rorty's disclaimer about assigning to any one level a "deeper" meaning than any other: "From a pragmatist angle, this whole notion of privileging a level and putting it forward as a foundation of inquiry is one more unhappy attempt to save the notion of truth as correspondence" (12).

28. I prefer to talk in terms of "encounters some problem" rather than, say, "captures her fancy," in order to emphasize a choice available to her. The latter rhetoric could imply some foundationalist "fancy" waiting to be touched. I ascribe a feminist voice—"she"—quite deliberately throughout my argument about pragmatism. I do this to suggest pragmatism as an alternative to the male-dominated language of business and science, a language that Miller and Gilligan urge us to challenge.

29. I use the word "story" for a specific reason. Telling stories has acquired a pejorative meaning in social science discourse. Throughout the analysis, I use four terms interchangeably: "story," "narrative," "account," and "interpretation."

30. The key point is that a story is called into question by some discontinuity, or threat, to a person's guiding life story at any given time. Stories, in other words, can beget other stories. This is what Martin Packer describes as a "perspectival" feature of any story: "From one point of view it may seem sensible, whereas from another it may not. From one perspective an action has one meaning, from a different perspective it has another" ("Hermeneutic Inquiry in the Study of Human Conduct," *American Psychologist* 40, no. 10 [1985]: 1086). A story, in other words, can be interesting precisely because it can take on multiple meanings from which a storyteller can choose. Thus another way to understand this book is as a commentary on what strategic management researchers do with the contexts, which can be comprised of stories, in which persons choose to move.

31. This storytelling search is what Bruner seeks to discuss in terms of "possible worlds" (*Actual Minds*, 25–43). See Miller, *Toward a New Psychology of Women*, regarding stories told in a genre of domination (and subordination). See also S. Tepper, *The Gate to Women's Country* (New York: Bantam, 1989), for an account replete with men and women whose choices are conditioned, if not at times obliterated, through historical and cultural circumstance.

32. Kirk and Miller imply that social science researchers deny their interpretive activities because interpretive reasoning, in contrast to the Popperian method of objective reasoning, is more timid and less "scientific": "In another sense, 'objectivity' refers to taking an intellectual risk—the risk of being demonstrably wrong" (*Reliability and Validity*, 10). Think of my argument here as an acceptance of the gauntlet thrown down by Kirk and Miller. I will show that their chosen argument, in the context of the questions that I choose to raise, can be interpreted as demonstrably wrong. Kuhn, by contrast, adds an interpretive element to his account of "normal science." He argues that scientists are not selfless, transparent agents. Rather, "an apparently arbitrary element, compounded of personal and historical accident, is always a formative ingredient of the beliefs espoused by a given scientific community at a given time" (Kuhn,

Structure of Scientific Revolutions, 4). Moreover, Kuhn speaks to the drives of the individual scientist in a way that no dyed-in-the-wool positivist would admit: "Bringing a normal research problem to a conclusion is achieving the anticipated in a new way. . . . The man who succeeds proves himself an expert puzzle-solver, and the challenge of the puzzle is an important part of what usually drives him on" (36).

33. For an entertaining discussion of some metaphors of "hard" science, see Rosmarin, *Power of Genre,* 8–9. Conversations with Todd Hostager have been quite beneficial for me on this point. A recent variation on this search for Nature is the so-called naturalistic inquiry proposed in Y. Lincoln and E. Guba, *Naturalistic Inquiry* (Beverly Hills, Calif.: Sage, 1985). Lincoln and Guba propose an approach that is similar, in many respects, to the interpretive argument that I am reconstructing from Rorty, Rosmarin, Bruner, and Packer. But Lincoln and Guba take a very different position with regard to how they believe a researcher "knows" something: "[The naturalist] prefers to have the guiding substantive theory emerge from (be grounded in) the data because *no* a priori theory could possibly encompass the multiple realities that are likely to be encountered; because believing is seeing and [the naturalist] wishes to enter his transactions with respondents as neutrally as possible" (46 [Lincoln and Guba's emphasis]). Lincoln and Guba are searching for a discourse with Nature and thus want to pay homage with as "neutral"—presumably, though, reverent to Nature—a discourse as possible. Such "natural" dialogue is sharply at odds with the kind of interpretive approach whereby a researcher knows that she starts with a history of preferred interpretations that she cannot, and does not want to, escape. Lincoln and Guba can be understood to express a distinctly "nonneutral" preference, but they must deny this for their story to make sense.

34. Rorty, "Texts and Lumps," 15.

35. I follow the explanation of language as a pattern of conventions given in D. Lewis, *Convention: A Philosophical Study* (Cambridge, Mass.: Harvard University Press, 1969), 5–51. Language can be interpreted alternatively, of course, as some foundational set of symbols, or utterances, or sounds. As a pragmatist, I make no claim that Lewis's is an eternally secure meaning of language. Rather, his account is one that enables me to work through problems like the one that occupies me in this book.

36. Rorty, *Consequences of Pragmatism,* 199.

37. Ibid., 100. The objection is to "tool" as something inert and impervious to a user's influence.

38. A telltale sign in this regard is the priority given to empirical studies in the editorial policies of the *Strategic Management Journal, Academy of Management Journal, Administrative Science Quarterly,* and company. The positivist scientist, deferring to Nature's voice, commits what Fish calls a "total and debilitating relativism" that is also contradictory: "While relativism is a position one can entertain, it is not a position one can occupy. No one can *be* a relativist, because no one can achieve the distance from his own beliefs and assumptions which would result in their being no more authoritative *for him* than the beliefs and assertions held by others" (*Is There a Text,* 319 [Fish's emphasis]).

39. See R. Yin, *Case Study Research: Design and Methods* (Beverly Hills, Calif.: Sage 1984), 35–41. The emphasis on reliability suggests that a Popperian scientist *prefers* to operate on the assumption that researchers are "naturally" *un-*

reliable as observers of Nature. They must therefore check on one another's dependability, a curious Orwellian theme.

40. See Rorty, *Consequences of Pragmatism*, 94. This raises an interesting possibility that Ralph Ellison's *Invisible Man* could be read as a commentary on contemporary social science. See R. Ellison, *Invisible Man* (New York: Random House, 1952). Even when social scientists acknowledge that researchers are at least translucent, by making reference to others' works, those works are not the subject of inquiry. So this typical and begrudging acknowledgment takes the barren form of, for example, "*L* can be explained in terms of *P* (Tinker, 1916; Evers, 1929; Chance, 1914; Tinker et al., 1914)." What Tinker said, in particular, is apparently irrelevant. It is only important that he said it. Thus Tinker, Evers, and Chance are almost invisible as persons in this discourse.

41. Rorty, *Consequences of Pragmatism*, 94.

42. For an introduction to critical legal studies, see R. Unger, *The Critical Legal Studies Movement* (Cambridge, Mass.: Harvard University Press, 1986). The "critical" debate about legal truths can be carried forward in non-Marxian terms as well. See, for example, J. Frug, "Henry James, Lee Marvin, and the Law," *New York Times Book Review*, 16 February 1986, 1, 28–29.

43. Rorty, *Consequences of Pragmatism*, 92.

44. Rorty notes: "Pragmatism views knowledge not as a relation between mind and an object, but, roughly, as the ability to get agreement by using persuasion rather than force" ("Texts and Lumps," 11). Fish talks about this in terms of "shared agreement" as an alternative to an independently "authoritative" text: "Thus, while there is no core of agreement *in* the text, there is a core of agreement (although one subject to change) concerning the ways of *producing* the text" (*Is There a Text*, 342 [Fish's emphasis].

45. Bruner, *Actual Minds*, 122. I write Chapter 4 in this spirit. Bruner provides a "constructivist" account of human action, adapted from the arguments of Nelson Goodman (97, 159). Kuhn provides such an account of books written at one time about physical optics (*Structure of Scientific Revolutions*, 13). Constructivist accounts are more frequently appearing in management research. See, for example, L. Smircich and C. Stubbart, "Strategic Management in an Enacted World," *Academy of Management Review* 10, no. 4 (1985): 724–736; and even I. Maitland, J. Bryson, and A. Van de Ven, "Sociologists, Economists, and Opportunism," *Academy of Management Review* 10, no. 1 (1985): 59–65. Not all such accounts are alike, however. Little is gained if constructivist arguments are mere preludes to new forays into foundational truths. In this regard, see D. Gilbert, Jr., "Management, Persons, and the Business Novel" (Paper presented at the Annual Meeting, Academy of Management, New Orleans, Louisiana, August 1987).

46. See, for example, Smircich and Stubbart, "Strategic Management"; M. Calas and L. Smircich, "Using the 'F' Word: Feminist Theories and the Social Consequences of Organizational Research" (Paper presented at the Annual Meeting, Academy of Management, Washington, D.C., August 1989); and R. E. Freeman and D. Gilbert, Jr., *Corporate Strategy and the Search for Ethics* (Englewood Cliffs, N.J.: Prentice-Hall, 1988), 2–20, 158–175.

47. Fish, *Is There a Text*, 368.

48. We could thus explain failures at so-called participatory management

programs in terms of a prior disposition by managers to preserve a status quo language that precludes joint action.

49. That history, in turn, can be understood as a product of autonomous persons joining and departing a community. Louis Gottschalk observes elegantly: "Every man is . . . a historian having to compose, if only his own thoughts, his own history for his own understanding" (*Understanding History: A Primer of Historical Method,* 2nd ed. [New York: Knopf, 1969], 27). Bruner argues that each person commences such historical writing within a context: "What is 'given' or assumed at the outset of our construction is neither bedrock reality out there, nor an a priori: it is always another constructed version of a world that we have taken as given for certain purposes" (*Actual Minds,* 97). Those who claim to conduct "grounded" research seem to deny their own history or, in Bruner's words, their "certain purposes." Kuhn similarly eschews such a denial of starting place, which he pictures in terms of shared agreements about paradigms (*Structure of Scientific Revolutions,* 10–22).

50. Consider, as one of a host of examples, the current classification scheme used for professional minor league baseball. In the not-too-distant past, the most proficient players played at the AAA level, and the least proficient played at Class D. This made sense for many years, for a variety of reasons explained in K. Kerrane, *Dollar Sign on the Muscle: The World of Baseball Scouting* (New York: Simon and Schuster, 1984). One could read Kerrane's story as a commentary on the difficulty that many parties encounter in connecting the past and present stories that constitute baseball scouting. For a long period of time, the "AAA–D" story was a useful alternative to an earlier historical context when players were more difficult to find and engage in contractual relations. More recently, those in the baseball community altered the scheme to the point where A is the "lowest" level. This interesting Orwellian twist on language—where A is "bad"—can be understood in relation to the historical pattern of problems faced by persons in this community over almost a century. In short, the pragmatist argues, in effect, "We got here with a history that we cannot shake."

51. The difference can be interpreted as a gulf between persons as variables and persons as sources of measurement for variables that are detached from persons. See Gilbert, "Business Ethics." Clifford Geertz observes that those adopting the measurement approach seem bent on "turning culture into folklore and collecting it, turning it into traits and counting it, turning it into institutions and classifying it, turning it into structures and toying with it" (*The Interpretation of Culture* [New York: Basic Books, 1973], 29).

52. This contrasts sharply with the argument made by Donald Seibert and William Proctor, for example. Seibert and Proctor argue that a mature person must decide once, and once and for all, about a "personal philosophy of life." To do otherwise is to waffle, a sign of weakness. See D. Seibert and W. Proctor, *The Ethical Executive: A Top C.E.O.'s Program for Success with Integrity in the Corporate World* (New York: Simon and Schuster, 1984), 36. For an extensive counterargument, see Freeman and Gilbert, *Corporate Strategy.*

53. See Rorty, *Consequences of Pragmatism,* 92. What Kuhn does is reject one horizontal perspective and argue for another in historical terms: "Perhaps science does not develop by the accumulation of individual discoveries and inventions" (*Structure of Scientific Revolutions,* 2).

54. See Yin, *Case Study Research,* 47–53.

55. The literary genre of lonely scientist can follow from this, as interpretable, for example, in S. Lewis, *Arrowsmith* (New York: New American Library, 1961).

56. See Rorty, "Texts and Lumps," 7. From this assumption, we can understand a genre in which writers make villains of the lonely scientist, as Ayn Rand does with her character Dr. Robert Stadler. See A. Rand, *Atlas Shrugged* (New York: Signet, 1957), 990–993. The movie *Ghostbusters* can be understood as a satirical variation on this same theme about the scientist–hero.

57. H. Barnes, *An Existentialist Ethics* (Chicago: University of Chicago Press, 1985), 9.

58. Coles, *Call of Stories,* 90. Coles can help us understand that the mere act of using literature and "the liberal arts" in a community of persons talking about, say, management, is not necessarily a humanist practice. If we read various genres of literature merely to honor and idolize the status quo, we have missed an opportunity to become better readers and people. See D. Gilbert, Jr., "Management, Literary Criticism, and What We Could Say About the Matter of Control Over Others" (Paper presented at the Social Issues in Management Research Workshop, Annual Meeting, Academy of Management, Anaheim, California, August 1988).

59. Miller, *Toward a New Psychology of Women,* 114.

60. Ibid., 111. Miller discusses this ethical point in the following terms: "Despite all our commonality, each of us, each day, creates our own particular attempt to put the picture together, as it were."

61. By now, it should be clear that I have articulated these four questions in terms that are not only familiar to social scientists, but also "friendly" to their position. I have, to put it somewhat differently, created a genre with these four questions as a means of contrasting a pragmatist language and a positivist language about research. This is the general idea of the analysis that I conduct in Chapters 3, 4, and 5.

62. Rosmarin, *Power of Genre,* 4. Rosmarin discusses "theory" as an antonym for pragmatist interpretation, that is, theory as the medium through which Nature is seen.

63. What we could say here, however, is that the positivist scientist has simply ignored persons without any explicit justification for that act of omission and denial. Nietzsche minces few words in this regard: "They are all advocates who resent that name, and for the most part even wily spokesmen for their prejudices which they baptize 'truths' " (*Beyond Good and Evil,* 12–13). Quite prominent among such well-known prejudices in management research and organization science is the premise that you and I pose major decision-making difficulties for organizational leaders.

64. Alternatively, the well-read Kantian scientist could argue deftly that ethics is simply one more source of foundational truths to be mined through scientific methodology. Pick up an issue of the *Journal of Business Ethics* or *Academy of Management Journal* and you will likely run across an article in each issue that presents "ethics research" in this sense. For a rich discussion of this matter of enduring ethical truths that lie beyond a person's creative choice, see A. MacIntyre, *After Virtue: A Study in Moral Theory,* 2nd ed. (Notre Dame, Ind.: University of Notre Dame Press, 1984).

65. Consider, for example, the recent call for papers for a special *Strategic Management Journal* issue about "strategy content": "The first special issue will focus on theoretical and theory-based empirical work on strategy content." There is little mistaking the scientific drift here. To the pragmatist, a theory is simply another kind of story, no more privileged than any other story as a candidate for our application to the problems that we confront in our lives.

66. There is no finish line in this pragmatist story. We simply create better stories to solve our problems as they appear and unfold.

67. J. Elster, *Ulysses and the Sirens: Studies in Rationality and Irrationality,* rev. ed. (Cambridge: Cambridge University Press, 1984), 4.

68. I employ a means of argument here that Rorty terms "rational reconstruction." See R. Rorty, "The Historiography of Philosophy: Four Genres," in R. Rorty, J. Schneewind, and Q. Skinner, eds., *Philosophy in History* (Cambridge: Cambridge University Press, 1984), 49–56. The idea is that we can chart our progress in creating increasingly useful stories if we engage others who, while not necessarily prone now to speaking our language, could be "reeducated"—persuaded—by our story to do so. Rorty thus writes of hypothetical conversations with the "mighty dead" philosophers.

69. I have no one specific in mind as I name my characters, so any correspondence between my characterizations of persons who pursue these kinds of research and actual persons is coincidental. Nonetheless, I do choose each of these names as a small way of thanking privately those who have supported my research as fellow pragmatists.

70. Again, I do not intend to pattern LaFleur after the story of anyone I know. Still, I am well acquainted with the context of this particular story. A note of gratitude can be read between the lines.

71. See P. Miller, "Tornado!" *National Geographic* 171, no. 6 (1987): 690–715; W. Reifsnyder, *Weathering the Wilderness: The Sierra Club Guide to Practical Meteorology* (San Francisco: Sierra Club Books, 1980); and "Stalking the Savage Storm," *U.S. News & World Report,* 24 July 1989, 48–55.

72. Although the orthodox management scientist might be tempted to claim that I am guilty here of "reductionism," I stand guilty only in the context of the kind of stories that he chooses to tell. That story, in particular, has little if any room for individuals. Hence, by comparison, my story is told at a level of analysis that, in relation to the management scientist's designs for a "grand theory," is "reduced" in scope. What we must keep in mind is that his kind of story is no more or less privileged than is my genre about researchers' choices. We simply are pursuing different kinds of problems for different purposes. On a pragmatist view, he is as eligible as I am to be called on the carpet of the critic who asks, "What does your story do for you and the persons in the community it reaches?"

73. Michael Keeley makes the point that organization theorists often uncritically tend to collaborate, as evident in the stories that they produce, with the managerial elite at a given firm. M. Keeley, *A Social-Contract Theory of Organizations* (Notre Dame, Ind.: University of Notre Dame Press, 1988). For a critique of the unstated search for power to which social scientists can succumb, see W. Woodworth, "The Politics of Intervention Theory: Ideology in Social Science" (Ph.D. diss., University of Michigan, 1974). I thank Gordon Meyer for bringing this dissertation to my attention.

74. I do not mean to imply any kind of vertical relationship here between language and genre, whereby one is a "deeper" level of meaning than the other. Rather, we can think of one as a commentary related to the other. I follow Rosmarin, who claims that a genre is "the critic's heuristic tool" (*Power of Genre*, 25). That tool can be applied *in* a language, as Rorty puts it.

75. In that customary language of science, such a storm is "identified." See "Stalking the Savage Storm," 51.

76. Booth urges us to think about this kind of language, as with any language, as a genre of masquerade: "We must never forget that though the author can to some extent choose his disguises, he can never choose to disappear" (*Rhetoric of Fiction*, 20).

77. There is reason to question whether "global business" is a language distinguishable from other business world languages, with its own special set of problems at the heart of a discourse. A literary critic could make a significant contribution in this context someday soon, given the rush to "internationalize" business school curricula.

78. Note that the language of socialization is hardly value-free. One implication is that immigrants must adapt to American customs. For a discussion about alternative genres of the "American way" that social historians are telling these days, see M. Kazin, "The New Historians Recapture the Flag," *New York Times Book Review*, 2 July 1989, 1, 19, 21.

79. Rorty observes that we could also choose not to engage in such a discussion if we want instead to understand "that there have been different forms of intellectual life than ours" ("Historiography of Philosophy," 51). He refers to this act of leaving our intellectual ancestors "alone" as "historical reconstruction." If that is the only kind of permissible historical inquiry, however, then we can never critique a "great dead writer" in the context of our lives and concerns. Hence, we also need to "converse" with our intellectual ancestors—via rational reconstruction—in search of stories that descend from our ancestors' stories.

80. Consider the two different meanings of the verb "table" in legislative discussions on the North American continent. Canadian parliamentarians and United States legislators find it in their respective interests to agree on a meaning that is local to their communities but contradictory to the meaning used in the other community. Neither meaning is correct, in some universal sense. Thus persons in these two communities might face the prospects of a frustrated dialogue when they cross the "boundaries" between their communities.

81. The attribution of gender to "unscientific" belief might not be coincidental. Regarding the (male) language of science, see Miller, *Toward a New Psychology of Women*, 56.

82. In this way, an aggregate barometer on "business ethics," for example, can carry a trace of human meaning, but little more. A key pragmatist question is this: Why is it important that you know that 34 percent of left-handed, baseball-loving, Pennsylvania house painters value XYZ strongly? Regarding the "science" of business ethics, see Gilbert, "Business Ethics."

83. Regarding the failure of utilitarians to "take seriously the distinction between persons," see Rawls, *Theory of Justice*, 27.

84. Weather forecasters frequently try to engage us in conversation—for example, "Carry an umbrella tomorrow"—but they arrange their stories in such

a way that we cannot respond to them as storytellers. Their advice, although appreciated, is not part of a discourse with us. We are excluded from the meteorologist's stories and, hence, community. Note how a naturalist, who can tell a story in terms of your role and mine in an ecosystem, begins to outdo the meteorologist in pragmatist terms.

85. Meteorologists *could* tell a pragmatist story in terms of me as, say, a "rainmaker." But they would need to turn their stories about climatic phenemona inside out to tell that kind of story.

86. This raises an interesting possibility for a genre of management research: reading biographies and autobiographies as "data" rather than the typical "data instrument" approach of social science.

87. LaFleur has, in short, generalized her story to pertain to her and her subject's life. It is curious to note that the term "comparable worth," as applied in contemporary discourse about labor markets, is used as a genre about comparably worthy *jobs,* not persons.

88. My historian father, Daniel R. Gilbert, Sr., has helped me understand why "could" is the appropriate message here, as modern historical research has been encroached upon by social science.

89. I follow Miller and Rosmarin here in giving reasons for my argument in a Hegelian way. As Miller puts it: "Growth requires engagement with difference and with people embodying that difference." (*Toward a New Psychology of Women,* 13). See also Rosmarin, *Power of Genre,* 46.

90. Regarding "possible worlds," see Bruner, *Actual Minds,* 11–43.

91. The popularity of multiple regression analysis, in search of a greater and greater explanation of deviation from Nature, follows from this belief.

92. A key implication of pragmatism, then, is that meanings can be "up for grabs." Furthermore, the meaning of a concept can, on a pragmatist account, be explained as "stable" insofar as persons in a community continue to find their own respective reasons for agreeing to that meaning. For an account tinged, in part, with a fear of such a contingent understanding of meaning, see MacIntyre, *After Virtue.* For an account that emphasizes the usefulness of such stable meaning, see Kuhn, *Structure of Scientific Revolutions.*

93. A contemporary example of this is the growing community of "social issues in management" researchers who, by and large, apply classical positivist methodology to a class of "social," as opposed apparently to "business," cases.

94. For one example, see the Rely Game analysis in Freeman and Gilbert, *Corporate Strategy,* 91–105. Explaining that kind of humanist analysis to members of the orthodox strategic management research community was no walk in the park. Our effort there was, in part, to break the grip of the assumption that *role* determines a person's behavior. Regarding Rill, in particular, see "Putting the 'Anti' Back into the Antitrust Division," *Business Week,* 19 June 1989, 64, 68, 70.

95. J. Hillis Miller discusses the need to act consistently in this regard in terms of an "ethical moment" that reader and writer alike can experience. See J. H. Miller, *The Ethics of Reading: Kant, de Man, Eliot, Trollope, James, and Benjamin* (New York: Columbia University Press, 1987), 4, 43. On a similar note, Packer reminds researchers: "As social agents ourselves, we always find meaning in a course of action, not by abstracting from it a logical structure but by understanding what human purpose and interests the action serves" ("Herme-

neutic Inquiry," 1086). In no small way, this issue comes down to a researcher's choice to act in good faith with respect to persons in his audience. As examples of anticommunity beliefs that dominate certain management research quarters, consider the lesser status commonly accorded invited works and "commissioned" histories.

96. By conducting the analysis in the customary language of strategic management research, I give Strategy through Process a "home field advantage." If Strategy & Justice can outperform Strategy through Process on this turf, then so much the worse for the meaningfulness of contemporary strategic management research.

97. In my rational reconstruction project, then (see note 68), I arrange for a conversation among a certain group of prominent, very much alive strategic management researchers.

98. I draw primarily on Rawls and Gauthier here. For a brief introduction to a contractarian moral genre, see, in particular, Gauthier, *Morals by Agreement*, 17–20.

99. I place my justification, in other words, in the context of a community in which I can join scientists in a discussion about possible languages for validity, reliability, and generalizability. Again, as Rosmarin notes, a pragmatist can find precisely as many genres as she needs to make her point (*Power of Genre*, 25).

100. This is only to say that management scientists give meaning to their data in a different language that is used to solve a different problem.

101. For this reason, I set myself up for criticism inasmuch as I sketched a relatively bare genre in Chapter 1—with reference to Drucker, Katz and Kahn, and others—about the necessary demise of persons in organization science. In other words, I argued "validly" but, in the scientist's terms, rather unreliably with respect to the texts written by those researchers. I *could* make that genre more substantive if that were necessary to strengthen my point there in some crucial way, which is not the case.

102. Bruner, *Actual Minds*, 123 (Bruner's emphasis).

103. It does not, however, follow from my pragmatist account of generalizability that the next step is to develop a taxonomy—a social scientist's favorite project—of Strategy through Process. I create Strategy through Process as a genre that helps me argue about the vast shortcomings, in humanist terms, of contemporary strategic management research. Strategy through Process is an option that I choose to employ, in other words. Taxonomies are optional, too. If, in the course of your joining me in a community "convened" to discuss the issues that I pose, you get the urge to start drawing taxonomic charts and the like, stop yourself. That act will impede, if not end, our dialogue.

104. More generally, I apply a case research method here, where replication—a pragmatist's kind of generalizability—serves as a key criterion for defending a particular study. See Yin, *Case Study Research*, 48–53.

105. As Yin carefully explains, to ask about sampling is to ask an inappropriate question of a case researcher and, hence, a pragmatist researcher (ibid., 39–40, 48–53).

106. I do, in a literal sense, take a strategic management researcher's text out of the context of his time and place and purpose. But I very carefully create a context—the Problem of Strategic Management in Chapter 3—within

which to relocate his text. If such an act were impermissible, then no critical discussions are possible. In fact, if my act of "reading out of context" is not permitted, then so, too, is the effort of *any* researcher—pragmatist or not—to develop a literature review within which his work can be situated. Indeed, to relish research as an interpretive discourse is to accede to having one's arguments taken out of one context and reconstructed in another. For an entertaining rendition of this line of reasoning, see the comments about "encoding" and "decoding" attributed to the fictitious Morris Zapp, in D. Lodge, *Small World: An Academic Romance* (New York: Warner Books, 1984), 29–30.

107. Fish, *Is There a Text*, 356.

108. Kirk and Miller argue that Popperian science "properly contrasts the scientific enterprise with others (such as art or ethics) in which practitioners do not routinely subject their theories to that sort of empirical risk, or their egos to the potential of battery not only by the arguments of intellectual adversaries but also by the demonstrative refutation of the empirical world" (*Reliability and Validity*, 11). I elected to write Chapter 2 with a particular genre that can provide "demonstrative" evidence that the Kirk–Miller perspective on rigor is nothing more than one option, and a timid one at that.

Chapter 3

1. See S. Lewis, *Babbitt* (New York: New American Library, 1961), 100. I use STP with the permission of First Brands Corporation, which holds a registered trademark for STP automotive products.

2. I create this possible forum on the postmodern premise that we create truths through an ongoing discourse with one another. I follow the arguments of Richard Rorty here, in particular. See R. Rorty, "Texts and Lumps," *New Literary History* 17, no. 1 (1985): 1–16. Conversations with Thelma Lavine, Linda Smircich, and Robbin Derry have been particularly helpful to me in this regard. My intent throughout the practice of placing corporate strategy in twilight is to make a favorable case for the corporate strategy concept by casting that twilight on the "home turf" of strategic management research.

3. I consider Strategy through Process to be a further development of, and one justification for, the premises of the unnamed genre with which we critically analyzed strategic management research in D. Gilbert, Jr., E. Hartman, J. Mauriel, and R. E. Freeman, *A Logic for Strategy* (New York: Harper & Row, 1988), 5–6. This link is one sense by which I claim to give Strategy through Process a fair hearing in twilight.

4. I have no particular persons in mind as I identify the characters in this story. Any resemblance is thus coincidental. There are, of course, clear reasons for choosing these names. I played for the Red Devils. Rocket is a cat.

5. Once again, I have no particular person in mind as a model for Beleaguered. My brief story is a composite of events unfolding at a variety of colleges and universities, including Bucknell. One way to interpret this pattern of turmoil is in terms of the unwillingness of Greek-letter society supporters to self-critically consider the meanings of their efforts, particularly as they affect others.

6. This story is likewise a composite tale about the complexity of managing a local telephone company.

7. In other words, I find little use for the well-known distinction between long-term and short-term concerns. If we choose to understand persons in a pragmatist, literary sense, then we can choose to tell stories about their lives in terms of a past connected to a present connected to a future. Alternatively, we can saddle ourselves with an idiosyncratic conception of personhood if we make use of the temporal distinction that many management researchers idolize.

8. It is common practice among writers in the business media to talk about strategy in such insular terms. See, for example, "NCR Is Finding Out that No Strategy Works Forever," *Business Week*, 30 January 1989, 80–81. Interestingly, NCR executives have quietly pulled back from their self-proclaimed concern with stakeholders, a concern that would have been one avenue to escape the temptation to think about strategy as something NCR perpetrates on the rest of the world. I commented on this same kind of story line in D. Gilbert, Jr., *"The Deal of the Century: The Breakup of AT&T,* by Steven Coll; *Chronicles of Corporate Change: Management Lessons from AT&T and Its Offspring,* by Leonard A. Schlesinger, Davis Dyer, Thomas N. Clough, and Diane Landau; *The Fall of the Bell System: A Study in Prices and Politics,* by Peter Temin, with Louis Galambos; *Disconnecting Parties: Managing the Bell System Break-Up: An Inside View,* by W. Brooke Tunstall"* (book review), *Academy of Management Review* 14, no. 1 (1989): 107–110.

9. By this interpretation of personal benefit in a web of relationships with others seeking their own gains, I set up the possibility that we can talk about corporate strategy in a different way. Specifically, that alternative language does not turn on the ethical egoism implied by the popular theme of "getting one's own act together" (see note 8). See, in this regard, R. E. Freeman and D. Gilbert, Jr., *Corporate Strategy and the Search for Ethics* (Englewood Cliffs, N.J.: Prentice-Hall, 1988), 158–170.

10. I develop this connection between values ("reasons for acting"), belief ("value of acting"), and action from D. Davidson, "Actions, Reasons, and Causes," *Journal of Philosophy* 60 (1963): 685–700. With this connection between decision and action, I set myself apart from the decision–action distinction that Henry Mintzberg prefers to use to defend his story about "strategy formation." H. Mintzberg, "The Design School: Reconsidering the Basic Premises of Strategic Management," *Strategic Management Journal* 11 (1990): 171–195.

11. K. Andrews, *The Concept of Corporate Strategy,* rev. ed. (Homewood, Ill.: Irwin, 1980), 46. For an account that praises the pragmatist promise of Andrews's arguments, see Gilbert, Hartman, Mauriel, and Freeman, *Logic for Strategy,* 39–54.

12. I am performing case study research here, with my interest in replicating ("cast my interpretation more widely") this conception of strategy. In this regard, I follow R. Yin, *Case Study Research: Design and Methods* (Beverly Hills, Calif.: Sage 1984), 48–54.

13. For another critical consideration of the arguments made by Chandler and Barnard, see Gilbert, Hartman, Mauriel, and Freeman, *Logic for Strategy,* 10–13.

14. A. Chandler, Jr., *Strategy and Structure: Chapters in the History of the American Industrial Enterprise* (Cambridge, Mass.: MIT Press, 1962), 15.

15. A. Chandler, Jr., *The Visible Hand: The Managerial Revolution in America* (Cambridge, Mass.: Belknap Press, 1977), 12.

16. Chandler, *Strategy and Structure*, 383–396.

17. Ibid., 13.

18. Ibid., 385.

19. C. Barnard, *The Functions of the Executive,* Thirtieth Anniversary Edition (Cambridge, Mass.: Harvard University Press, 1968), 189, 196–199, 231–234.

20. Ibid., 241.

21. Ibid., 57.

22. Likewise, this generic concern with "individual satisfaction" can be understood as an intellectual ancestor of the stakeholder genre of strategic management research. One telltale sign of the absence of meaningful critical discourse in strategic management research is the peripheral place assigned to Barnard's work. Furthermore, upon comparing Barnard's arguments with the orthodoxy in contemporary strategic management research, one could conclude that little progress has been made in the latter over the past fifty years. That conclusion, of course, turns on a premise that Barnard has something useful to "say" to us, a position that I am defending.

23. Mintzberg has extended the reach of his "strategy formation" genre to include this physiological metaphor about the corporation ("Design School," 172–179). For a critique of such unquestioned synthesis, see Gilbert, Hartman, Mauriel, and Freeman, *Logic for Strategy,* 153–159. One wonders, from a pragmatist perspective, why so-called ecological perspectives on corporate strategy have any worldly relevance for decision-makers to whom those perspectives are aimed. In other words, Mintzberg's typological, or taxonomic, efforts can make a great deal of sense if we choose to believe that persons' decisions at the corporation make little, if any, difference. The choices are ours.

24. Chandler, *Strategy and Structure,* 13.

25. This diversity is but one condition, since I also want to demonstrate the concurrence between my interpretation and the writings of other strategic management researchers. I follow this Hegelian strategy in the spirit of A. Rosmarin, *The Power of Genre* (Minneapolis: University of Minnesota Press, 1985).

26. I thus literally remove these twelve "voices" from their isolated contexts and join them in a new interpretive context that I create. This act of purposefully specifying contexts for discourse, and then drawing on specific texts to enrich that discourse, is developed in the spirit of what Rosmarin calls an "expressly deductive genre criticism" (ibid., 23–25). By creating the Problem of Strategic Management with the purpose in mind of eventually critiquing Strategy through Process, and defending the premises of the Problem of Strategic Management with a reading of these twelve texts, I provide in effect one justification for the three principles that we deduced in Gilbert, Hartman, Mauriel, and Freeman, *Logic of Strategy,* 5–19. In short, I offer one justification here for our assertion of those criteria.

27. H. I. Ansoff, *The New Corporate Strategy* (New York: Wiley, 1988), 5 (Ansoff's emphasis).

28. Ibid., 5–6.

29. Ibid., xviii.

30. I have chosen to read and interpret three of Harrigan's arguments in this regard. See K. Harrigan, *Strategies for Declining Businesses* (Lexington, Mass.:

Lexington Books, 1980); *Strategic Flexibility: A Management Guide for Changing Times* (Lexington, Mass.: Lexington Books, 1985); and *Managing for Joint Venture Success* (Lexington, Mass.: Lexington Books, 1986). I choose the last with particular regard to her commentary about relationships with actors—such as venture partners—in the firm's environment.

31. Harrigan, *Strategies for Declining Businesses*, 2.

32. Harrigan, *Strategic Flexibility*, 1.

33. L. Hrebiniak and W. Joyce, *Implementing Strategy* (New York: Macmillan, 1984), 28 (Hrebiniak and Joyce's emphasis).

34. Ibid., 29 (Hrebiniak and Joyce's emphasis).

35. P. Lorange, *Corporate Planning: An Executive Viewpoint* (Englewood Cliffs, N.J.: Prentice-Hall, 1980), 4. See also R. Vancil and P. Lorange, "Strategic Planning in Diversified Companies," *Harvard Business Review*, January–February 1975, 81–90.

36. R. H. Miles, *Coffin Nails and Corporate Strategy* (Englewood Cliffs, N.J.: Prentice-Hall, 1982), xix.

37. R. E. Miles and C. Snow, *Organizational Strategy, Structure, and Process* (New York: McGraw-Hill, 1978), 7 (Miles and Snow's emphasis).

38. Ibid., 18.

39. Ibid., 11.

40. M. Porter, *Competitive Strategy: Techniques for Analyzing Industries and Competitors* (New York: Free Press, 1980), xiii.

41. Ibid., 34.

42. J. B. Quinn, *Strategies for Change: Logical Incrementalism* (Homewood, Ill.: Irwin, 1980), 8 (Quinn's emphasis).

43. J. B. Quinn, H. Mintzberg, and R. James, *The Strategy Process: Concepts, Contexts, and Cases* (Englewood Cliffs, N.J.: Prentice-Hall, 1988), xi.

44. A. Rappaport, *Creating Shareholder Value: The New Standard for Business Performance* (New York: Free Press, 1986), xiv.

45. Ibid., 11–12.

46. D. Schendel and C. Hofer, "Introduction," in D. Schendel and C. Hofer, eds., *Strategic Management: A New View of Business Policy and Planning* (Boston: Little, Brown, 1979), 6.

47. My interpretive approach is a "horizontal" attempt to extend the interpretation of the Problem of Strategic Management in numerous directions. I thus proceed in the spirit of a horizontal search for truth, as discussed in R. Rorty, *Consequences of Pragmatism* (Minneapolis: University of Minnesota Press, 1982), 92.

48. By "ethical" I mean that this story line can be interpreted as a commentary about some subjects that interest those engaged in ethical inquiry. Most prominent among those subjects are persons, their aspirations, and their relationships with one another. Certainly, other lines of inquiry can cover a similar territory with a different language. Thus my ethical genre holds no unerring or eternal priority. It is simply, and powerfully, useful for my ends.

49. The point is that I interpret Strategy through Process in the "friendly" venue of the Problem of Strategic Management, using the language with which strategic management researchers are familiar and comfortable.

50. Once again, I deliberately use the feminine pronoun when referring to the pragmatist researcher. I do this consistently to emphasize that the prag-

matist and feminine voices are outsiders to the dominant language and discourse in strategic management research and management science more generally.

51. Some researchers are prone to call such common understandings "paradigms." On a pragmatist account, what counts are the ongoing searches for personal meanings through discourse.

52. My efforts here can be understood as a variation on the practice of "rational reconstruction" for philosophical discourse. See R. Rorty, "The Historiography of Philosophy: Four Genres," in R. Rorty, J. Schneewind, and Q. Skinner, eds., *Philosophy in History* (Cambridge: Cambridge University Press, 1984), 49–56.

53. J. B. Miller, *Toward a New Psychology of Women,* 2nd ed. (Boston: Beacon Press, 1986), 140.

54. Ibid.

55. For an entertaining, informative, but not pragmatist, account of the language used by economists, see D. McCloskey, *The Rhetoric of Economics* (Madison: University of Wisconsin Press, 1985).

56. Note that in all these cases, the *stability* of certain meanings is clear. Yet we need not automatically explain such stability in terms of some deep structure of the world or mind. Thomas Schelling makes this point masterfully. Jerome Bruner, on the contrary, cannot quite bring himself to eschew a foundationalist explanation. In particular, he infers from "possible worlds" a natural structure of literary forms. See T. Schelling, *Micromotives and Macrobehavior* (New York: Norton, 1978); and J. Bruner, *Actual Minds, Possible Worlds* (Cambridge, Mass.: Harvard University Press, 1986), 159.

57. For two recent surveys of the boundaries commonly presumed true for strategic management research, see J. Grant, ed., *Strategic Management Frontiers* (Greenwich, Conn.: JAI Press, 1988); and J. Fredrickson, ed., *Perspectives on Strategic Management* (New York: Harper & Row, 1990).

58. L. Fahey and H. K. Christensen, "Evaluating the Research on Strategy Content," *Journal of Management* 12, no. 2 (1986): 168.

59. Ibid., 168–170, 180–183.

60. A. Huff and R. Reger, "A Review of Strategic Process Research," *Journal of Management* 13, no. 2 (1987): 211–236.

61. Ibid., 211.

62. Put bluntly, strategy content and strategy process are two optional ways of talking. Each concept can be worthwhile insofar as persons find use for it in their associations and discourses. I do not, however, find the distinction meaningful for my purposes here.

63. Andrews, *Concept of Corporate Strategy,* iv.

64. Schendel and Hofer, "Introduction," 17.

65. Quinn, Mintzberg, and James, *Strategy Process,* xxii.

66. Lorange discusses implementation in terms of implementing a strategic planning system, which is a more limited conception than the one advocated by Hrebiniak and Joyce. See Lorange, *Corporate Planning,* 11, 211, and P. Lorange, *Implementation of Strategic Planning* (Englewood Cliffs, N.J.: Prentice-Hall, 1979).

67. M. Porter, *Competitive Advantage: Creating and Sustaining Superior Performance* (New York: Free Press, 1985) 3.

68. Ibid., 33–61.

69. Rappaport, *Creating Shareholder Value,* 11.

70. Quinn, *Strategies for Change,* 8.

71. This convergence on a shareholderless story should hardly be surprising. These three arguments draw on contemporary organization science where few persons, shareholder or not, are deemed relevant.

72. Andrews, *Concept of Corporate Strategy,* 79.

73. Harrigan, *Managing for Joint Venture Success,* 193.

74. Harrigan, *Strategies for Declining Businesses,* 1.

75. See, for example, the bibliographies in Porter, *Competitive Strategy* and *Competitive Advantage.*

76. What can be meaningful here, I claim, is the new understanding(s) that we can develop by means of this single story line. Thus Strategy through Process is clearly a literary device that takes on meaning in the context of persons who write about corporate strategy and act on the basis of those writings. In another time and place for interpretive discourse, Strategy through Process might serve no useful purpose.

77. I use the word "proviso," rather than "assumption" or "premise," only to emphasize the widespread de facto argument among my group of twelve that this is how a contemporary strategic management researcher *should* think. When it comes time to critically assess Strategy through Process, I set aside the distinction among provisos, assumptions, and premises.

78. By this logic of strategy acquisition, the distinction between strategy formulation and strategy formation—a distinction that Mintzberg takes to be crucial—becomes unimportant. See H. Mintzberg, "Strategy Formation: Schools of Thought," in Fredrickson, *Perspectives on Strategic Management,* 105–235; and "Mintzberg Design School." One way to talk about corporate strategy without using Mintzberg's distinction is reconstructed in Gilbert, Hartman, Mauriel, and Freeman, *Logic for Strategy,* 127–143.

79. For an account of the "birth" of the RHCs, see W. B. Tunstall, *Disconnecting Parties: Managing the Bell System Break-Up: An Inside View* (New York: McGraw-Hill, 1985).

80. I create this case from a variety of published sources in the business press. I have not discussed these issues with anyone at Bell Atlantic Corporation. That step is not necessary for what I intend to do with this case.

81. See *Bell Atlantic 1988 Annual Report* (Philadelphia: Bell Atlantic, 1988), 4.

82. Ibid., 30–33. For 1988, local service accounted for almost 40 percent of Bell Atlantic revenues. The ratios for 1986 and 1987 were also in the neighborhood of 40 percent.

83. See, for example, L. Fish, "Rivals Challenge Bell Local Service," *Philadelphia Inquirer,* 11 June 1990, C1, C9; and J. Lopez, "Bells Feel Heat from Upstarts in Fiber Optics," *Wall Street Journal,* 27 December 1989, B1, B4.

84. For an informative discussion of the history of pricing practices in the telecommunications industry, see P. Temin, with L. Galambos, *The Fall of the Bell System: A Study in Prices and Politics* (Cambridge: Cambridge University Press, 1987). I am grateful to Edward Block at AT&T for bringing this study to my attention. It is significant to note that in the 1988 Bell Atlantic annual report, the scenes extolling Bell Atlantic products and services deal in each case with institutional, not residential, customers (*Bell Atlantic 1988 Annual Report,* 9–10, 13–14, 17–18, 21–22).

85. J. Keller, "Cellular Phones Dial Digital for Growth," *Wall Street Journal*, 14 May 1990, B1, B7.

86. J. Lopez and M. Carnevale, "Phone Firms Are Becoming Poles Apart," *Wall Street Journal*, 9 February 1990, B5; S. Gannes, "Behold, The Bell Tel Cell War," *Fortune*, 22 December 1986, 97–98, 102.

87. A. Gnoffo, "Ringing in New Year, New Chief for Bell," *Philadelphia Inquirer*, 2 January 1989, E1.

88. Executives at the Bell RHCs blame the continued oversight by U.S. District Judge Harold Greene for their lack of financial incentives to accelerate network enhancements. See, for example, the Bell Atlantic advertisement entitled "Can you imagine living in a country that limits the flow of information to its students? You do" (*Richmond Times-Dispatch*, 19 January 1990, A7). For an overview of Greene's role in this story and related stories, see "Should the U.S. Free the Baby Bells?" *Business Week*, 12 March 1990, 118–128.

89. See, for example, C. Sims, "AT&T Is Granted Greater Freedom to Set Its Prices," *New York Times*, 17 March 1989, A1, D4; and K. Bradsher, "Freer Rein on AT&T Is Proposed," *New York Times*, 9 March 1990, D1, D4.

90. The irony here is that the "level playing field" metaphor was reportedly used by AT&T executives, prior to the 1984 divestiture, with regard to warding off AT&T competitors. For an account of the AT&T role in the information services marketplace, see C. Sims, "Judge Will Allow AT&T to Publish Electronic Data," *New York Times*, 29 August 1989, 1, 34; and M. Carnevale and J. Lopez, "Many Waiting for AT&T's Electronic Publishing Move," *Wall Street Journal*, 2 August 1989, B1–B2.

91. See, for example, "Should the U.S. Free the Baby Bells?" 125; R. Smith, "California Rule on Phone Rates May Aid Trend," *Wall Street Journal*, 12 October 1989, B1, B6; and B. Davis, "Many States Deregulate Telephone Rates, Hurting Residential Users in Short Run," *Wall Street Journal*, 19 September 1986, 21.

92. See, for example, A. Gnoffo, "A Growing Call for Rate Shifts," *Philadelphia Inquirer*, 20 March 1989, D1, D7; L. Fish, "Bell Admits Abuses Were Widespread," *Philadelphia Inquirer*, 14 September 1989, A1, A4; and R. Zausner, "Bell to Pay $41.8 Million Over Sales Pitches," *Philadelphia Inquirer*, 11 April 1990, B1, B7.

93. See, for example, C. Sims, "The Baby Bells Scramble for Europe," *New York Times*, 10 December 1989, sec. 3, 1, 8–9; and "The Baby Bells Take Their Show on the Road," *Business Week*, 25 June 1990, 104–106. With specific regard to Bell Atlantic, see M. Carnevale, "Ameritech, Bell Atlantic Will Operate Under Little Restraint in New Zealand," *Wall Street Journal*, 15 June 1990, A4; "Bell Atlantic Corp., US West Set Venture with Czechoslovakia," *Wall Street Journal*, 21 June 1990, B2; L. Fish, "Bell Wins Contract in Argentina," *Philadelphia Inquirer*, 29 June 1990, C10, C16; and L. Fish, "Bell Rings Abroad for Expansion," *Philadelphia Inquirer*, 2 July 1990, D1, D8.

94. Lopez and Carnevale, "Phone Firms Are Becoming Poles Apart."

95. J. Lopez, "New Telephone Services Fail to Connect," *Wall Street Journal*, 23 May 1989, B1; R. Smith, "People Got Hooked, But Then Abandoned, Telephone 'Gateways,' " *Wall Street Journal*, 15 March 1990, A1, A8.

96. See, for example, Lopez, "New Telephone Services."

97. Gnoffo, "Ringing in New Year," E6.

98. *Bell Atlantic 1988 Annual Report*, 19–20.

99. See, for example, "The Tangle of Problems Hanging Up NYNEX," *Business Week*, 19 February 1990, 124–130.

100. J. Lopez, "Bell Atlantic Hopes to Cut 1,200 Jobs in Consolidation," *Wall Street Journal*, 15 September 1989, A7.

101. John Grant refers to this pair of activities as the "basic organizing paradigm" of strategic management research in J. Grant, "Strategy in Research and Practice," in Grant, *Strategic Management Frontiers*, 7. Check any strategic management textbook, including Quinn, Mintzberg, and James, *The Strategy Process*, for evidence of the wide concurrence with Grant's assertion.

102. See, for example, D. Hambrick and A. Cannella, "Strategy Implementation as Substance and Selling," *Academy of Management Executive* 3, no. 4 (1989): 278–285.

103. This proviso can be interpreted as a restatement and extension of the Expert Corollary in Freeman and Gilbert, *Corporate Strategy*, 150. More generally, I intend my efforts at placing corporate strategy in twilight as one pragmatist justification for the claims made in *Corporate Strategy and the Search for Ethics*. I am grateful to Robert Solomon and Edwin Hartman for their assistance in distinguishing between (1) the possible connection between ethics and strategy and (2) the reasons for talking about that connection. I wrote this book primarily with the latter concern in mind.

104. With reference to Table 3.1, Andrews, *Concept of Corporate Strategy*, viii, 170.

105. With reference to Table 3.1, Ansoff, *New Corporate Strategy*, vii, 91, 231.

106. With reference to Table 3.1, Harrigan, *Strategic Flexibility*, 3; *Strategies for Declining Businesses*, 50; and *Managing for Joint Venture Success*, 4.

107. With reference to Table 3.1, Hrebiniak and Joyce, *Implementing Strategy*, 29, 3.

108. With reference to Table 3.1, Lorange, *Corporate Planning*, 12, 8.

109. With reference to Table 3.1, Miles, *Coffin Nails*, 256. See also Miles's comments about the "primary responsibility of strategic managers" (50) and "the quality of executive leadership" (193).

110. With reference to Table 3.1, Miles and Snow, *Organizational Strategy*, 21, 20, 153. Regarding the imperative that future managers concern themselves with "*how* decisions should be made," as opposed to the meaning of those decisions, see also 164–165.

111. With reference to Table 3.1, Porter, *Competitive Advantage*, xv, and *Competitive Strategy*, ix, xiv.

112. With reference to Table 3.1, Quinn, *Strategies for Change*, 181, 58. Note also the discussion about who is involved in the "real integration" of strategy components (57).

113. With reference to Table 3.1, Quinn, Mintzberg, and James, *Strategy Process*, 21, xiii.

114. With reference to Table 3.1, Rappaport, *Creating Shareholder Value*, 100, 101.

115. With reference to Table 3.1, Schendel and Hofer, "Introduction," 1, 6, 14.

116. Once again, I am concerned here with the language that strategic management researchers working in the Strategy through Process genre, and their counterparts in the business media, use for spinning stories about corporate strategy. I do not attribute this hostile perspective to anyone at Bell Atlantic.

117. With reference to Table 3.2, K. Andrews, *The Concept of Corporate Strategy*, 3rd ed. (Homewood, Ill.: Irwin, 1987), 36, 39.

118. With reference to Table 3.2, Ansoff, *New Corporate Strategy*, 173, 14, 15.

119. With reference to Table 3.2, Harrigan, *Strategies for Declining Businesses*, 32, 33, 50. Note that even though Harrigan urges us to think in more collaborative terms—of which joint venturing is one vehicle—her argument still places this new version of the organization—the joint venture—against hostile forces beyond the firm and venture. This very limited sense of collaboration thus does not contradict her "contribution" to the proviso in question here (*Managing for Joint Venture Success*, 13).

120. With reference to Table 3.2, Hrebiniak and Joyce, *Implementing Strategy*, 38.

121. With reference to Table 3.2, Lorange, *Corporate Planning*, 12, 4.

122. With reference to Table 3.2, Miles, *Coffin Nails*, viii, 49.

123. With reference to Table 3.2, Miles and Snow, *Organizational Strategy*, 18. See also their comments about how "inefficient" organizations struggle to adapt (3).

124. With reference to Table 3.2, Porter, *Competitive Advantage*, 228, and *Competitive Strategy*, 3–4, 17.

125. With reference to Table 3.2, Quinn, *Strategies for Change*, 9.

126. With reference to Table 3.2, Quinn, Mintzberg, and James, *Strategy Process*, 955, 294–295. All but the first excerpt are taken from a passage by Mintzberg.

127. With reference to Table 3.2, Rappaport, *Creating Shareholder Value*, 12, 60.

128. With reference to Table 3.2, Schendel and Hofer, "Introduction," 6–7, 12.

129. With reference to Table 3.3, Andrews, *Concept of Corporate Strategy*, rev. ed., 24, 25, 25 (Andrews's emphasis).

130. With reference to Table 3.3, Ansoff, *New Corporate Strategy*, 234 (Ansoff's emphasis).

131. With reference to Table 3.3, Harrigan, *Strategic Flexibility*, 72, and *Managing for Joint Venture Success*, 13 (Harrigan's emphasis).

132. With reference to Table 3.3, Hrebiniak and Joyce, *Implementing Strategy*, 41 (Hrebiniak and Joyce's emphasis).

133. With reference to Table 3.3, Lorange, *Corporate Planning*, 6, 284.

134. With reference to Table 3.3, Miles, *Coffin Nails*, 255.

135. With reference to Table 3.3, Miles and Snow, *Organizational Strategy*, 3, 153.

136. With reference to Table 3.3, Porter, *Competitive Advantage*, 3.

137. With reference to Table 3.3, Quinn, *Strategies for Change*, 137, 145.

138. With reference to Table 3.3, Quinn, Mintzberg, and James, Strategy *Process*, 516.

139. With reference to Table 3.3, Rappaport, *Creating Shareholder Value*, 81.

140. With reference to Table 3.3, Schendel and Hofer, "Introduction," 11, 12.

141. This ethical commentary on Strategy through Process extends the commentary expressed by Freeman and Gilbert as the First Hypothesis of Strategy

Process, the Second Hypothesis of Strategic Process, and the Value-Free Hypothesis of Strategic Process (*Corporate Strategy*, 150). In effect, I combine all three hypotheses in the form of the first premise of Strategy through Process as an ethical genre.

142. Ibid., 12–20.

143. In other words, I make it possible for persons who work in a language of ethics to engage in dialogue with persons who work in a language of strategic management research. As one piece of evidence for the contemporary chasm between these two languages, consider the program announcement for the 1990 Strategic Management Society conference on "Strategic Bridging: To Meet the Challenges of the Nineties." Nothing in that program remotely suggests a bridge between these two languages.

144. This is to say that I deliberately crafted my Bell Atlantic case to be interpretable in terms of the three premises that follow. Note how the research "veil" worn by the orthodox social scientist would prevent him from entertaining even the thought of placing himself "in" the story that he tells.

145. The premise implies further that a primary part of this specialized task is to create congruence between employees' aims and corporate purpose. I omit this implication from my statement of the Injunction Premise because the language of Strategy through Process precludes these "other" employees from agency in the strategy acquisition process.

146. *Bell Atlantic 1988 Annual Report*, 4.

147. My point is that, *by the logic of the Strategy through Process story*, such private deliberations are out of bounds for Smith and associates. I assume that they do, in fact, deliberate about their own lives all the time! But this is only to say that the Strategy through Process story is suspect on this point.

148. With reference to Table 3.4, Andrews, *Concept of Corporate Strategy*, rev. ed., 16, 85.

149. See R. E. Freeman, D. Gilbert, Jr., and E. Hartman, "Values and the Foundations of Strategic Management," *Journal of Business Ethics* 7, no. 11 (1988): 821–834.

150. With reference to Table 3.4, Andrews, *Concept of Corporate Strategy*, rev. ed., 44, 97.

151. With reference to Table 3.4, Ansoff, *New Corporate Strategy*, 32, 234, 211, 213 (Ansoff's emphasis).

152. With reference to Table 3.4, Harrigan, *Strategies for Declining Businesses*, 50; *Strategic Flexibility*, 3, 5; and *Managing for Joint Venture Success*, 193.

153. With reference to Table 3.4, Hrebiniak and Joyce, *Implementing Strategy*, 7–8, 15.

154. With reference to Table 3.4, Lorange, *Corporate Planning*, 52, 138, 168.

155. With reference to Table 3.4, Miles, *Coffin Nails*, 254, 243.

156. With reference to Table 3.4, Miles and Snow, *Organizational Strategy*, 14, 94–95. See also their comments about the value of controlling persons' behaviors (6).

157. With reference to Table 3.4, Porter, *Competitive Strategy*, xviii, 41.

158. With reference to Table 3.4, Quinn, *Strategies for Change*, 90, 74.

159. With reference to Table 3.4, Quinn, Mintzberg, and James, *Strategy Process*, 18, 18, 959. The first two excerpts are from a passage by Mintzberg.

160. With reference to Table 3.4, Rappaport, *Creating Shareholder Value*, 20, 6, 174, 101–102.

161. With reference to Table 3.4, Schendel and Hofer, "Introduction," 14. They qualify "first" as a starting point in an interactive process.

162. D. Schendel and C. Hofer, "Organizational Goals and Goal Formulation," in Schendel and Hofer, *Strategic Management*, 54.

163. This premise necessarily follows from the Struggle Proviso for Strategy through Process to remain a coherent story at a single firm. I take the specific notion of "impediment" from Miller, *Toward a New Psychology of Women*, 87. Miller discusses impediment in terms of a male aversion to affiliation.

164. It is interesting to note how the warfare metaphor is commonly used both by writers in the business media and by a number in my group of twelve. Members of both groups could be considered partners in a community that turns on a language of warfare, in other words. This intriguing convergence likely sends a troubling message to the orthodox strategic management researcher, who sees himself as a scientist working "above" what journalists do. The breadth of this unlikely community is worth critiquing further.

165. I develop this interpretation of prudence from T. Beauchamp, "Ethical Theory and Its Application to Business," in T. Beauchamp and N. Bowie, eds., *Ethical Theory and Business*, 3rd ed. (Englewood Cliffs, N.J.: Prentice-Hall, 1988), 3–5.

166. I make a grammatical case against Strategy through Process in D. Gilbert, Jr., "Strategy and Justice" (Ph.D. diss., University of Minnesota, 1987), 237–242. I thank William Evan for his helpful commentary in this regard.

167. With reference to Table 3.5, Andrews, *Concept of Corporate Strategy*, 3rd ed., 48–49, and *Concept of Corporate Strategy*, rev. ed., 89.

168. With reference to Table 3.5, Ansoff, *New Corporate Strategy*, 234, 103.

169. With reference to Table 3.5, Harrigan, *Strategies for Declining Businesses*, 34, and *Strategic Flexibility*, 29.

170. With reference to Table 3.5, Hrebiniak and Joyce, *Implementing Strategy*, 38, 39.

171. With reference to Table 3.5, Lorange, *Corporate Planning*, 1, 284, 119, 2.

172. With reference to Table 3.5, Miles, *Coffin Nails*, 49, 52, 92, 52.

173. With reference to Table 3.5, Miles and Snow, *Organizational Strategy*, 20, 81, 57, 29.

174. With reference to Table 3.5, Porter, *Competitive Strategy*, 70, 70, 70, and *Competitive Advantage*, 531. One can count dozens of military references (*Competitive Strategy*, 75–107).

175. With reference to Table 3.5, Quinn, *Strategies for Change*, 46, 47.

176. With reference to Table 3.5, Quinn, Mintzberg, and James, *Strategy Process*, 14, 17. I take these two excerpts from a passage by Mintzberg.

177. With reference to Table 3.5, Rappaport, *Creating Shareholder Value*, 60, 84.

178. With reference to Table 3.5, Schendel and Hofer, "Introduction," 13.

179. I develop this premise from the conception of institution provided in P. Selznick, *Leadership in Administration: A Sociological Interpretation* (New York: Harper & Row, 1957).

180. In this regard, see the very different stories told about the Bell System in S. Kleinfield, *The Biggest Company on Earth: A Profile of AT&T* (New York: Holt, Rinehart and Winston, 1981); and A. von Auw, *Heritage & Destiny: Reflections on the Bell System in Transition* (New York: Praeger, 1983).

181. With reference to Table 3.6, Andrews, *Concept of Corporate Strategy*, rev. ed., 46, 106.

182. With reference to Table 3.6, Ansoff, *New Corporate Strategy*, 173, 235 (Ansoff's emphasis).

183. With reference to Table 3.6, Harrigan, *Strategic Flexibility*, 147. See also her comments about avoiding "volatile competition" (45).

184. With reference to Table 3.6, Hrebiniak and Joyce, *Implementing Strategy*, 104.

185. With reference to Table 3.6, Lorange, *Corporate Planning*, 284.

186. With reference to Table 3.6, Miles, *Coffin Nails*, 255.

187. With reference to Table 3.6, Miles and Snow, *Organizational Strategy*, x, 18–19, 3.

188. With reference to Table 3.6, Porter, *Competitive Advantage*, 1, 3, 9.

189. With reference to Table 3.6, Quinn, *Strategies for Change*, 164, 190–191.

190. With reference to Table 3.6, Quinn, Mintzberg, and James, *Strategy Process*, 607, 607.

191. With reference to Table 3.6, Rappaport, *Creating Shareholder Value*, 12, 94.

192. With reference to Table 3.6, Schendel and Hofer, "Introduction," 6, 16.

193. D. Schendel and K. Cool, "Development of the Strategic Management Field: Some Accomplishments and Challenges," in Grant, *Strategic Management Frontiers*, 27.

194. J. Fredrickson, "Introduction: The Need for Perspectives," in Fredrickson, *Perspectives on Strategic Management*, 2. In a similar vein, see P. Shrivastava and G. Lim, "A Profile of Doctoral Dissertations in Strategic Management: A Note," *Journal of Management Studies* 26, no. 5 (1989): 536–538.

195. I take time to discuss this thirst for a paradigm only because it serves as a ready foil for my interpretations of the Problem of Strategic Management and Strategy through Process genres across my group of twelve. I find the matter of paradigm, in the sense that Schendel, Cool, and Fredrickson apparently want to honor it, uninteresting per se. At the least, their efforts at finding a paradigm for strategic management researchers to idolize can be understood as the very kind of deterrent to self-criticism that Nietzsche criticizes. The thirst for a paradigm certainly seems to be one more attempt to place strategic management research "beyond mankind."

196. Schendel and Cool, "Development of the Strategic Management Field," 31.

197. Ibid., 27.

198. D. Hambrick, "The Adolescence of Strategic Management, 1980–1985: Critical Perceptions and Reality," in Fredrickson, *Perspectives on Strategic Management*, 250.

199. Put somewhat differently, the fragmentation story is optional. We need not worry about the presence of a paradigm, if we prefer.

200. Rosmarin, *Power of Genre*, 25.

Chapter 4

1. Note that the possibility of telling an alternative story as a device for critical analysis is missing from the ostensible critique in J. Fredrickson, ed., *Perspectives on Strategic Management* (New York: Harper & Row, 1990). The criteria by which strategic management research can be improved are, by that account, familiar measures for "fine-tuning" that research—for example, more theory, more data. Richard Daft and Victoria Buenger assert, in this regard: "Strategic management scholars can avoid accepting a level of research analysis too far below the complexity of the empirical world being investigated" ("Hitching a Ride on a Fast Train to Nowhere: The Past and Future of Strategic Management Research." in Fredrickson, *Perspectives on Strategic Management,* 102).

2. T. Kidder, *The Soul of a New Machine* (New York: Avon, 1981), 182.

3. I do not, however, mean to imply that the concept of strategy is confined to matters of purpose at the corporation. We can talk about military strategy, baseball strategy, and so on. I make the connection between strategy and purpose simply to place the analysis in the context of strategic management research, which traditionally focuses on the corporation. I do this, in turn, to accord Strategy through Process a favorable opportunity to be defended in humanist terms.

4. For an informative introduction on this count, see T. Beauchamp, "Ethical Theory and Its Application to Business," in T. Beauchamp and N. Bowie, eds., *Ethical Theory and Business,* 3rd ed. (Englewood Cliffs, N.J.: Prentice-Hall, 1988), 41–49.

5. I wrote this chapter as a substantial and pragmatist revision to what I termed "an alternative account of strategy" in D. Gilbert, Jr., "Strategy and Justice" (Ph.D. diss., University of Minnesota, 1987). In a pragmatist sense, I regard "Strategy and Justice" as a genre that can be reinterpreted for purposes and uses other than my critical aims here.

6. H. Barnes, *An Existentialist Ethics* (Chicago: University of Chicago Press, 1985); D. Gauthier, *Morals by Agreement* (Oxford: Clarendon Press, 1986); J. Rawls, *A Theory of Justice* (Cambridge, Mass.: Harvard University Press, 1971).

7. In search of a thorough opportunity to explain and critique the concept of autonomy, I have my students contrast Ayn Rand's characters—most prominently, Howard Roark, Dominique Francon, and Gail Wynand—with a host of characters including Sinclair Lewis's George Babbitt, F. Scott Fitzgerald's Jay Gatsby and Daisy and Tom Buchanan, and Rand's Peter Keating. See A. Rand, *The Fountainhead* (New York: Bobbs-Merrill, 1947); S. Lewis, *Babbitt* (New York: New American Library, 1961); and F. S. Fitzgerald, *The Great Gatsby* (New York: Scribner, 1925).

8. This conception of personhood is intended to contrast sharply with the search for a set of fixed virtues that more than a few commentators seek to uncover and attach to business executives. See, for example, D. Seibert and W. Proctor, *The Ethical Executive: A Top C.E.O.'s Program for Success with Integrity in the Corporate World* (New York: Simon and Schuster, 1984); and J. Casey, *Ethics in the Financial Marketplace* (New York: Scudder, Stevens & Clark, 1988). I eschew the virtues genre of business ethics discourse for my ends here, in part because that discourse provides a second-order focus on persons' transactions compared to, for example, a Rawlsian interpretation.

9. Barnes, *Existentialist Ethics,* 14.

10. For a memorable account of the human costs of not asking this question, see R. Ward, *Red Baker* (New York: Washington Square Press, 1985).

11. Barnes, *Existentialist Ethics*, 9.

12. Ibid., 27.

13. T. Schelling, *Micromotives and Macrobehavior* (New York: Norton, 1978), 14.

14. I include this last example to emphasize that neither corporate "boundaries" nor the door to the executive suite is impervious to this kind of interpretation about autonomy.

15. For an extended discussion of the opportunities in, and the costs of, human conflict, see J. B. Miller, *Toward a New Psychology of Women*, 2nd ed. (Boston: Beacon Press, 1986); and T. Schelling, *The Strategy of Conflict* (Cambridge, Mass.: Harvard University Press, 1960).

16. I keep self-interested persons *and* their associations in the same story, in other words. I do this by specifying a person's autonomous actions as the pertinent *level* of analysis and specifying both (1) each person's relationships with specific others and (2) the subsequent terms of those relationships as the pertinent *units* of analysis. The upshot is that we need not collapse individual action into a collective entity, as organization scientists are wont to do. Nor must we rule out self-interest when we talk about joint human efforts, as the advocates of altruism prefer. The focus on the terms of association—such as ethical principles—make altruism an unnecessary assumption.

17. See Rawls, *Theory of Justice*, 31. I explicitly include this condition in anticipation of the skeptic's complaint that individual autonomy necessarily breeds hostile relations among persons. Oliver Williamson's axiomatic interpretation of opportunism is a well-known example of such skepticism. See O. Williamson, *Markets and Hierarchies: Analysis and Antitrust Implications* (New York: Free Press, 1975). Although not often interpreted in such terms, Rand's Howard Roark character in *The Fountainhead* can be understood as an autonomous agent who values, seeks out, and acts to contribute to a community of autonomous persons. Roark's community includes Mallory, Dominique, and Mike, for example. Rand's Ellsworth Toohey, for example, is denied entry into that community since he openly makes it his project to undermine others' projects, most notably those pursued by Roark.

18. Gauthier, *Morals by Agreement*, 9.

19. I am grateful to Thelma Lavine and James Buchanan for their suggestions in this regard, made during the 1987 Liberty Fund Conference, "Wealth, Liberty, and Morality," in Fairfax, Virginia.

20. Rawls, *Theory of Justice*, 92–93.

21. Ibid., 126–130.

22. Ibid., 127.

23. In this way, the concept of scarcity is activated in a pragmatist sense that pertains to the specific relationship in question. In that context, we can then explain joint action as a function of those specific persons' "strategic behaviours," and not some "parametric" condition, as Jon Elster puts it. See J. Elster, *Ulysses and the Sirens: Studies in Rationality and Irrationality*, rev. ed. (Cambridge: Cambridge University Press, 1984), 18–28.

24. Rawls, *Theory of Justice*, 4.

25. Ibid., 3–6.

26. Ibid., 528, regarding a "just society."

27. Ibid., 48.

28. In this regard, Rawls makes the distinction between the concept of justice and many conceptions of justice. He argues that we all share the former, even as our discourses are enlivened by disagreement over the latter: "Men disagree about which principles should define the basic terms of their association. Yet we may still say, despite this disagreement, that they each have a concept of justice. . . . Thus it seems natural to think of the concept of justice as distinct from the various conceptions of justice" (ibid., 5).

29. Ibid., 31.

30. Ibid., 499.

31. Ibid., 513.

32. See Rawls's discussion connecting and contrasting the right and the good (ibid., 31–32, 446–452).

33. Rawls elegantly critiques a utilitarian conception of justice for devaluing this notion of distinctive identity: "Utilitarianism does not take seriously the distinction between persons" (ibid., 27; see also 448).

34. I intend that these stories serve as cases with which I can replicate the general usefulness of the three premises. In this regard, I follow R. Yin, *Case Study Research: Design and Methods* (Beverly Hills, Calif.: Sage, 1984).

35. Both the telecommunications and airlines stories are created from published materials in the business press. I have talked with none of the persons whom I mention. That contact is not necessary for the purposes at hand.

36. Drivers Smith, Jones, and Wilson are products of my imagination and driving experiences. I am indebted to Carol Jacobson for her useful commentary about this case.

37. Any resemblance between Stripes and a living, whistle-carrying person is coincidental. I do, nevertheless, create Stripes's comments to recognize those few referees, with whom I have been associated, who believe that the game is not played for them alone.

38. I deliberately intend that the player guarding East slips in this story. I do so to make the point that there is nothing in the Strategy and Justice genre to guarantee a desirable outcome by virtue of simply *having* a sense of purpose. The common observation "They failed; therefore their strategy was wrong" operates on a much more deterministic conception of strategy. That conception is dubious if we entertain an interpretation of our lives that makes room for serendipity. I thank Robert Frank for conversations, during the conference mentioned in note 19, that helped me work out this line of thought. He likely still does not agree with me.

39. Note that Brick's comments can be interpreted in terms of the value that he places on a kind of just context, wherein players from each team can excel in their own ways. I attribute this statement to Brick—a statement rarely heard in the language of coaching bravado—as a disguised tribute to those coaches of mine who have approached their craft with this particular sense of justice.

40. I do not mean "refund" in the literal sense of a cash rebate. Rather, I use the term to indicate a lesser future bill that will be forthcoming from the local telephone companies for local access. See M. Carnevale, "Phone Firms Ordered to Cut Access Rates," *Wall Street Journal,* 22 June 1990, A3; and "F.C.C. Trims Phone Charges," *New York Times,* 22 June 1990, D8.

41. K. Bradsher, "AT&T Sets Long-Call Rate Cuts," *New York Times*, 29 June 1990, D3.

42. J. Keller, "In Computer Industry, No One Is Laughing at AT&T's Effort Now," *Wall Street Journal*, 12 January 1990, A1, A4; J. Keller, "AT&T Profit Fell 6% in Second Quarter on Higher Payments to Local Companies," *Wall Street Journal*, 20 July 1990, A3; J. Keller, "AT&T Increases Rates for Service Used by Businesses," *Wall Street Journal*, 17 July 1990, C10. Allen knows that there are other demands for cash at AT&T. See, in this regard, K. Bradsher, "Equipment Drags on AT&T," *New York Times*, 1 July 1990, sec. 3, 10.

43. J. Guyon, "Stung by Rivals, AT&T Is Fighting Back," *Wall Street Journal*, 30 June 1989, B1.

44. "Bob Allen Is Turning AT&T into a Live Wire," *Business Week*, 6 November 1989, 140–141, 144, 148, 152.

45. C. Sims, "Regulatory Victory for AT&T," *New York Times*, 27 October 1989, D1, D3.

46. Ibid.

47. "Bob Allen Is Turning AT&T into a Live Wire"; "Sounding More and More Like a Three-Man Band," *Business Week*, 23 April 1990, 30.

48. "Bob Allen Is Turning AT&T into a Live Wire," 144, 148.

49. For an entertaining history of MCI, see L. Kahaner, *On the Line: The Men of MCI—Who Took on AT&T, Risked Everything, and Won!* (New York: Warner Books, 1986).

50. M. Carnevale, "After a Weak Start, MCI Battles AT&T with Growing Vigor," *Wall Street Journal*, 12 May 1989, A1, A9; M. Carnevale, "MCI, in New Phone War Skirmish, Files Suit over AT&T Ad Claims," *Wall Street Journal*, 11 October 1989, B7.

51. A. Nichols, "MCI to Buy 25% Stake in Infonet for $27.5 Million," *Wall Street Journal*, 19 January 1990, C12; "MCI Credit Rating Is Downgraded," *New York Times*, 3 July 1990, D4; M. Carnevale, "MCI Posts Drop of 11% in Net for 4th Quarter," *Wall Street Journal*, 31 January 1990, A2; J. Keller, "MCI's 2nd-Quarter Net Climbed 18% but Revenue Data Cause Stock to Fall," *Wall Street Journal*, 20 July 1990, A14; J. Lopez, "MCI Decides to Offer Payout Semiannually," *Wall Street Journal*, 8 May 1990, C9.

52. M. Carnevale, "FCC Opens Study Today of Competition Within Long-Distance Telephone Sector," *Wall Street Journal*, 8 March 1990, A4.

53. "The Smooth Operator Making Connections at the FCC," *Business Week*, 23 April 1990, 45.

54. K. Bradsher, "MCI to Acquire Telecom USA," *New York Times*, 10 April 1990, D1, D4; M. Carnevale, "Telecom USA Gets MCI Bid of $1.25 Billion," *Wall Street Journal*, 10 April 1990, A3.

55. "People Aren't Laughing at U.S. Sprint Anymore," *Business Week*, 31 July 1989, 82–83, 86; C. Sims, "Sprint Picks Up Steam, at Last," *New York Times*, 11 June 1989, sec. 3, 4; C. Sims, "AT&T Sues MCI; Says Rival Switched Clients," *New York Times*, 11 January 1990, D5; J. Markoff, "MCI Sues AT&T over Ads," *New York Times*, 11 October 1989, D4.

56. Markoff, "MCI Sues AT&T over Ads"; J. Roberts, "United Telecom to Acquire GTE Stake of 19.9% in US Sprint for $500 Million," *Wall Street Journal*, 18 April 1990, A10.

57. *1988 United Telecom Annual Report* (Kansas City, Mo.: United Telecom,

1988), 2–5; R. Daniels and J. Keller, "United Telecommunications Shares Plunge on 55% Drop in 2nd-Period Net," *Wall Street Journal*, 18 July 1990, A3; J. Keller, "United Telecom's 2nd Period Dive Spurs Six Lawsuits," *Wall Street Journal*, 23 July 1990, B2; K. Bradsher, "United Telecom's Profit Down 55.1%; GTE Gains," *New York Times*, 18 July 1990, D5.

58. *1988 United Telecom Annual Report*, 24–25.

59. R. Rose and R. Harris, "United Places a Huge Order for Boeing Jets," *Wall Street Journal*, 27 April 1989, A3, A6; "$3 Billion United Deal for Boeing 767 Jets," *New York Times*, 20 May 1989, 37.

60. R. Henkoff, "Bumpy Flight at McDonnell Douglas," *Fortune*, 28 August 1989, 79–80.

61. Rose and Harris, "United Places a Huge Order."

62. "Planemakers Have It So Good, It's Bad," *Business Week*, 8 May 1989, 34–36; "How Boeing Does It," *Business Week*, 9 July 1990, 46–50; A. Ramirez, "Boeing's Happy, Harrowing Times," *Fortune*, 17 July 1989, 40–44, 48; E. Weiner, "McDonnell's Less Costly New Jet," *New York Times*, 14 February 1990, D7.

63. R. Stevenson, "Battling the Lethargy at Douglas," *New York Times*, 22 July 1990, sec. 3, 1, 6; R. Wartzman, "McDonnell Will Cut up to 17,000 Jobs, Many in Long Beach, Calif., Before '91," *Wall Street Journal*, 17 July 1990, A3–A4.

64. K. Bradsher, "UAL Deal: Cast of Main Characters," *New York Times*, 19 September 1989, D17; " 'The United Job Is History-Making,' " *Fortune*, 2 July 1990, 53–54; "Heads You Win, Tails I Lose," *Business Week*, 2 April 1990, 30–31; "Still Trying to Land UAL," *Business Week*, 20 November 1989, 28–29; J. Valente, "In the Takeover Age, Pilots Union Forges a New Role for Labor," *Wall Street Journal*, 30 June 1989, A1, A4.

65. "The Heat Is On Airline Deals," *Business Week*, 2 October 1989, 32.

66. "American Aims for the Sky," *Business Week*, 20 February 1989, 54–55, 58; S. Greenhouse, "Airbus Reaches Cruising Speed," *New York Times*, 5 July 1989, D1, D7.

67. A. Ramirez, "How Safe Are You in the Air?" *Fortune*, 22 May 1989, 75–76, 80, 84, 88; R. Harris, "As Boeing Focuses on Fire-Control Flaws, Safety Issues Widen," *Wall Street Journal*, 11 April 1989, A1, A16.

68. Rose and Harris, "United Places a Huge Order."

69. Ramirez, "Boeing's Happy, Harrowing Times"; "How Boeing Does It"; R. Rose, "Boeing Co. Plans Plant Expansion for 737, 757 Jets," *Wall Street Journal*, 16 March 1989, C9; D. Jefferson, "Boeing to Get Loan of Workers From Lockheed," *Wall Street Journal*, 8 March 1989, A2.

70. "Who Pays for Peace? Many Companies and Towns Are on a Knife's Edge," *Business Week*, 2 July 1990, 64–70.

71. J. Valente and R. Smith, "UAL's Unions, 5 Banks Discuss Buy-Out Effort," *Wall Street Journal*, 9 July 1990, A3; J. Valente and R. Smith, "UAL Unions Woo Boeing, GE in Bid to Get Backing for Buy-Out of United," *Wall Street Journal*, 21 June 1990, A4; J. Valente, "UAL Buy-Out by Unions Faces Possible Setback," *Wall Street Journal*, 18 June 1990, A3, A12.

72. A. Nomani and R. Harris, "UAL Suspends Talks for Purchase of New Aircraft," *Wall Street Journal*, 6 July 1990, A2.

73. J. Cushman, "Support for Airline Deregulation," *New York Times*, 14 February 1990, D1, D22; "The Frenzied Skies: Ten Years After Deregulation, Air-

lines Are Still in the Throes of Change," *Business Week,* 19 December 1988, 70–73, 76, 80; K. Labich, "Should Airlines Be Reregulated?" *Fortune,* 19 June 1989, 82–84, 88, 90.

74. B. O'Brian, "American Air Expands into Three Continents, But Not So Smoothly," *Wall Street Journal,* 8 June 1990, A1, A4; A. Nomani and T. Georges, "American Near Liftoff to Tokyo," *Wall Street Journal,* 11 June 1990, B1, B4; A. Salpukas, "Airlines' Big Gamble on Expansion," *New York Times,* 20 February 1990, D1, D6; E. Weiner, "For Airlines, a Heated Push into the Pacific Rim," *New York Times,* 7 January 1990, sec. 3, 6.

75. "Boxed in by Trump: American's Crandall Has Few Options," *Business Week,* 23 October 1989, 54–56.

76. J. Hirsch, "American Plans to Buy 185 Planes," *New York Times,* 23 March 1989, D4; A. Salpukas, "McDonnell Douglas Gets Big Plane Orders," *New York Times,* 8 February 1989, D1, D5.

77. For a more extensive discussion of persons and projects, see R. E. Freeman and D. Gilbert, Jr., *Corporate Strategy and the Search for Ethics* (Englewood Cliffs, N.J.: Prentice-Hall, 1988), 158–174.

78. L. Lomasky, "Personal Projects as the Foundation for Basic Rights," *Social Philosophy & Policy* 1, no. 2 (1984): 43.

79. One can, of course, find it useful in another discourse to not distinguish between persons and, say, trees and rocks when it comes to matters of rights. See, for example, C. Stone, *Earth and Other Ethics* (New York: Harper & Row, 1987).

80. I say "prima facie" to exclude those projects that foreclose one or more persons' rights to pursue projects of their own. Regarding what he terms the "priority of justice" and "interests requiring violation of justice," see Rawls, *Theory of Justice,* 31.

81. I should note that I take a narrow definition of McGowan's projects here, by talking about only his corporate projects. So, at first glance, the Projects Premise appears to cover the same territory as the Specialization Proviso. But even with this narrow ascription of projects, there are two key distinctions. First, these are McGowan's projects, not the "corporation's." Second, his pursuit of these projects leads him into association with others pursuing their projects. That pattern of associations among autonomous project pursuers simply does not have a place in the Strategy through Process story.

82. Of course, Shrontz does not develop the 777 all by himself. But the point of the Projects Premise is that we can identify a person in terms of the pursuits in which she or he has an enduring interest, where that interest eventually leads to relationships with others. Note as well that I first identify Shrontz in terms of his corporate projects, not his role at Boeing. See note 81.

83. J. Keller, "US Sprint's Troubles Come Amid Ferment in Long Distance Field," *Wall Street Journal,* 31 July 1990, A1, A7.

84. By the Projects Premise, we can extend the scope of a person's projects as far as we choose. The relevant bound, then, is not determined in response to the question How many projects? but with the question With what situations are we interested? Thus, for example, if we want to talk about potential competitors in the long-distance business, we might want to consider how McGowan's pursuits intersect with those of the presidents of the Bell RHCs, which are barred from providing interstate long-distance services.

85. In this regard, I depart from the popular concern in organization science with transactions as a unit of analysis on which measurements are taken. I am not setting the stage for measuring the standardization, routinization, coordination, specialization, centralization—and any other aspect of the "-tion" genre of organization science—of a transaction. By Strategy & Justice, a transaction is interesting as a source of meaning for a person.

86. With regard to "the unity of the individual's past, present, and future," see Barnes, *Existentialist Ethics*, 14, ix, 15.

87. If we want to talk about central authority, or sovereign power, I create a story here with which we can interpret such notions as simply another kind of contractual agreement, tacit or explicit.

88. "How 'Sam the Hammer' Could Nail the Airlines," *Business Week*, 26 June 1989, 126–127.

89. By the logic that I am developing here, we can interpret that issue in terms of relationships between Brick and, say, a particularly vocal public-address announcer. In a larger sense, the Projects Premise provides a cue to start looking for intersections of projects among specific persons. On a pragmatist account, this is preferable to attributing action to collectives or parameters of Nature.

90. I draw extensively on C. Fried, *Contract as Promise: A Theory of Contractual Obligation* (Cambridge, Mass.: Harvard University Press, 1981).

91. On a pragmatist note, we can build cases as expanding webs of bilateral relationships, keeping persons in the story at all times. See, as one example of such a perspective, R. E. Freeman, *Strategic Management: A Stakeholder Approach* (Cambridge, Mass.: Ballinger, 1984).

92. For a discussion of the irrelevance of the firm's boundaries, see S. Cheung, "The Contractual Nature of the Firm," *Journal of Law and Economics* 26 (1983): 1–21.

93. I take a very different conception of contracts than does Ian Macneil and other collectivists. Macneil argues, with respect to contracting among persons: "We shall start at the beginning. In the beginning was society. And ever since has been society. . . . If we wish to understand contract, we must return from our self-imposed intellectual isolation and absorb some basic truths. Contract without the common needs and tastes created only by society is inconceivable" (*The New Social Contract: An Inquiry into Modern Contractual Relations* [New Haven, Conn.: Yale University Press, 1980], 1). The congruence between Macneil's assumptions and those chosen by organization theorists is clear.

94. I carefully frame these questions to express a very different rhetoric for strategic management inquiry. Note, for example, that none of the questions is a "How?" query. Hence, questions about process—*How* does X do this?—are not part of this genre. Note, as well, that these questions are not "friendly" to the premises of neoclassical perfect competition. On that well-known account, competitors are obliged not to pay attention to their neighbors. See D. Gilbert, Jr., "Corporate Strategy and Ethics," *Journal of Business Ethics* 5, no. 2 (1986): 137–150.

95. The clear implication here is that acting on strategy can be usefully understood as an exercise in coping—that is, in being purposefully prepared for an uncertain future—as opposed to exercises in control or prediction.

96. Gauthier makes this point lucidly, whereby persons can contribute to

community by honoring duties toward one another: "Duty overrides advantage, but the acceptance of duty is truly advantageous" (*Morals by Agreement*, 2).

97. See Gauthier's discussion of Hobbes's Foole (ibid., 158–170).

98. For a distinction between this conception of responsibility and the conception of corporate social responsibility "beyond mankind," see Freeman and Gilbert, *Corporate Strategy*, 88–105. The continuing encouragement of William Frederick has been remarkable in this regard.

99. Regarding the actions of a "constrained maximizer," see Gauthier, *Morals by Agreement*, 167–170. Gauthier makes the key point that an autonomous person *prefers* to participate in a pattern of mutual self-constraint. But she does not sacrifice her projects in interaction with a maximizing looter (169).

100. We can agree on many conceptions of empowerment, of course. Promise-keeping is one example. One way to think about the ethical norms by which we commonly associate is the notion of "common morality." See C. McMahon, "Morality and the Invisible Hand," *Philosophy & Public Affairs* 10, no. 3 (1981): 247–277. For an application of McMahon's thesis, see also Gilbert, "Corporate Strategy." To the pragmatist, responsibility is a concept that we can define through discourse. It need not be merely a trait "hard-wired" into our brains.

101. Thus the Responsibility Premise creates an opportunity, through contractual relationships, for persons to derive mutual benefits. The premise does not guarantee such an outcome, however. Persons thus must "take seriously" the search for terms of association, as I articulate in the premise.

102. In formal terms, I created the freeway case as a coordination problem in the language of game theory. See, for example, A. Schotter, *The Economic Theory of Social Institutions* (Cambridge: Cambridge University Press, 1981); and D. Lewis, *Convention: A Philosophical Study* (Cambridge, Mass.: Harvard University Press, 1969).

103. In this way, my Strategy & Justice genre contrasts with the so-called collective action genre of organization theory. Often credited as creator of that genre, John Commons clearly states a case for collective control over persons: "Collective action means . . . liberation and expansion of individual action; [it] is literally the means to liberty. . . . The appropriate statement, avoiding fictions, is collective action in control of individual action" (*The Economics of Collective Action* [New York: Macmillan, 1951], 34, 56). The juxtaposition of liberty and control might not be so ironic in the arguments of those who have adapted Commons's thesis.

104. This conception of responsibility returns ethical discourse to persons' lives. The popular alternative is to consider responsibility as some aggregate parameter. See, for example, M. Magnet, "The Decline & Fall of Business Ethics," *Fortune*, 8 December 1986, 65–66, 68, 72.

105. The utilitarian takes a very different view of responsibility. He argues that voluntary self-restraint is itself subject to the test of whether such action contributes to the greater social good.

106. On a utilitarian view, such as that which Macneil articulates, contractual roles are interchangeable and contracts are "tradable" if some measure of aggregate "good" is advanced. Note that such a conception turns on a weak and second-order conception of a person's empowerment.

107. I fully intend a distinction between joint action and collective action.

The former, I have argued, deals with a story line that preserves each person's project-centered identity. The latter has little to do with persons as persons.

108. J. Bruner, *Actual Minds, Possible Worlds* (Cambridge, Mass.: Harvard University Press, 1986), 122.

109. Thus we can continue to talk about "corporate purpose" as an ex post descriptor. But on that interpretation the notion has no explanatory worth.

Chapter 5

1. I am questioning, in other words, whether those strategic management researchers whose stories are faithful to the Strategy through Process logic are providing the recipients of those stories—for example, managers and students to whom those stories are communicated—with interpretations that those persons can use in their lives. The issue is whether a *place is created* in those stories for those specific persons who are expected to act on the stories that they hear. Once again, I arrange this pragmatist critique on the well-worn "home field" of strategic management researchers: the Problem of Strategic Management. If Strategy through Process cannot satisfy humanist criteria on its home field, then the "paying customers" have good reason to leave the stadium before the game is over.

2. This is not to say that strategic management researchers must cease altogether their creation of stories by the logic of Strategy through Process. But I do clearly mean to suggest that such storytelling efforts cannot be convincingly defended as worldly interpretations. Hence, a strategic management researcher can continue to tell such stories much as an astronomer tells stories about planets, stars, and galaxies. The astronomer makes no claim that his stories hold places for persons as they create meaning for their lives. Yet his stories are no less intriguing. They serve a different purpose. In short, there is a place for stories about the Strategy through Process genre "in the stars" but not in the worldly forums of teaching, consulting, and so on.

3. I first ran across this interpretation of "twilight" in my days at NCR Corporation. A product designated for obsolescence was "twilighted" in terms of lesser, and more expensive, maintenance services. I am grateful to R. Elton White, Lewis Van Antwerp, and Robert Gaines for my education in what amounts to Nietzschean field-engineering policies.

4. J. Marquand, *Point of No Return* (Chicago: Academy Chicago, 1985), 248.

5. G. Walker, *The Chronicles of Doodah* (Boston: Houghton Mifflin, 1985), 48–49. A comparative critical reading of Walker's novel and anything having to do with "managing corporate culture" could raise some questions about the pragmatist worth of the "culture" fascination. I have encouraged my students to think about the same kind of chilling conclusion through a critical comparison between S. Milgram, *Obedience to Authority: An Experimental View* (New York: Harper & Row, 1974), and any "authoritative" tabloid sold at supermarket checkout stands.

6. Moreover, I defend this claim with Strategy & Justice, a story that does not even begin to resemble a story told in the orthodox language of strategic

management research. This suggests just how ripe Strategy through Process is for the picking.

7. Note, by contrast, the formal and structural criteria for worthy research stories advocated in D. Whetten, "What Constitutes a Theoretical Contribution?" *Academy of Management Review* 14, no. 4 (1989): 490–495. Whetten's passing reference to anything remotely human—that is, the "Who" question (492–493)—holds only for a collective of persons. His "seven criteria" (494–495) could apply as readily to organization theory as to astrophysics. This is, of course, what organization scientists and many strategic management researchers want us to believe about their crafts.

8. Once again, I use the feminine voice throughout the chapter whenever I refer to a person practicing according to a pragmatist, humanist perspective.

9. Consider, by contrast, the following passage that Lawrence Hrebiniak and William Joyce choose to write about the determination of certain objectives in the strategic decision-making process: "This step represents the point in the planning process at which strategic objectives are developed for the operating units and are then translated into specific, short-term measures of performance. Focusing first on strategic objectives, it is helpful to picture the long-time existence of autonomous divisions or businesses that comprise the primary structure of the organization. Strategy formulation includes portfolio analysis and related issues of resource allocation at the corporate level. But strategy formulation also occurs at the divisional or business level. In the case of *existing* businesses or divisions, strategy formulation at the corporate and subunit levels may occur virtually simultaneously, but the former is clearly more global, whereas the latter reflects more limited local concerns" (*Implementing Strategy* [New York: Macmillan, 1984], 13). Not *one single person* is mentioned in this passage.

10. Generations of management researchers have interpreted the writings of Herbert Simon as justification for holding such fallibility against persons. Conversations with Lance Kurke have been helpful in this regard. He likely still does not agree with me.

11. See, in this regard, the account of Galt's Gulch, in A. Rand, *Atlas Shrugged* (New York: Random House, 1957).

12. Once again, a person's endeavor is a candidate for legitimacy status. We can affirm such legitimacy by critically appraising the effects of that pursuit on others' respective pursuits, from the contractarian genre that I adapt here.

13. For a discussion of equal status in terms of rights and corresponding duties, see R. E. Freeman and D. Gilbert, Jr., *Corporate Strategy and the Search for Ethics* (Englewood Cliffs, N.J.: Prentice Hall, 1988), 44–60.

14. My point is that even the canonical status of human decision-making limitations can be optional, open to critique, and even found deficient in rudimentary ethical terms.

15. Note how frequently the stated impetus for writing books and articles about corporate strategy follows from the supposedly errant, foolish, and uninformed understandings of corporate executives. See the writings of Kathryn Rudie Harrigan, for example, in this regard.

16. It is true that certain models of organization provide for debate among a variety of interested parties and internal coalitions. Often cited in this regard is the "political process" model in R. Cyert and J. March, *A Behavioral Theory of*

the Firm (Englewood Cliffs, N.J.: Prentice-Hall, 1963). Yet Cyert and March are interested in explaining attributes of the firm, and next to nothing about distinct persons. For this reason, the Strategy & Justice genre is like the Cyert and March genre only in terms of multiple actors engaged in discourse about strategy at the firm. After that, the stories are quite different. I could have readily critiqued the Cyert and March story in a "group of thirteen."

17. See, for example, Robert Burgelman's more complicated rendition of Chandler's basic distinction between strategy formulation and implementation. See R. Burgelman, "A Process Model of Internal Corporate Venturing in the Diversified Major Firm," *Administrative Science Quarterly* 28, no. 2 (1983): 223–244.

18. This claim can be interpreted as her claim to a right. In this way, the concept of right can bolster the concept of project at the individual level of discourse.

19. I make use, in my case stories about the telecommunications and airline industries, of the Projects Premise with only a limited cast of characters—that is, well-known executives and regulators. I do this only to preserve the "level playing field" for Strategy through Process. Even without introducing the broader cast of actors eligible for the Projects Premise story, I show that the Projects Premise outdistances the Injunction Premise in humanist terms. A next project for me is to tell such an expanded story in the context of a corporation or other institution.

20. Lorange notes the worth of a planning system for assisting with the "transferability of strategic skills from one manager to another." See P. Lorange, *Corporate Planning: An Executive Viewpoint* (Englewood Cliffs, N.J.: Prentice-Hall, 1980), 9. This interpretation of management skills as a commodity is consistent with the Strategy through Process logic. It could, in fact, be identified as a fourth proviso.

21. In other words, I have provided an account that separates the level of meaningful action (distinct persons A, B, etc.) from the unit of meaningful action (contracts between A and B, A and C, etc.).

22. The popularity of such a language in the business press is widespread. Among many expressions, see the discussion of "killer competitors" in B. Saporito, "Companies that Compete Best," *Fortune,* 22 May 1989, 36–44; and the SkyTel advertisement depicting a shark, "If He Were a Businessman, You Can Bet He'd Use SkyTel." In that advertisement, the copy begins: "The laws of business are not unlike the laws of nature. There are those who eat. And those who are eaten" (*Wall Street Journal,* 8 May 1990, A18). A critical analysis of the warfare language in the popular media and in strategic management research—beginning with the writings of Michael Porter and Harrigan—might lead us to conclude a broad convergence between these two ostensibly separate communities of writers.

23. D. Gilbert, Jr., and R. E. Freeman, "The Flight from Meaning: A Critical Interpretation of the Management Classics" (Paper presented at the Critical Perspectives in Organizational Analysis Conference, Baruch College–CUNY, New York, September 1985).

24. That sustained emphasis can be traced, through critical reading, across a century to the writings of Henri Fayol, Charles Babbage, and Frederick Tay-

lor. The more coherent that sustained interpretation, the more confidently we can conclude that administrative science has made little progress in a century-long use of the machine metaphor for management discourse. Ibid.

25. One such new posture merits a swift critique. The "shareholder value" approach, advocated by Alfred Rappaport, can be interpreted as an attempt to heavily circumscribe a person's interests. By that approach, projects are merely translated into financial terms. Accordingly, Rappaport's use of "stakeholder" is gratuitous and deserves not to be taken seriously for humanist reasons. See A. Rappaport, "Let's Let Business Be Business," *New York Times*, 4 February 1990, sec. 3, 13.

26. Again, my point deals with the logic of Strategy through Process. Surely persons at Bell Atlantic mingle with persons "outside" that company. It is just that the logic of Strategy through Process obscures that social interaction.

27. For a critique of this relationship with an environment of signals and parameters, see J. Elster, *Ulysses and the Sirens: Studies in Rationality and Irrationality*, rev. ed. (Cambridge: Cambridge University Press, 1984).

28. For a captivating story about the distance between persons in the context of a number of institutions, most notably the family and the firm, see Marquand, *Point of No Return*.

29. The account is sterile insofar as contracts can be interpreted as mere building blocks—and thus sources of measurement—for some larger entity "beyond mankind," such as the firm. One well-known modern genre of such a sterile contract is Oliver Williamson's story about transactions as vehicles for crafting efficient organizations. See, for example, O. Williamson, "The Economics of Organization: The Transaction Cost Approach," *American Journal of Sociology* 87, no. 3 (1981): 548–577. Williamson's unit of analysis, like mine, is the contract, but he places the level of action at the corporate entity.

30. I follow John Rawls's conception of mutual advantage. See J. Rawls, *A Theory of Justice* (Cambridge, Mass.: Harvard University Press, 1971).

31. Rawls discusses this in terms of the utilitarian's penchant for separating the "right" terms of association from the "good" of any one person.

32. Thus I call into question the very notion of "organizational effectiveness" as some meaningful independent standard of advantage. See D. Gilbert, Jr., "Michael Keeley, *A Social-Contract Theory of Organizations*" (book review), *Journal of Business Ethics* 9, no. 9 (1990): 45–49.

33. Note that consideration of questions of ethics is not even remotely at issue in J. Fredrickson, ed., *Perspectives on Strategic Management* (New York: Harper & Row, 1990). This tradition of silence endures.

34. A popular manifestation of this logic is the concept of corporate culture. I can provide a story about corporate culture in terms of shared meanings that distinct persons find useful at the confluence of contracts as well. But the similarity ends there. It is worth noting that the popular conception of corporate culture seems quite similar to the practice of "capitalizing culture" that Sinclair Lewis satirizes in *Babbitt* (New York: New American Library, 1961), 212.

35. It is the sorry prospect for denial of managerial responsibility that makes the "stakeholder" concept worthwhile as an ethical, as opposed to a decision-making process, commentary on the modern corporation. See D. Gilbert, Jr., "Business Ethics and Three Genres of Stakeholder Research" (Paper presented at the Quality-of-Life/Marketing Conference, Blacksburg, Virginia, November

1989). For a connection between the stakeholder concept and distributive justice, see R. E. Freeman, *Strategic Management: A Stakeholder Approach* (Cambridge, Mass.: Ballinger, 1984), 249.

36. This fit between a single identifiable firm and the composite environment is a widely used theme in the business press. See, for example, R. Guenther, "Chase Manhattan Bank Reaps Profit from New Leveraged Buy-Out Strategy," *Wall Street Journal*, 25 October 1988, A20; L. Fisher, "Shift in Strategy at Wells Fargo," *New York Times*, 14 December 1988, D10; S. Swartz and M. Winkler, "Salomon Claims Its Turnaround Strategy Is Paying Off," *Wall Street Journal*, 8 February 1989, A9; and R. Harris, "Boeing Plans Major Overhaul of Its Strategy," *Wall Street Journal*, 14 April 1989, A4. I have referred elsewhere to this rhetoric in terms of the "self-sufficient firm." See D. Gilbert, Jr., "The Mystery of the AT&T Divestiture," in R. Grover, ed., *Proceedings*, 30th Annual Conference, Midwest Academy of Management (Bloomington, Ind.: Midwest Academy of Management, 1987).

37. Clearly, self-constraint can come in many varieties. See, with regard to "common morality," Freeman and Gilbert, *Corporate Strategy*, 55–60.

38. My comments here refer to the Strategy through Process story line and not any actions taken, or not taken, by Smith and associates.

39. I thus choose my alliterative trio deliberately. Each premise begins with the letter *I*, to designate the telltale signature of the ethical egoist. The logic of ethical egoism creates little meaningful room for others, a condition that I attribute to Strategy through Process. For a discussion of ethical egoism, see T. Beauchamp, "Ethical Theory and Its Application to Business," in T. Beauchamp and N. Bowie, eds., *Ethical Theory and Business*, 3rd ed. (Englewood Cliffs, N.J.: Prentice-Hall, 1988), 16–21.

40. The implication, then, is that the modern story line about "the person versus the collective" is optional. That is, if it contains little hope for persons seeking meaning in their lives, we have literary, pragmatist, humanist, and ethical reasons to create and share through discourse a more favorable interpretation about our interactions.

41. I am decidedly not seeking balance here. There is no need for balance—the idolatry of which can all too easily impede critical discourse—if the issue is the comparative worldly usefulness of two genres about persons acting at the corporation.

Epilogue

1. A rare departure from the tradition of ignoring critical inquiry is P. Shrivastava, "Is Strategic Management Ideological?" *Journal of Management* 12, no. 3 (1986): 363–377. Even then, Shrivastava responds affirmatively en route to making a case for doing better theoretical, and nonpragmatist, work in strategic management research.

2. Strategy through Process can be eminently useful for stories about organizations that are created akin to geologists' stories about glaciers. Geologists can entertain and awe us with accounts that hold no place for us as autonomous interpreters of our own lives. And no one worries about that, for good reason. The geologist never claims that he provides such a narrative. Researchers using the logic of Strategy through Process encounter pragmatist difficulties

when they attempt to use their stories as vehicles for dialogue with persons who are asked to act on those stories. Put somewhat more unusually, Strategy through Process could serve as a budding genre of natural science.

3. I employ a "faint light" metaphor simply to say that there are many projects that can follow from the obsolescence of Strategy through Process and the comparative promise of Strategy & Justice. Conversations at Bucknell with Douglas Sturm, Douglas Candland, Jeffrey Turner, Mary Evelyn Tucker, Mary Hill, Gordon Meyer, Larry Shinn, and Gary Steiner—humanists all—and Isabel Lopez, Cathy O'Brien, Leonard Panzer, Jacqueline Hudson, Sandy Kelk, Lisa O'Dell, and Rachel Levenkron—humanists all—helped me begin to sketch an agenda in this regard.

4. R. Rorty, *Consequences of Pragmatism* (Minneapolis: University of Minnesota Press, 1982), 92.

5. I take the trump metaphor from A. Goldman, *The Moral Foundations of Professional Ethics* (Totowa, N.J.: Rowman and Littlefield, 1980).

6. C. Gilligan, *In a Different Voice: Psychological Theory and Women's Development* (Cambridge, Mass.: Harvard University Press, 1982), 29; J. B. Miller, *Toward a New Psychology of Women,* 2nd ed. (Boston: Beacon Press, 1986), 136.

7. My principal source regarding conventions is D. Lewis, *Convention: A Philosophical Study* (Cambridge, Mass.: Harvard University Press, 1969).

8. I am grateful to John Rutland for his encouragement in this endeavor.

9. One such interpretive effort could involve the derivation of other premises of Strategy & Justice. Another effort could expand the "group of twelve" to a "group of one hundred." What I do not have in mind, however, is an interpretive quest for the management researcher's pet project: the taxonomy. Rather, my aim is to encourage interpretations that prove useful for the considerable project of humanist storytelling.

10. D. Gilbert, Jr., "Management, Literary Criticism, and What We Could Say About the Matter of Control over Others" (Paper presented at the Social Issues in Management Research Workshop, Annual Meeting, Academy of Management, Anaheim, California, August 1988). I have also benefited from conversations with my colleagues in the Humanities and Management Study Group at Bucknell, particularly, Gordon Meyer, Timothy Sweeney, John Miller, and James Gillespie.

11. Thus my reference to "we" can apply as readily to our family relationships as to our activities in the conduct of strategic management research. On a pragmatist account, these two settings differ only in that we might use different languages, or patterns of meaning, for each. In this way, strategic management research can remain a distinctive enterprise, if we choose.

12. Note the context-rich expression here, as opposed to the context-free consequence of scientific research about corporate strategy and the modern corporation.

13. An ancestor to this notion of protected pursuits is the concept of "strategic duty," with which William Roering and I once toyed. Conversations with Barbara Edwards aided us at that time.

14. Accordingly, I could have designated the Responsibility Premise as a "self-governance premise." I choose the former because "responsibility" can more clearly and readily be attributed to an individual decision-maker, whereas "self-governance" can too easily be construed as a collective effort.

15. With regard to conventions, see, for example, Lewis, *Convention;* E. Ullman-Margalit, *The Emergence of Norms* (Oxford: Clarendon Press, 1977); and A. Schotter, *The Economic Theory of Social Institutions* (Cambridge: Cambridge University Press, 1981). With regard to the cost of avoiding critical questioning in a corporate context, see A. Kantrow, *The Constraints of Corporate Tradition: Doing the Correct Thing, Not Just What the Past Dictates* (New York: Harper & Row, 1987).

16. Note that my focus on conventions as means is quite different from a concern with, say, the processes of convention formation.

17. Thus if we want to talk about "corporate culture," we can interpret it as the *result* of joint action by autonomous persons, and not some parameter of a nonhuman corporate entity. But this possibility also suggests that "corporate culture" is redundant and unnecessary, since we can already address specific shared understandings as specific conventions.

18. Lewis, *Convention,* 36–42.

19. My inclusion of tacit kinds of conventions opens the door to all sorts of business relationships where coordinated behavior can be mutually beneficial, even if communication is costly. One such case involves market competitors. In that regard, conventions about antitrust law set the context for competitors' joint efforts at coexisting with one another. Michael Porter uses the notion of "good competitor," which has promise in this regard, Porter's "membership" in my group of twelve notwithstanding. See M. Porter, *Competitive Advantage: Creating and Sustaining Superior Performance* (New York: Free Press, 1985), 212–218.

20. Lewis, *Convention,* 42.

21. A rich study of conventions that are rarely questioned—a conventional practice, at that—can be read in J. Marquand, *Point of No Return* (Chicago: Academy Chicago, 1985).

22. Nor, on a pragmatist account, must that agreement be the product of innate psychological traits that we carry. Belief in "psychological trait" can, of course, be interpreted as another convention.

23. Lewis, *Convention,* 41.

24. Note that the concept of mutually conditioned choice that creates a convention does not apply if LaFleur sends her cards regardless of who did or did not send cards to her. In that case, we have reached a context where the concept of convention cannot help us.

25. This case is adapted from T. Schelling, *Micromotives and Macrobehavior* (New York: Norton, 1978), 31–33.

26. I name the characters here with no intended resemblance to any specific persons. This story is told as a composite, nonetheless, of my cross-border experiences at NCR Comten Canada. John Tomlinson and Lynda Phinney helped me make sense of this matter.

27. To a pragmatist, of course, a matter of semantics is a matter of utmost importance. For a discussion of the difference between semantics and the syntactical structure of language, see J. Searle, *Minds, Brains, and Science* (Cambridge, Mass.: Harvard University Press, 1984), 28–41.

28. I am grateful to Mariann Jelinek and Ian Maitland, two who should know, for their encouragement in my efforts to shape this story.

29. One implication, then, is that multiple conventions can prove useful for assisting the parties to a given relationship. More formally, this multiplicity of

solutions is a prominent feature of a kind of game known as a coordination problem. See Schotter, *Economic Theory,* 15.

30. See R. Axelrod, *The Evolution of Cooperation* (New York: Basic Books, 1984). Axelrod seeks a structuralist explanation of cooperation. I do not.

31. The upshot is that the concept of convention can be usefully employed in quite "local" contexts. This further ensures the possibility of keeping distinct persons in a story about the corporation. In the same local vein, the recently banned versions of so-called rap music have been defended as kinds of local conventions. The argument there is that these musicians have merely adapted a centuries-old kind of counterlanguage convention coined by African slaves as a means of disguising their conversations in the presence of slave "masters." Moreover, and controversially, the terms of disguise are precisely those that others find irritable, for example, meaning "good" while saying "bad." Of course, the concept of language conventions as something local to a group of persons runs counter to the apparent aims of legislators seeking a single Orwellian language convention.

32. Put differently, John Commons's concept of sovereign force that controls, and liberates, individual behavior in contractual relationships is optional. See J. Commons, *The Economics of Collective Action* (New York: Macmillan, 1951).

33. If anything, the current "rap music" controversy cited in note 31 suggests the futility of worrying about a sovereign language authority.

34. I could extend the story to include Stern as another autonomous character who has certain available choices about interpreting the traffic laws. Stern could choose, for example, to pay very close attention to Driver Jones's behavior, and less to Driver Wilson's, on the premise that a driver seeking to enter the freeway could be a more proximate cause of damage and injury. In this way, I can interpret "the law" here in terms of this man's choices.

35. Hence, we need not interpret "the law" as some natural, determinative force. In this sense, my critique shares kinship with critical legal studies and also the public-choice genre of inquiry about government actors.

36. The issue is thus not how many contracts constitute a "complete" story about human action at the corporation. Rather, the pertinent question is Which issue involving which persons and their contracts do we seek to interpret? I provide an interpretation of activity at the firm in terms of contracts *and* distinct persons. As a consequence, my aims differ from the theory-building endeavors in Schotter, *Economic Theory;* Lewis, *Convention;* and Schelling, *Micromotives.*

37. Lewis interprets vicarious reasoning as follows: "In order to figure out what you will do by replicating your practical reasoning, I need to figure out what *you* expect *me* to do" (*Convention,* 27).

38. I adopt the "names and faces" approach from the characterization of "stakeholder" in R. E. Freeman, *Strategic Management: A Stakeholder Approach* (Cambridge, Mass.: Ballinger, 1984).

39. Note that my questions are decidedly not about processes of decision-making. I use the "what" interrogative deliberately here. Strategic management inquiry need not be synonymous with stories about processes, structures of processes, and so on.

40. I carefully frame this story in terms of the possibility, not the guarantee, that persons can gain mutually. In this way, I leave room for confusion about

one another's moves, complications arising from third-party relationships, serendipity, and so on.

41. Note once again that these questions are stated in terms of effects, not processes. Moreover, both questions imply the need to introduce persons in terms of the history of their projects and resulting contracts. Put somewhat differently, Strategy & Justice can support a biographical genre about human interaction at the corporation.

42. I begin to construct such an interpretation of a web of contracts in terms of foreground and shadow games in D. Gilbert, Jr., "Strategy and Justice" (Ph.D. diss., University of Minnesota, 1987), 304–305, 348.

43. We can understand this extension, according to the stakeholder map in Freeman (*Strategic Management*, 55), in terms of multiple concurrent stakeholder relationships (along multiple radii in the map). By contrast, the preferred interpretation of multiple relationships is a highly aggregated one in Strategy through Process. By Strategy through Convention, we need not sacrifice attention to other persons when we move the analysis from single contract to a story about multiple bilateral relationships.

44. One example of such a radical revision is the "Hawaii Best Company" case written by Ram Charan. I am grateful for his permission to teach this case on several occasions.

45. For an extended discussion of this distinction between questions, see D. Gilbert, Jr., "Business Ethics and Three Genres of Stakeholder Research" (Paper presented at the Quality-of-Life/Marketing Conference, Blacksburg, Virginia, November 1989).

46. For an example of a pluralist fascination ("How many meanings?"), see G. Morgan, *Images of Organization* (Beverly Hills, Calif.: Sage, 1986).

47. For an accessible introduction on this point, see R. Rorty, "Texts and Lumps," *New Literary History* 17, no. 1 (1985): 1–16.

48. In other words, I infer from the actions taken across my group of twelve their respective preferences that others accept their strategic management research stories. The significant actions here include writing, teaching, and consulting. One consequence of this interpretation, then, is the conclusion that all research can be understood in normative terms. This can render irrelevant, in turn, the conventional distinction between normative and "descriptive" research. Put somewhat differently, critical inquiry can flush descriptive inquiry from its hiding place.

49. Discussions with Rein Peterson have been particularly useful to me, with regard to the concept of power. Nonetheless, I suspect that he finds little use for my line of argument here.

INDEX